Alphabetical

By Color

40+ Years as the 'Clark Kent' of Library Science

Dale Carpenter M.L.S.

Alphabetical by Color:
40+ Years as the "Clark Kent" of Library Science

Copyright 2023 by Dale Carpenter. All rights in all formats reserved. No part of this publication may be reproduced, stored, distributed or transmitted in any form or by any means, electronic, mechanical, photocopying, recording, scanning, or otherwise, without prior written permission of the publisher.

Published in the United States of America by Lies Told Press, LTD. - Non-fiction division.

Lies Told Press, LTD. is a non-profit company helping authors and artists publish and market their works. All profits, except for what is needed to keep us running, go directly back to the authors and artists. Lies Told Press, LTD. books are available at www.Lulu.com.

Bookworm designed and drawn by AniLee. All rights reserved. Copyright 2023.
Cover design by Dale Carpenter with input by AniLee. Copyright 2023.

Carpenter, Dale
Alphabetical by Color: 40+ Years as the "Clark Kent" of Library Science

ISBN 978-1-7332714-8-6 print
ISBN 978-1-7332714-9-3 ebook

1. Librarianship. 2. Library Science. 3. Librarianship – Vocational guidance. 4. Librarians – Career development. 5. Library management and operation. 6. Library personnel and positions.

Z682.N452   2023
020.23

Books by Dale Carpenter

Non-fiction

Computer Software Evaluation: Balancing User's Needs & Wants

Electronic Sludge: Humor From the World Wide Web

Email From the Librarian

Hitchhiking in America: Using the Golden Thumb

If I Was Organized, I'd Be A Librarian

Lyrics Without Music

Needs & Wants: The History of a Corporate Needs Analysis Project

Fiction

She Thinks Not of Me

Alphabetical by Color
40+ Years as the
"Clark Kent" of Library Science

Introduction and Disclaimers	3
Before I Was a Librarian	5
Graduate School - 1979	14
What Graduate School Does Not Teach but Should	16
Binghamton Public Library - 1980 to 1982	19
Starting a New Library Job or Taking Over a Library	21
Managing Your Manager	31
Singer Link Flight Simulation - 1982 to 1987	35
Attending Conferences & Professional Meetings	43
Business Cards are Essential	55
Management	57
Industries and Working in Them	65
Solo Librarian Versus a Library Network	68
Bendix and Allied-Signal Aerospace - 1987 to 1996	70
Cost of Cutting a Purchase Order and a Check	80
Allied-Signal Total Quality Library Network Team	86
Non-Disclosure Letters & Outside Work Letters	104
Library Marketing & Publicity	108
Surveys on Ways to Improve Service	122
AT&T and Lucent Technologies - 1996 to 1998	131
Lucent Newsletters & Readers Responses	137
Reporting Your Worth, Money and Budgets	152
Communication	163

Alphabetical by Color 2

Financial Planning for Librarians	165
Manchester Intl. & Right Management - 1998 to 2003	167
The Medicines Company - 2004 to 2013	184
Position Descriptions	195
Library Planning	200
Consultation Work & Other Jobs - 1985 ongoing	202
Woodbourne Correctional Facility - 2016 to 2018	204
New York State Fire Academy - 2018 to 2021	206
Job Skills You Need	210
Accomplishments & Failures	217
The Special Library Association Has Lost Its Way	221
Where to From Here	224

Appendixes:

Bibliography	226
A Sort of a Full Resume	227
Contacting Recruiters	237
Policies (POL) & Standard Operating Procedures (SOP)	247
Creating a Library From the Ground Up	257

Alphabetical by Color – 40+ Years as the "Clark Kent" of Library Science

Introduction

Hi, I'm Dale Carpenter. In my 40 plus years as a librarian I have worked in academic, corporate, government, private, public, and special libraries and had sex in several of them. I'd like to share some of my experiences, good and bad, and some knowledge I've learned along the way.

Like my first book "Hitchhiking in America: Using the Golden Thumb", this one came about by someone saying "Dale, you should write a book". At a conference a group of us librarians were discussing how to handle difficult patrons and I had just related a couple of my experiences. I am not going to remind the person who told me to write a book because she would probably want a free copy.

I first wrote this book thinking it could be used in a course on practical librarianship. I set it aside for 6 months and re-read it. It was very dull, like almost all college level textbooks I have read. I trashed that version.

This version is loaded with real world experiences and common sense. It might never be used for teaching a course, but you will have much more pleasure reading it. And I think you will find it more useful.

Disclaimers

This book was written using notes I made and copies of materials such as emails I saved while working in the positions and industries described. All events are told from my point of view. Other people may have their own memories and interpretations of the events and situations described. If they want to express those opinions, let them do it in their own book.

I have not mentioned the complete names of most individuals with whom I worked. Mostly it is to protect their privacy. Other times it is to protect their stupidity or the stupidity of the company policies they were following or enforcing. My co-workers at the companies will know which is which.

This is not an autobiography. I have always tried to keep my personal and professional lives separate. Most aspects of my life are not included because they are not relevant to my career as a librarian. I have included events, situations and employment in which I experienced and learned something which helped my career as a librarian.

I have been reading about, studying, and collecting notes on management and work-related issues for a long time. Many thoughts and ideas were heard at professional conferences. If some writing in here sounds like some other person's writing, I would not be surprised. I have given credit where I can.

The Title

Ed S, my first manager at Bendix, rushed into the Library with his worried, "troubles coming" look on his face. "Dale, next week upper management from AlliedSignal Aerospace is touring the plant and we have to make our areas look good. What can you do with the Library?" "We'll do what we can, Ed." "Could you do something with the books, maybe? They'd look better if all the same colors were together."

"Oh, arrange them alphabetical by color?" "Yea, they would look better." "I'll see what I can do." Ed rushed off to worry about something else. The group from headquarters never came near the Library.

So **"alphabetical by color"** became one of my key phrases for an idea which sounds good but upon detailed examination has no merit and adds no value. I have often used it since that day in describing idiotic corporate, government, and political ideas, plans and projects.

Before I Became a Librarian

I cannot remember a time in my life when I was not reading. I have a photo of me as a toddler sitting on the living room floor looking at a book. My parents tell me from the time I could move, I was always reaching for books.

I grew up on a working farm owned by my great-grandmother in upstate New York. It was a New England colonial style built in the 1850's, with three stories, and 18 rooms. Great grandma lived in one side of the house and we lived in the other. When I was young, I would wake up and go visit her before the rest of my family was awake. She shared her collection of books which included great English writers such as Dickens and Shakespeare, religious books from all the world's religions, and many popular novels of the 1800s & 1900s.

On a farm there are always chores. Throughout the year there was the feeding of our chickens, pigs, and for a while beef cattle. In the spring we planted a garden, weeded, and hoed it throughout the summer, and in the fall harvested the crops and canned or froze them. Springtime we tapped maple trees and boiled the sap to make maple syrup. Throughout the year we picked apples, crab apples, cherries, chokecherries, strawberries, blackberries, raspberries, and wild mushrooms. In the winter we shoveled snow and brought coal up from the cellar for the coal burning furnace to heat the house. I learned early there is always work to do and once you get it done, then you can play.

"To ensure domestic tranquility" my parents created charts listing all the chores and who was to do them each day. The children's names were rotated around the chart so no one could claim they worked harder than anyone else. There were no "boy chores" or "girl chores", there was just work to be done. One day you might be feeding livestock or cutting the grass and the next day doing laundry or vacuuming the house. This simple chart introduced us children to the concepts of fairness, division of labor and event completion tracking, skills which proved very useful in my life and profession.

Now when I hear or see someone marketing their "new" "task manager" or "project tracker", either paper or electronic, I want to tell them my parents had created one for our family by the time I was eight years old. They are not creating something new, only different.

Since we took turns doing both "inside" and "outside" chores, we had skills in multiple areas and people have often been surprised when I do something they do not except me to do. Sew on a button, iron clothes, change a baby's diaper, bake a cake, tune a car engine, run a chainsaw or other machinery, etc.

Often instead of waiting for janitors, housekeeping, or maintenance, I did things I wanted done by myself. At the New York State Academy of Fire Science I relocated 19 filing cabinets twice; erected six units of library shelving with end caps, top caps and nuts and bolts. I also moved 2 steel shelf units (42" by 16" by 7' with 7 shelves each) from the basement up to the Library. Since they didn't fit into the elevator, I had to take them apart and put them back together again. And hung 16 posters. It needed to be done so I did it.

My parents did not have much education, having left school when young to earn money for their families but there were always books in the house and we were always reading. If I asked what a word meant or what something was, the answer was 'Go look it up in the dictionary or the encyclopedia'. I might not know how to pronounce a word (still don't for many), but I learned a lot.

I never understood, and still don't, why schools make students read materials in which they have absolutely no interest. Jane Eyre? What the fudge do I care about women in Great Britain in that time? Luckily, "Kim" by Rudyard Kipling was also in the book of 4 English novels. Now there was a story that interested me. I forced myself to read Jane before I read Kim.

If the teachers let the students find, read and report on something they were interested in, they would develop a love of reading. And maybe someday the students would read Jane Eyre.

In my teens, I worked construction in the summer. This could be anything from carrying supplies at the worksite, hauling cinder blocks, cleaning smoke damage from rooms, painting, or nailing together walls. Doing this made me interested in building so I took mechanical and architectural drafting in high school. I made money by drawing plans when local neighbors and organizations needed plans to get a building license from the town.

I learned a lot from the owner of the building and remodeling company. He insisted on leaving a clean worksite at the end of every day. He said it made the customers feel better about your work and it helped keep the work site safe. Also we could start work right away the next morning without having to clear anything out of the way. He, if any customer complained, offered to re-do a job so they were satisfied. But he also told them it would increase the time to finish the job and perhaps add more cost. He let them make the decision. I have tried to follow these examples during my career.

In junior and senior high school I had a wide range of interests. I wrestled and played soccer, participated in art, drama and the audio-visual club and took both college and vocational focused classes. I was friends with students in all social groups, the 'brains', 'jocks', 'motorheads', 'artists, 'nerds', and troublemakers. Why not? They are all interesting.

And many of them had different tastes in literature. It was common for us to loan and trade books to each other. Most of them were not on the state "approved reading list" but we didn't care. We wanted adventure, danger, romance, sex in our books. I still do.

I joined the Army right after high school. My father and his father had served during the Second World War and it was something I wanted to do. I also knew the G.I. Bill would help pay for college. I was also anxious to see a bit more of the world. My individual specialty in the service was surveying and I was attached to an artillery unit. I also went through jump school and served as a paratrooper with the 82nd Airborne Division. I had told the Army I was willing to serve anywhere in the world so in their wisdom they posted me to Fort Bragg, North Carolina. My two buddies (one married and one engaged) who had gone through survey training and jump school with me were sent to Germany. They wanted to stay stateside. Just shows you the Army doesn't give you what you want.

I was introduced to the concept of "There is a right way, a wrong way and the Army way." Guess how things were done in the Army. It might not be easiest, or most efficient, or least expensive, but whatever it was, it was done the Army way.

Gee, I wonder how often in my work career I was introduced to the concept of "There is a right way, a wrong way, and our Company way." Again, perhaps not the best, cheapest, and certainly often not the smartest, but that was the way things were going to be done. You ever run across this corporate mentality?

I did some hitchhiking while in high school since we lived a distance outside of town. I did a lot while in the Army, hitchhiking from North Carolina to various places. You meet a lot of interesting people while hitchhiking. One time I got a ride with a tractor trailer hauling vegetables up the east coast. To speed him along, I helped unload crates of broccoli while in my army dress uniform at a warehouse in Baltimore. The warehouse workers asked me why I was helping. I said the faster he gets back on the road the sooner I get home to see my girl. Then everybody helped moved those crates. Several my experiences are in a book called "Hitchhiking in America: Using the Golden Thumb", available at Lulu.com.

Ghosting is the act of disappearing when there is work to be done or looking busy when someone is needed to do a job. I learned a bit more about this in the Army. A squad from our company was assigned to the coal yard for several weeks. We were to pick up all the pieces of coal which missed the chutes when the coal was unloaded from the train cars. A very dirty job. We showed up for the first couple days, then started taking our time getting to the coal yard. We found out another unit was also sending a squad to that assignment so we would make sure the other squad had shown up, then go hide in the woods all day. It worked great for almost two weeks until our unit called the coal yard asking for one of us.

Ghosting is very useful in the corporate world. If I have something to deliver to a client, I take the longest way to get to their work area and the longest way back to the Library. I always carry a folder or a binder and stop and read all the bulletin boards. And talk to whoever I met in the hallways. This is a good way of being seen, having people know you are willing to bring their information to them, and a good way for wasting time. And an excellent way to find out what is going on in the company.

The upper front pockets on the Army field jackets were just the right size to fit a standard size paperback book. Whenever we went to the field for training exercises, I always carried books to read. I did get kidded about reading all the time, but I just kidded back and said I wanted to be smarter than you dopes.

Once I was reading a Louis L'Amour western and got kidded about it. I explained how L'Amour had traveled all over the west while growing up and if he described a place, he had been there. I said listen to this and started to read the description of a gunfight between one man and several others. When I stopped before the end of the gunfight, everyone wanted to know how it turned out. I told them I would loan them the book and they could read it for themselves. Jim, who was from Texas, borrowed the book, read it and then asked for more. I got him reading books, something he said he had never done before.

Being a veteran has helped greatly in my career. It has given me extra credit when being considered for a position. I assume employers thought I was more mature and capable because I had been in the Army. HA. Some co-workers, also veterans, understood what I had been through, so we had a common bond. Some co-workers, hearing I had been a paratrooper, assumed I was crazy. A paratrooper is viewed either one of two ways. He could be viewed as adventurous and brave, or he could be viewed as crazy or stupid. A good reputation to have either way.

Since I love to read, I was often at the post library. The librarian asked if I planned to attend college after I got out and when I said yes, suggested I take the College Level Examination Program (CLEP) tests. If you pass these tests on common knowledge such as math, English, and history, you receive credits which are accepted by colleges. I took a series of them which gave me 18 credit hours. I also received 4 credits for physical activities, so I never had to take any gym course in college.

After getting out of the Army I moved to the Gulf Coast of Florida and lived near Ft. Myers. I found a small bungalow to rent and a job as an engineer at a TV station, WINK-TV in Ft. Myers. My job was to load videotapes on videotape machines, load 8mm and 16mm film into film projectors, and load slides into slide projectors. The lead engineer in the main control board would remotely turn on these machines so the materials on the tapes or films or slides would play and be broadcast. I helped in production of news broadcasts and anything else the station needed. This was a very good introduction to the backstage processes required for television production.

I moved back to upstate New York for college. I attended SUNY Geneseo and majored in speech communication. I did not have to take the basic requirement courses, thanks to the CLEP, and therefore could indulge in a wide variety of elected courses. Indians of North America; Fiction Writing; Photography; Exploring Alternate Futures of the World; Personal Finance; Nature of Human Potential; Design Fundamentals; Ethno-Nonverbal Communication; Printmaking; and History of China are a few of the electives I took. Taking a wide variety of courses, I met a lot of people who were majoring in different fields.

While in college I worked part time in a tobacconist store, part time in bars and restaurants, and as a band technician for several rock-n-roll bands. I also volunteered with Kino, the organization which brought films to the camp campus, and worked for a short time as a DJ at the college radio station, WGSU.

I met some very interesting individuals and made some great friends while at Geneseo. I have kept in touch with several and still communicate and visit with them. Some people are astonished when they find out I still am in touch with friends I made over 40 years ago. "If you want to keep your friends, you have to work at staying in touch." I tell them. I write letters, I call, and I email them. Sure, sometimes they don't respond right away or even for half a year. But we work at it because our friendship is important.

other too much. And quite often work problems are brought home and personal problems come into the workplace. This has been difficult for me because I have met several women at work places with whom I think I would've had a good relationship.

During this time I was haunting the local libraries. My great curiosity and love of learning would get me interested in various subjects and I would research them. Knowing this my friends often asked me to find information. I would help someone, and they would mention it to others and these others would ask me to help them. It was getting so I was spending more time finding information for other people then I was spending on my own pleasure. I started refusing to help people by claiming to be too busy. Until one day a guy offered to pay me to find information for him. "What? I can make money doing what I love to do? Satisfy my curiosity and help people? Okay, pay me."

One day Mary, one of the reference librarians, said I had a knack for it and why didn't I become a librarian. I asked what the requirements were, and she and I had a talk about library science, and the various career paths for librarians. As a librarian I could help other people, indulge my curiosity, and love of learning, and increase my earning potential. It sounded good to me.

I researched colleges which granted a library science degree and which ones I could afford, and applied to SUNY Geneseo.

"A little learning may be a dangerous thing, but a lot of learning may turn out to be even worst. I have tried to know absolutely nothing about a great many things, and, if I do say so myself, have succeeded fairly well."
Robert Benchley

Graduate School – January through December 1979

"You will learn more in the first year on the job than we can ever teach you here". Paul Studer, one of the library school professors told us this in his first class. He was right. I would say 50% to 70% of the materials they taught have never been used in my career. And they never gave instruction in some useful skills such as budgeting, marketing, negotiation, and writing publicity materials.

I believe your personal organizational skills are most important. Second are your relational skills, how you relate to other people in all levels of life. Third, is your creativity, if you can come up with workable creative solutions to problems. For example, I have a knack for creating search structures for online database searching which other people do not seem to have. People would come to me with a search request and during the reference interview, I could see they would not get the results they need with the terms they had. I rework their search and amaze them with the results.

Graduate school was very interesting. There were individuals who had gone from high school, to college and directly into graduate school so they were in their early 20s. Most of these people had never held a job. Some said they worked in their high school library and liked it so much they were making it a career. There were other individuals who had raised a family, and now were going to graduate school and they were in their 40s. I was in my late 20s. I saw I had far more varied and extensive life experiences than most of these people. Also I was the only military veteran.

On-Line Data Bases was a very interesting course. Remember, this was in 1979 and the Internet was less than 20 years old. The World Wide Web (WWW) was not created until 1994. (IT REALLY PISSES ME OFF WHEN PEOPLE SAY INTERNET WHEN MEANING THE WWW!! THEY ARE NOT THE SAME!!) We learned COBOL (Common Business Oriented Language) and wrote programs. We punched the program onto punch cards, ran them through a compiler onto magnetic tape and then ran the program on the computer mainframes.

The online data base searching was done using a dial up modem over a 300 baud phone line. The output went to a thermal paper dot matrix printer. Back then, each data base often had its own way of coding and it seemed you had to learn a different language for each data base. It came easily to me for some reason, and I found myself loving it and helping other students. Having done data base searching at this early date gave me an advantage in the workplace.

I was Geneseo's library school delegate to the first White House Conference on Information Science. This was a great introduction to what happens at a conference. I found it great fun, intellectually stimulation and overwhelming. It made me want to attend every conference I could.

I also joined the Special Libraries Association (SLA) during library school and have stayed a member for these last 40 years.

As with my undergraduate schooling, I attended graduate school year-round. I started in January and finished in December with 36 credits. Most of the professors and the school's human relations department said they had never heard of anyone finishing in one year. I was one of the last people to obtain a Master's Degree in Library Science from Geneseo since New York closed their graduate program in 1981.

During graduate school, I worked in the school's Fraser Library, mostly as a periodical librarian. Since I often closed the library at night, the other workers and I would party afterwards. Sometimes it was uptown in a bar, sometimes in the library. I found out another student was going to celebrate her birthday so I brought in a bottle of inexpensive champagne. We ended up celebrating naked in one of the back offices. College sure is fun sometimes.

> "I never let my schooling interfere with my education."
> **Mark Twain**

What Graduate School Does Not Teach but Should

Certain knowledge and skills I found very useful in my career, no matter if it was in industry, academia, or government. These should be taught to all librarians.

A course on general business practices which explains the functions and interrelationships of all company departments: -- For example, how does accounting and finance keep track of all the money flowing through a company? How do they find out about and approve expenditures for each department? What are all the ways accounting and finance can do this: line-item budgeting, project budgeting, etc.? What are the state and federal laws (in a general sense) regulating how a company must report their finances? Such a course will help librarians navigate their budgeting process once they get into a job.

Money budgeting and finance for a library: -- How to create and follow a budget, how to tie your budget into department and company's strategies and plans.

The ability to draw a flowchart: -- How do you determine and demonstrate step-by-step processes so you can communicate them and improve them? You draw a flowchart. The flowchart must contain every step and event which moves a process from start to finish. Only by simplifying, speeding up or eliminating steps in a process can you speed up the delivery of materials or information.

The writing of policies and standard operating procedures (SOPs). -- You need to be able to write up policies and SOPs which will work to manage the functions of a library and be enforceable. I have seen too many policies and SOPs which do not work because they have no method by which to enforce themselves. Or the policies and SOPs are too general and vague and do not precisely state what is to be done in a situation.

Report writing: -- What you want to report dictates the focus of the writing. Write clear, concise, and aimed at the reader's level and interest. You must write reports which legibly state what was done and how it was done it within a certain time. Or a report in which the librarian

Alphabetical by Color

states what they want to do, why they want to do it and the resulting benefit. If you can't state these facts in a clear manner, you can't gain support and get what you need.

Communication improvement skills: -- How you may best inform and influence your coworkers, your management and your customers.

A presentation skills course: -- This must be geared to everyone's personality and mannerisms to show and teach them how to use their strengths to present themselves. This would be useful in job interviewing, reports to management, and communicating with library users.

A course on how to market and publicize the library and the librarian: -- It would stress the constant "Hello, the library is here to help you" message as well as the "Look what we recently did" message. It would remind the librarian to always have a "30 second elevator" speech with which to pass on tidbits of what the library is doing to help.

How to how to plan, organize and run a meeting to get what you want accomplished: -- How to hold meetings effectively to make sure everyone has a chance to offer their ideas in a non-threatening environment and in such a way, no one will dominate the meeting.

Information gathering skills for meetings, questionnaires and surveys: – You need to know how to gather the precise data and numbers to support your goals for the library. That is why I have included several surveys for you to use.

Product comparison: -- How you can evaluate and rank services and products.

Priority ranking and time management skills: -- How you can determine what is most important and how to organize the time to do it.

Vendor negotiation skills: -- This will include the economics of buying and selling products and services and how to work with vendors to get the best deal for you and the company.

Measurements and metrics: -- What they are, how to compile them and use them. You need them to communicate with management to show productivity and customer satisfaction.

Skills assessment: -- How you can determine how skilled you or another person is in a specific area.

And of course WWW and Internet security basics: -- How to safety use email, computer communications and safely exploring the WWW and the Internet.

Lynda W. Moulton made a powerful argument for improving the competencies of special librarians in "Under Assault? Offense, the Best Strategy". This was published in the Spring 1995 issue, Vol. 18, No. 2, of Library Management Quarterly. She says, and I quote "This is also a call to library school professors who have never worked in corporate America, who don't know what it means for an information professional to understand the essence of his/her corporation's business technology." She talks about activities librarians should consider abandoning (such as over precise inventory of books and rigid loan periods) and activities we should add (such as developing a refined vocabulary of index terms relevant and accurate to your industry.) This was true in most of my corporate positions. The Dewey Decimal and Library of Congress cataloging systems never had the precise "jargon" terms used in each industry.

Library schools should drill into their students these proverbs:

What you do is more important than how you do everything else.

Doing something well does not make it important.

Binghamton Public Library – 1980 into 1982

After graduate school I found a job as a page at the Binghamton Public Library. A page is about the lowest level person working in a library. Most of your tasks consist of re-shelving books and shelf reading to make sure the books are in the proper order. Sometimes you do help patrons if you see they're having difficulty, but most of the time they go to the reference librarians.

The pages also did basement duty where we would get books from the reserve section of the library and the microfilm of older magazines and newspapers. We pages noticed every month two men would come into the library basement and look through the daily newspapers for the past month. They copied information from some papers. We found out they copied down all the new birth announcements so companies could mail the parents product information. Other researchers did the same with real estate sale listings so they could try and sell products to the new owners.

I, as did all the other staff, dealt with the people who used the library. The homeless who used the bathrooms to wash up and shave. The people who napped in the reading rooms. The people who had to be watched so they didn't tear pages out of the newspapers and magazines. And the weird one who followed women wearing skirts and would lay on the floor in the next aisle and try to look up their skirts.

As well as the 'normal' people who expected us to remember a book they read a year ago so they could recommend it to their friends.

An interesting event happened on February 5, 1981. There was a fire in the State Office Building (SOB) in downtown Binghamton. All our mail was delivered to the SOB and part of my duties was to bring it from the SOB to the Library. I walked over, entered the building, went downstairs to the mail room and talked to the staff while getting the mail. There was an electrical fire smell everywhere. I found out later polychlorinated biphenyls (PCBs) were involved in the fire and the building was contaminated with PCBs. It took 13 years to clean the building. I have had no ill effects from the exposure but some people have remarked I glow faintly in the dark.

The New York library system is civil service based. Which means every position has a test for it given by the state and the state keeps a list of those individuals, ranked by test scores, by which they hire for positions. In my opinion, a very stupid way to hire. I know plenty of people who are very intelligent and have very good common sense but are not good at taking tests. They have difficulty writing out, in a logical coherent manner, their knowledge. They may be able to verbalize it but not write it down. Taking a written test penalizes them.

And just because you have the knowledge to pass a test does not mean you will be good in a position. You could have terrible people skills. And some of the tests ask you to list your relevant experience in a position. How can you get experience if you must pass a test which grades you on what experience you have? A classic Catch-22 situation.

At that time there were so many names on the list for beginning level librarians, the test was not to be given for several more years. There was no way I was going to be hired off the New York civil services lists for public librarians.

**"There is a big difference between
certification and qualification.
Al Gregory**

Starting a New Library Job or Taking Over a Library

Why am I placing this chapter here before I've even told you about my professional librarian positions? So you can see what I've done and what I have learned from each position.

I evolved this process from working in many different professions and industries. It works everywhere.

You first look at three areas:
- relationships with other members of the library staff and your manager.
  - the inventory of the library; and
  - contacts with your customers and the corporate culture.

You start with two-way communication.

Who are the people who work in the library? You should give them a summary of your background and experiences. Then have a conversation with each person to gain an idea of their personality, job details, skill level, and background. Are any of them professionally trained librarians, educated in any other fields, or have other valuable skills? If you are working in a chemical or pharmaceutical company, having someone with a chemistry background is priceless. I had one clerk who was a shopping demon. Loved to get bargains and knew where the best buys were to be had. People come in to ask her questions and ask for directions and then used local maps to plot their trip to the store. They use the library's resources, they get counted as a patron. They also used Consumer Reports, one of our often-requested resources.

Oh, speaking of communication. At my job with the New York State Academy of Fire Science, someone said "We don't know anything about you, Dale." I made a large display on poster board and hung it in the Library's windows. It has a copy of my MLS degree, a photo of me taken while I was in the Army out on field maneuvers, a photo of me landing a parachute, and copies of two of my books. "Hitchhiking in America: Using the Golden Thumb", and "Computer Software Evaluation: Balancing User's Needs and Wants". A paragraph on the poster reads   "Dale Carpenter served in the 82nd Airborne Division, has hitchhiked over 30,000 miles in the US, has a Master's Degree in Library Science and has written several books, including these two."

This has led to many interesting conversations.

The resources held by the library determines how well it can serve its patrons. You need to do a physical survey of everything. After this, you can determine if the resources are enough, if the resources are arranged and cataloged in an efficient manner, what you need to obtain, and what might be discarded. You will perform these tasks:

Explorer & Discover, Learner, Cataloger, Sorter, Shelver & Boxer, Trasher, and Web Spinner.

These are the functions I perform in a new job. Don't rush in to do them. Take your time scouting out your library, its resources, and corporate functions.

While you are doing this, the staff might get nervous thinking you are going to be making drastic changes. You don't want them reading your notes and coming to false conclusions. Take everything, the maps and the listings and notes you make, home every day.

-- **Explorer & Discoverer** -- You must go peeking and poking into every area of the library. All the shelves, closets, boxes, file cabinets, desks, everything under the library's control. Write things down on a pad of paper. You will use this list as a first inventory of what the library contains. Put the lists into electronic form later and compare your lists with any existing inventory lists you find.

At the NYS Academy of Fire Science I downloaded from the computer a shelf listing of our holdings. Then I did a book by book, shelf by shelf inventory using the paper listing. We were missing over 12.5% of our holdings. After six months, I did another shelf-by-shelf inventory which confirmed the first one. This gave me a great insight into what the library contains, what circulates the most and what sections need to be updated. And what areas get stolen the most.

Alphabetical by Color

Since you need to remember where things are, you must map the library. If you can't find a floor map, make a quick sketch, and write down where things are. It doesn't have to look like an architectural drawing, it could look like a child's sketch as long as you can record the information.

What does the library have now in the way of resources? What books, what magazines, what information, what people, what space, etc.? Whatever you have isn't enough. I had a person store computer printouts in the Bendix Library saying he needed them. This went on for two years and he looked at them only three times by my count. One July 1st he found them piled on his desk with a note saying the Library has no room to store any materials but their own.

Make a survey of what you have. I look at every reference book, the date of publication, what year we bought it, and who has ever borrowed it. This gives an idea what the depth of each area is, and where it might need improving. One former librarian left a handwritten list of what periodicals the library had. Just titles, not the years. It was incomplete. I generated one from the bibliographic computer system, incorporated the years we held and listed the missing issues.

What junk is being kept in the library? Is it historical or did no one ever get around to throwing it out? In the Bendix library we had a list of what engineers signed out what lab notebook back in the 1940's. Somehow, I doubt this has any significance now. We had scrapbooks of newspaper clippings from the '50s, '60s, and '70s about the company. These came in handy when Bendix was involved a lawsuit about toxic waste dumping. You should view all of this with a very critical eye. Keep company newspapers. Boxes of old paper with a letterhead the company doesn't use anymore, recycle.

-- **Learner & Student** -- Spend time learning the systems and processes in use at the library. It may be a different computer system or software than one you're used to. It may be a different check-in or checkout process. There will always be something new to learn. And the only way to learn is to get on and ride. Ask the expert's working there to help you. Ask one of them to sit down with you when they can spare the time. I spent many an evening after work playing with the computer system, just so I could find my way around without crashing it or being embarrassed in front of a patron.

Usually I stay late at work two or three days a week for the first two or three months at a new job so I can learn the software systems and explore the library's holdings. And I might go in on a Saturday or Sunday. I would often meet co-workers on the weekend I never saw during the week. It is a good way to expand your contacts.

How are you going to catalog and control your resources? Is there a cataloging system in place? If so, what is it? Is it something you can learn on your own or do you need to call for instruction from outside? If it is a program written in-house, ask for an afternoon of tutoring from one of the people who created it. If it is a program purchased from outside the company, where are the reference and training manuals? Can you learn from those or should you arrange for training from outside the company?

At each job, I wrote down the steps and processes as I taught myself the quirks of the in-house library system. I later used those notes to create helpful "How to Search and Find" guides we posted by the public computers.

Ask your staff about the process and procedure for ordering and purchasing materials. If no staff, ask the administration department or the finance department. Tell them you want to learn this so you can help them make it as easy as possible. As they explain it to you, write down each step for future reference.

– **Cataloger** -- When you find out what is in the library, you must put it in some form of order. What sort of order doesn't matter, if you and the staff can find items when they are needed. Usually sorting by subject matter works best. Sometimes it's easy, all books on history go there, all books on waterwheels over here. But where does a book on the history of waterwheels go? If you do not know the field well when you start, let this go until you are a bit more comfortable and knowledgeable. Or ask your staff to introduce you to a subject expert in that area and ask them to give you a quick course. At The Medicines Company, I first had to learn all about the drug development process, clinical trials, and how the

Food and Drug Administration evaluates and authorizes a drug's use before I was comfortable enough to evaluate materials.

Separate the duties of the professionals and the clerical staff. If you have talented clerical staff, you may be able to train them to take on some of the professional duties or tasks. Always document and track the duties and the tasks, and the time spent on them so you can report this to management. If the current staff is not doing this, sit with them and work up a chart so they can easily track what they do every day.

-- **Sorter** -- You'll be sorting and shuffling items about as you are cataloging and organizing items. Sometimes you will be moving things several times as you come across more of the same item and find the area you are putting them in is overflowing. I always find similar items in multiple places. Perhaps older magazine issues were put in boxes on top of the shelves or moved to some archive area somewhere. This is when the inventory list and map(s) you made come in handy, by reminding you where things are.

-- **Shelver & Boxer** -- Once things are organized put them put in boxes or in shelves, or racks, or filing cabinets. Any place where you can find them again and other folks won't mess up your system. And let everyone know there is a system and there are penalties for messing with it. Of course, if there is a system in place when you start, leave it alone until you come up with a better one and can convince your staff your system is better.

-- **Trasher & Garbageman** -- You will be trashing materials such as duplicates, things which just don't fit in the Library or are not needed. Be careful when you are doing this. The old guard will panic and believe you are throwing away worthwhile items. Or historically important information. A good way to do this is, if the janitors come at night after everyone else leaves, stay late. Tell people you are learning the computer system, or reading the procedures book, and when they have left, trash stuff. Ask the janitors or housekeeping or maintenance for a large trash bin and then wheel it out of the library to where they will take care of it. Old periodicals can be stacked with a "free" sign next to them.

After I had been at the Bendix library for over two years and decided the criteria to be used for discarding outdated or superseded books, I had a book give away.

Take your time before you start doing this. Your staff will panic if you start tossing things out the first week you start working there. And they will panic if you start looking in their desk right away, even though you are doing it to find out what supplies are available. Look in their desk after working hours.

This learning period cannot be done too quickly, for it would be folly to act before you know a lot about the library and its role in the company. Your patrons are both a pain in the neck and your greatest source of support. You must get to know them, their needs, desires, and job functions, so you can support their work. Let them know you consider them experts in their fields, and you will ask for their help and advice in improving the library. Determine if you are serving a diverse group with many interests or one homogeneous group, for this will affect how your library should grow. While getting to know your patrons, you should also learn about the surrounding departments and the groups which can be of aid to you and the library.

You, the librarian, are the expert. Regardless of what anyone says, you know best when it comes to running the library. Creating a library or taking one over must be approached informally, but thoroughly. Your planning should be relaxed and unhurried. Otherwise you give the impression of being on the edge of panic and not being professional. There is a great big support group of other librarians who have done what you are about to and who are always willing to help. Reach out to them.

-- **Web spinner** -- Tell the staff that every time an expert comes in, you should be introduced. An expert is anyone who uses a certain section a lot or orders a lot of books on a certain subject, or is a manager of a department, or is just a pleasant person. Tell the expert you'll be calling on them for help in their area of expertise. You can learn a lot by holding information audits with them and asking for their suggestions.

Alphabetical by Color

At Bendix, my manager Ed said the Library supported the Engineering Department. I soon realized employees from other departments were coming in for help. I made a concerted effort to reach out to all departments and offer them help. In return, I gained company wide support for the library. Ed brought up the issue of me providing service to other groups one day. I told him I didn't want him to get yelled at. I explained if I didn't help people from other departments, those people would go back and complain to their management. Then someone would come to me and ask why I wasn't helping other departments. Then when I told them you, Ed, told me not to help anyone, someone would yell at you. So I was doing this to protect my manager. Ed just nodded and walked off.

Who is the library's audience? Who are you working for or aiming at? Is it the public, a limited group with a specific interest, several groups with wide diversity of interest, or what? At Bendix, first I dealt mainly with engineers: mechanical, electrical, computer, stress, optical, all sorts of engineers. Later I worked to interest marketing and other groups with totally different needs and interest in the library.

Reach out to various department heads and request a meeting to ask how you can make their life easier. "What has the library been doing for you before?" "Would you please explain what your department does? Perhaps that might give me an idea of a way to help you?" "What can the library do to provide service and value to you and your department?"

One of the best questions I have ever come up with is "What is the one thing the library can do to provide the best value to you and your department or group?" Tell them they can think about it and get back to you later if necessary.

Make sure you take notes during these meetings so you can remember what each department manager said.

If you know your audience and their interests and have an idea of what you need to fill their information request, how are you going to get the resources you need and do not have? Where's the money going to come from? My recommendation is to ask your manager what sort of budget you have. If he says not to worry, don't worry. If they start to give you a song and dance about how poor the company is, and how tough times are, tell them right away you cannot provide services if the company doesn't provide money. Give them your first impressions of the reference section, periodicals, books, and computer hardware and software, but always say the library should have the best resources and you are positive the company employees needs them.

To me, starting a new job is like cooking a meal in a strange kitchen. You know how the stove, fridge, and microwave in your kitchen works, and you know where all the utensils, pots and pans and condiments are. In the new kitchen, their stove may be electric where as you are familiar with gas stoves. Their microwave may have a touch pad control and your old one has a dial. You cook with aluminum and they have all steel pots and pans. You feel lost or at the very least, confused.

So what if you are used to Windows and they use UNIX or some other cataloging program or software, which has happened to me more than once. Your typing skills are still with you and it will just be a short learning period until you are up to speed. Take some time to wander thru their spice rack, IE., the reference section, until you find the materials you are familiar with, notice what items they don't have, and savor and sniff the new spicy selections you are not familiar with.

It will take you a while to learn where everything is. That is good because it will give you the opportunity to ask questions. Ask why things are done the way they are, why items are kept in a certain place, why a procedure is done the way it is. Is it because a procedure calls for it or is it just habit? You can gently mention the way things were done at other places you worked at, not to say one way is better than another, just to state a different way of doing things. This will get your co-workers to explain why things are done the way they are and possibly thinking about new ways of doing it. And while your new co-workers are teaching you, they may ask themselves, why do we do this task this way and is this is the best way of doing it.

There is a good side to feeling and acting like an outsider. You can bring up issues members of the group might not, and by doing so, ask questions and offer explanations and suggestions for improvements and change. You will be excused for after all, you are new and don't have the mind ruts other employees have. I always ask why something is done in

Alphabetical by Color

a certain way, because it gives me the data to suggest improvements.

Let your manager and your staff know there will be a period during which you and they will work out the level of information you will need on different occasions. Sometimes you will need very detailed reports, other times you will just need a go/no go opinion from them.

This puts a positive spin on your transition by making them aware first, there will be a period of adjustment, and second, you want their cooperation in finding an appropriate level at which to report information.

Here is a sheet listing the ideas I had shortly after starting a job with Lucent Technologies in Whippany, New Jersey. You see I've come up with "Quick & Easy", "Medium Expenditure of Money and/or Time" and some "Long Term" projects.

Suggestions for the Whippany Library

Quick, Easy and Low-Cost Improvements

1. put 'LIBRARY' direction signs all over this floor to publicize & remind people we have a Library and this is where it is.
2. new OPAC searching hints signs – would help make it easier to search.
3. don't use 'Technical' in Library's name - people will think we only have technical stuff.
4. rewrite Library procedures & policies to: A. specify maximum number of books a person may have out at one time, B. specify maximum number of renewals (Circle (the circulation system) will have to be rewritten to prohibit renewals), C. specify penalties for not adhering to Library procedures.

Medium Effort Which Requires Spending Some Money and/or Time

5. divide video room in half. install a VCR/TV in one half so small groups can use it without disturbing single users on the other side. install VCR/TVs on other side with headphone jacks so up to 3 people can use facilities at one time.
6. run circulation reports for books and journals. remove any book which hasn't circulated in 10 years. cancel any subscription which

shows no or very low use in last 2 years.
7. divide back room in half with wall so security's file cabinets are still secure. use available space for something?

Long Term Efforts

8. weed collection using circulation reports and holding reports from other libraries.
9. create users group to meet once a quarter to offer suggestions on specific issues concerning library, what section of collection needs most improvement, how can we better serve users, etc.
10. track usage during evenings and weekends to see if library needs to remain open during those times.

Almost half of these ideas were implemented. Notice suggestion 1? While walking around the Whippany plant, I saw there were lots more signs pointing to the Cafeteria than to the Library. Now I know the Cafeteria is more important to a lot of people than the Library, and it gets used more, but there should be some signs pointing to the Library. I contacted Maintenance and asked how to add more signs. They said I could fill out a work request, have the department manager sign it and send it in. I filled one out, set it to Betty K, my manager. She ignored it.

I am looking at a November 1991 Plot Plan of the Lucent Murray Hill location. Shipping, Purchasing, Medical, Employment/Personnel, and the Cafeteria are located on the map. Not the Library. At Murray Hill the Library Network staff were located in Building 3, in Hallways 3A, 3B, 3C & 3D. I counted the number of times a department name was mentioned on an office door. The Library Network was named 3 times. The other department had their name up 45 times. That shows how much Nancy M, the Library Network Director, knew about marketing and publicity.

"The only thing that you absolutely have to know, is the location of the library."
Albert Einstein

Managing your Manager

The easiest manager to work for is one who is young and ambitious. All you must do is make them look good. (Always try to make your manager look good.)

We want managers which are supportive, helpful, wise, and know their way around the organization. We want staff who are ambitious, bright and have ideas. Good subordinates make good trouble for their bosses.

The purpose of your manager is to help you get things done which you can't get done by yourself by using the manager's leverage and power within the organization. You are entitled to your manager's time. It is unacceptable if your manager says they do not have time for you. You have as much time as your manager does. If they want to talk, stay, and talk. But you must have an agenda to talk about. Talk to your manager about what you are doing and what you want to be doing.

Organizations have problems. Don't present your manager a problem, present your manager a solution. A problem with a solution will move it off your manager's desk. Give your manager the credit for the idea.

Do not underestimate your manager's ability to forget. Confirm any verbal agreement with your manager in writing by paper or email. Specifically spell out what was agreed upon. Once you get approval, don't ask anymore, just go ahead and do it.

Most managers do not expect too much from the library. Many believe libraries provide nothing but paper storage and moving. Their assumption is libraries are good, but they don't know what the expectations of a great library are. Most people in an organization think the library is not important enough to worry about so they're not out to get you.

Most librarians work for non-librarians. These managers do not understand libraries, library products, or library services and do not think it is important to learn about them. Many do not want to know.

With a new manager, you should call a meeting as soon as possible. Explain this is the library, this is where it has been, here is where it is now, here is where it is going and where we want to go. You should discuss certain topics about the library and your position:
1. Vision & purpose: What do we want the library to do? What are the goals and how does each person involved support those goals?
2. Metrics: How do we and how will we measure successful completion of tasks? Both in the quantitative manner (by numbers) and in the quality manner (by adjectives such as good, fair & bad).
3. Ownership & Scope: What are the librarian's areas of responsibility and authority? Where it begins, what it covers and where it ends?
(I have always bent those limits. And sometimes just blown right by them.)

If your boss is only giving lip service to your ideas, ask to be there when they meet with their manager so you can present your ideas yourself. Give your manager two choices. Choices, not ultimatums. If they don't or won't accept your choices, they must give you the answer to the question 'why not?'.

You must develop the skills to manage your boss to gain their respect and to make them look good to all levels of management. Look at the personality and temperament of your boss. Are they an extrovert or introvert, soft-spoken or loud and brash, relaxed, or uptight? Determine the best way to approach your manager on various subjects. A good starting point would be to talk to their secretary, if they have one, and ask what the best way is to approach them.

My manager at Singer Link, Jim H, told me how I should be reporting my work. The conversation went something like this.

> "If you don't measure it, it can't be tracked and then you don't know if you are improving what you are doing. So write down what you do, how many times you did it, for how long and who you did it for. Write it down immediately after you finish so you don't forget the details. In the corporate world, numbers and statistics equal money."

I find it useful is to create a mental image of how I want my manager to act and support my efforts. I think up all the possible concerns, questions, and objectives people might come up with and develop positive responses to each one. I arrange to have all my ideas, supporting documents and information handy to answer any question. By imaging all the negatives, I gain the confidence to handle the discussion, no matter how it goes.

As a library manager, there are 2 different tasks you do. You must make your manager aware of this. 1, you are the librarian providing reference and research services. 2, you are the library manager overseeing the staff, doing collection development, budgeting, marketing, and every other management task. You can't do both at the same time. Divide and budget your time so both tasks get done.

Knowing one of my managers had an engineering background and was always wanting to hear the numbers, I was always prepared to provide a statistic to support the library. For example, I and my staff would always count how many reference questions or services we did each day. Then if I saw my manager the next day, I was ready to say, "Ed, the library answered 47 requests for information or services yesterday."

This showed I was aware of everything going on and we were collecting statistics for reporting to upper management. I was making him look good, therefore he will reciprocate making me look good.

You should begin with the end in mind. What I mean is, if you want to bring a new service in house or start a new service, think about the best way you can bring it up as a suggestion or request to your manager. What is the good of the service? Will it help save time or money? How will it make life or work easier for the employees?

After you have worked with a manager for a while, it is helpful to ask questions. Your first-year review is a good time. What am I doing that I should continue doing? What am I doing that I should stop? And what am I doing that I should change in some way? Tell your manager they may think about it if they do not have a ready answer. Most managers have never been asked to judge your performance in this manner.

Now a good manager should have these abilities and skills. They should have the technical skills to know if you are doing your job well. They should not micromanage you but empower you to do your job on your own. They should be results oriented, but still have interest and concern about their subordinate's well-being. They must have a clear vision and strategy for the group, be able to listen and share information. They also should help their subordinates with their career development. I have not had many managers who had all these abilities and skills.

Ten Essential Time Management Techniques

1. Tame email and the phone. I only look at email first thing in the morning, at lunchtime and at the end of the day. Immediate & important emails are answered at once, everything else is done at the end of the day. I let most of my calls go to the answering machine, listen to them at lunchtime or at the end of the day. I answer immediate & important call then. (Most calls and email are NOT both immediate & important.)
2. Minimize meetings. Most are time wasters. Find a strategy to avoid them or get out of them after your participation is done.
3. Be punctual and demand all others do the same.
4. Make and use lists. Paper does not forget. You do.
5. Know what your goal(s) is and focus all of your actions to move you toward your goal(s).
6. Create a folder system to aid your memory. Each of your projects should have 1 folder and all related materials are kept together in that folder.
7. Make appointments with yourself to work on a specific functions. Keep these appointments and work ONLY on that function. Blocking your time out prevents other from using up your time.
8. Plan and schedule your day to minimize unplanned and unproductive activities.
9. Avoid peak times. Don't go to the bank Friday during lunch hour or right after work. Don't food shop or go to the laundromat on weekends.
10. Always carry something to read or listen to during travel or wait times.

Singer Link Flight Simulation – 1982 to 1987

An aerospace company in Binghamton advertised for an "information specialist", and I applied, interviewed several times, and was hired. I found out later some individuals had wanted to hire a more experienced librarian but since the individual lived outside the area, they did not want to pay any relocation expenses so they hired me.

Singer-Link was the company. Their sewing machines brought in over 50% of sales. Their aerospace, marine systems and education sector was about 23% of sales and they also had divisions in air conditioning, power tools, furniture, controls and meters. I was joining the sector called Singer Link Flight Simulation. They built, maintained, and modified simulators for commercial and military aircraft and helicopters.

I reported into Special Projects, the group which did customization and modification of existing military simulators worldwide. I was hired as the first professional librarian and online database searcher for Singer Link in May 1982. At that time, some individuals were realizing the value of doing research using online databases. One day a week I would go to the company headquarters in Kirkwood and do online database searching. The rest of the week I was based in their Chenango Bridge facility controlling a locked room of classified and unclassified documentation.

I interviewed and was hired in May of 1982. The Human Relations Department called me on a Tuesday and offered me the position and I accepted. Thursday, George C., who was going to be my manager, called and told me the Special Libraries Association (SLA) was having their annual convention in June and it would be a good idea for me to attend. I went to Detroit for the convention. I lot of librarians I talked with said they had a hard time convincing their management coming to the SLA convention was worthwhile. When they found out I had worked for Singer Link less than 1 month and I got to go to the convention, they were astonished.

I went through a Department of Defense background security check and received training and a security clearance at the "Secret No Foreign" level. The United States may put modifications or upgrades on their aircraft which they do not provide to other countries. This material about the modifications or upgrades was then marked "No Foreign" meaning it was not to be shown to any foreign national.

The room I controlled had 12 locked filing cabinets and multiple shelves with documentation on the aircraft. Formerly it had been maintained by the department secretary "in her spare time". Of course you know secretaries have no spare time. The place was a mess. As the military did upgrades or modifications to their aircraft, the military and the manufacturers sent Singer Link pages with which to update the manuals. No one had put them in for a very long time. There were stacks of updates all around the room.

The first task was to put the manuals in order by the type of aircraft. For example, the F-4 Phantom fighter aircraft had several versions, F-4A, F-4B, F-4C, F-4D, F-4E, F-4F and so-on. Each version has their own set of documentation. For example we may have sold versions of the F-4B and F-4C to our allies while our aircraft were F-4F and F-4G levels. I had to put these manuals in order, put all the updates in order by date and then update all the manuals.

Since no one had been controlling the documents, there were some missing. An engineer who was working on the radar system for certain aircraft may have taken out those manuals and kept them at his desk. This meant the engineer was doing his job without the latest knowledge contained in the updates.

I immediately instituted a sign-out procedure for the manuals. This pissed people off. Some of them wanted to know why they needed to sign them out. Well obviously, if someone's looking for a manual we want to know where it is if it's not in the library. Also I told everyone, when updates come in, I need to find the manual to update it.

George C. received some complaints about the new sign-out procedure. He asked and I explained why I was doing it. He asked me to explain this in the next department meeting. I realized a little visual aid would add some emphasis to the point I needed to make. On the day of the department meeting, I filled a book cart with all the updates for one of the aircraft. I wheeled it into the meeting, getting a lot of funny looks. When George asked me to talk, I stood up, put my hand on the book cart

Alphabetical by Color

and said "These are all the updates for just the C-130 program. If you are working on the C-130 program and you have a manual you may be working with outdated information. If you turn in your work using outdated manuals, it's your fault. So the reason I'm asking you to sign out the manuals, is so I can find them and make sure you have the latest and most correct information to work with."

(Don't tell anyone but I padded out the C-130 updates with updates from other aircraft, which I put under the C-130 updates. Presenting an overflowing cart, rather than a full one, added emphasis to the point I was making.) After the demonstration, not too many people complained about the sign-out procedure.

This specialized library had technical materials for our department. There was a main library in the headquarters building. It was created and run by a department clerk which grew it into quite a respectable library. I believe at the time they had a total of three staff. Later, Singer Link was hiring a highly respected engineer who lived in Florida. As part of his hiring he told the company he wanted his wife to have a job. She was a teacher of French in high school. Singer-Link put her in charge of the library. And paid for her to go to graduate library school in Syracuse, including all tuition and travel expenses.

Eilene H. ran the library like she ran a high school class. The staff had to tell her what they were doing all the time. They could not leave the library to go to the bathroom, to the copier, or to lunch or to deliver a book or paper to anyone without getting her permission. I hope Singer Link got a lot of great work from her husband because Eilene made life difficult with her work and management styles.

This is called "The Peter Principle". "In every hierarchy, whether it be government or business, each employee tends to rise to his level of incompetence; every post tends to be filled by an employee incompetent to execute its duties." I have seen this a lot in individuals which move into management positions. I see it in teachers because they want to be in control. The worst managers I've ever had were librarians who moved into management and forgot the function of a library is to serve individuals. All they worried about was managing, budgeting, and management's opinions, not providing services to their customers.

Alphabetical by Color

The demand for online database searching grew so much I was going to headquarters two days a week. About 2 or 2 1/2 years after I'd started at Singer Link, the Special Projects department moved from Chenango Bridge to our Kirkwood headquarters. Shortly after a full-time database searcher was hired within the main library. I helped train this individual and was on standby to aid in searching if demand required.

The Special Projects group was re-organized at this time and now I reported to Jim H. I learned a lot from Jim. He wanted more formalized written reports than George. Two practices which I had been doing helped me greatly. The first was tracking everything I did each day. I take a pad of writing paper, mark the date on the left side of the paper and write down what I did. Who called me and what they called about, what projects I worked on, and so on. This gives me a written record I can refer to if someone asks. The second is a "Show Value Walk Around" list. Here is an example. It lists some recent work I have done and can mention to upper management when I see them in the hallways or elevators. Remember, if you don't blow your own horn to promote yourself, no one else will.

This is from March 2009 when I worked at The Medicines Company. It is a list of projects I recently finished or was currently working on. I use this as a memory jogger so I ALWAYS have something work related to mention to co-workers.

> **"What most adds or shows your VALUE and visibility to TMC?"**
> (This title which reminds me what to tell people to remind them of my value.)
>
> WALK AROUND AND BE SEEN
>
> DIALOG searching capabilities - create training session to show value of DIALOG access
>
> IDRAC searching capabilities - create training session to show value of IDRAC access
>
> Creating lunch and learn sessions on WWW resources, clinical trial data sites, etc. - 'Beyond Google: Searching the Web'; 'Science sites for your use'; '60 sites in 60 minutes'

Alphabetical by Color

Set up regulatory/compliance legislative monitoring effort. What sources: IDRAC, SCRIP, FirstWord, etc.?

Write articles for SLA chapter newsletters: how to work with recruiters; selecting software; practical library management

Plan for imaging regulatory documents onto server 21 CFR Part 11 compliant
When will IT get server compliant?
Put Regulatory Submissions on TeamSpace: need to talk with Amanda and Monica on structure

Re-write TeamSpace bio and add new photo - stress research skills and library creation and modernization

Add more to TeamSpace Library page: - RSS feeds, articles, links to websites

SMEADLINK: (Smeadlink is the name of the software program the VP of IT picked for the Library to use. It was NOT my choice. I'll explain later.)
Print regulatory document labels for recent submissions
Create Access database and move DDMAC Cleviprex documents into it

elevator speech with Glenn on money saving ideas:
- consolidate periodical and book ordering thru library
- use jobber like EBSCO for periodical ordering
- information architecture of TeamSpace

- re-write library SOPs, ask Stephanie what process is now and write library policy

Iron Mountain: (our off-site archives storage company)
- letter with new addresses & authorized account user names & only I may request boxes
- update Iron Mt database using old archive records
- pull old boxes from Iron Mt: compare and weed
- send New Zealand OPCAB records to Iron Mt
- ship Accounting & Drug Safety boxes in Library to Iron Mountain

Jim H also taught me a few other useful practices. Such as Finance does not like seeing amounts on expense reports which end in 0 or 5. I had turned in an expense report after I went to a SLA conference and put down a large amount for breakfast. Jim, in a private meeting, said no one spends over ten dollars on breakfast when traveling on company money and suggested I change it. I did. I also learned if I stayed at a hotel which had a breakfast included in the cost of the room, to later pick a receipt out of the trash when buying a mid-morning coffee at some place and use the receipt on my expense report for breakfast.

Jim once said, "I don't ask questions I don't want to know the answers to." A wise practice. Just like "Don't ask permission, just do it. If anyone complains, ask forgiveness."

Jim asked me to find and list all of the policies and procedures which were being used within Singer Link Flight Simulation. Such a list had never been complied during the company's history. Doing this brought me in contact with every company department and increased my image as someone who could provide help and knowledge.

Since this was back in the days before everyone got uptight about righteousness, we had some great Christmas parties. With alcohol. During working hours. In the plant. The first year after Special Projects moved to the Kirkwood plant, everyone talked about a guy from manufacturing who made and gave out rum balls. Okay, I thought, that is nice. The day of the party, I was at my desk and a guy walked up carrying two baking sheets. The smell of rum was overpowering. I could see the rum sloshing around on the trays. I took one and said thank you. He said take another. I did.

On paydays, especially if they came on a Friday, it was common to go out for lunch. Which usually included drinks. Not much got done those Friday afternoons.

Several people I knew from high school and the area worked for Singer-Link. Often I would go out to lunch with them. Sometimes it was the blue-collar workers from the manufacturing areas or sometimes it was the white-collar workers. This was a very good way to learn what was going on in all areas of the plant.

Alphabetical by Color

One day, a group of co-workers and I were going out to lunch and went past the desk of Linda R., an intelligent and personable blonde co-worker. One of the guys said the obvious and often used line, "Hey Linda, you know gentlemen prefer blondes." Not missing a beat, Linda replied "Yes, and blondes prefer gentlemen." Another guy said, "Well then, none of us have a chance." "Dale might." was the reply. Boy, did I get kidded about that.

I worked for Singer Link Flight Simulation from 1982 to 1987. I oversaw the move of the Library from Chenango Bridge to our Kirkwood headquarters. I created a documentation database for Special Projects. I controlled a secure room containing 12 locked file cabinets of classified documentation and multiple shelves of unclassified documents. I went through Department of Defense training courses on document security. Only the Security Department members and I had access to the documents and nothing was ever lost.

It was my habit to look at people's desk as I was walking around the building to deliver information or documents people had requested. Several times I saw, laying in the open on an unattended desk, classified documents which had been signed out from my library. If I saw this, I would pick up the document, carry it back and lock it up. I would leave a note on the desk saying I took the document. When the person came to pick it up, I would tell them they were very lucky I did not take the document down to Security and to report them. This would put a mark against their security clearance and if it happened more than twice, they stood a good chance of losing their security clearance and their job. I also told them I would get in trouble for letting them sign out a document and leave it unattended. So wasn't just their job, it was also my job. The word quickly got around I was very serious about the handling of classified documentation. And everyone who signed any out from my department had also better be very serious.

Because this plant dealt with classified materials and products, Security would search your purse, briefcase, or lunchbox when you left the building. After a couple years, Security would just wave me through without checking my briefcase. They knew I had a top-level security clearance but it did not feel right for me to be waved through when everyone else was being searched. I always stepped up and opened my briefcase.

One day I delivered some requested papers to a group and one of them said "Dale, you have a servant's heart." I did not know how to take that comment at that time. I first thought of it as a put-down. Now I know it is just my nature to be a helping individual. And by having this servant's heart and doing things which benefit others has often created a large deposit of favors I could call upon.

The economic situation in the late 1980s was such the defense and aerospace industries were not growing. I read about this in various business publications. I saw the company was letting go personnel and not hiring. I also saw a surge in leverage buyouts and realized Singer Link was a good candidate for a leveraged buyout. In a leveraged buyout, an investor buys enough stock in the company to take control of it and then sells off portions of the company to make a profit. Since Singer Link was a diversified company in several industries, it was a good candidate.

I started looking for another job. I told some coworkers why I was doing this and why I was convinced Singer Link was in trouble. My feelings were correct. I left Singer Link in June of 1987 and in October 1987 they were taken over in a leveraged buyout.

Since the industrial espionage case in which I participated (and was suspected of, at first) has not been declassified yet, I can not tell you about it but am planning to write a fictional version of it. I don't know why it has not been cleared, since the technology has been long surpassed, but it may be because of the individuals or the processes involved.

"A buck in books is worth a thousand in stupid."
Kim Kolakowski

Alphabetical by Color

Attending Conferences and Professional Meetings

There are many benefits of belonging to a professional association. Remind your managers they want everyone to improve their skills and gain new skills. By belonging to an association, you have access to the innovative knowledge of your profession.

Every year before I go to the annual Special Libraries Association convention, I determine what I wanted to focus on. When I was with Bendix and wanted to bring in specifications and standards on CD-ROM, I focused specifically on vendors who offered that product. Another year it was periodical vendors. I would always put in my convention travel request what I was focusing on and how many vendors would be there. I would specifically relate this to my job and how it would help the company.

You can use the time saved ploy. If there are 8 vendors at the conference and you talk to each one for half an hour, that is 4 hours. If those vendors came to talk to you at work, you would never spend only a half hour with them. Most likely it would be 1 or 2 hours. Tell your manager, instead of 1 or 2 days meeting with 8 vendors, you could spend half a day talking, getting a demonstration of their product or service, and gathering information. Then you would decide which ones to bring in house for a further meeting.

When meeting with any vendor, decide on 2 or 3 specific problems you want to discuss. Work out specific 'what if' questions to gather information. For example, does the machine use a special ink cartridge or paper or can it use any easily found cartridge or paper. Ask questions more than once to avoid canned replies. Take notes, you will forget less if you write it down. Visit early or late in the day because there are usually less people mobbing the vendors. Have any detailed literature mailed to you.

Other ways you may attain support from your company to attend conventions are:
- Inform your boss of specific sessions related to the company's current concerns and issues.

- Become a speaker or present a paper because many companies will pay if you are participating.
- Become active in the local chapter and show your boss the benefits of professional activities. Some companies will pay for your expenses.
- Write a report highlighting things you learned and how they relate to the company or industry.
- Give other libraries and librarians credit when they help to show how your participation pays in specific benefits. "The librarian I got this information from I met two years ago at SLA."
- Plan a working meeting if other librarians from your company are attending. Make sure everyone tells their manager about it. (I often draft up a report about what was discussed and share it with everyone who attended and my manager.)
- This is part of your professional development and is cost effective training to keep your organization competitive.
- It is a way to learn new ideas and apply them quickly for improved productivity.
- It is a way to investigate new sources and ways of packaging information provided to upper management.
- You might learn a new tool or technique which will more than pay for your attendance.

As part of negotiating for a new job, I always insist the company pay for my membership in professional societies and pay all expenses for a minimum of one conference a year.

One year when SLA was having their convention in New York City, I paid for a day pass and took the 2 Bendix library clerks for a walk through the vendor's booths. They were stunned, to say the least. They had never imagined there could be so many vendors of library products. I made sure to introduce them to the vendor representatives of the products we used and got them plenty of free handouts. They talked about the visit for weeks. Which was my idea, to spread the word about librarianship. I wanted to get my manager to the show but he begged off. Too bad.

Here are some write-ups I have used to justify my request to attend conferences. Go ahead, use them yourself.

Memorandum
Allied-Signal Aerospace Company
Bendix Guidance & Control Systems
To: M. McD
From: D. Carpenter
Subject: Special Libraries Association Annual Conference Special Libraries Association (SLA) holds its annual conference in early June. There are over 5000 attendees and over 400 exhibitors and vendors from around the world. The conference starts with a week-end of professional development programs. Some offered this year are:
- On You're Own But Not Alone: Management for the One Person Library
- The Library as Overhead: Cost Analysis, Cost Recovery Strategies and Charging Back
- Positioning for Success: Focusing on Your Customers and Your Future
- Librarians: Internet Information Professionals
- Patent Searching for Science & Technology
- Career Management for Information Professionals

The conference kicks off on Monday morning at 7 am with division business meetings. The day continues with information sessions, round table discussions, and presentations by experts in various fields. The exhibit hall opens at 10:30 and is open till 5:30, about the same time the sessions end. From 7 till 11 pm, divisions hold meetings or open houses for networking purposes. Tours to local libraries, businesses, and other places of interest to librarians take place on Thursday and Friday, as well as second offerings of the development courses.

Our AlliedSignal TQ team on Libraries and Information Resources has a meeting tentatively planned for June 14th, since many team members will be attending SLA. The working session will be to discuss common problems and share information about vendors and services. This is the only opportunity for us to meet in a group.

COMSTOW USER'S GROUP MEETING: I am the data base administrator for the Library software used plant wide. When the Vax's become accessible to all users, anyone will be able to search the Library's holdings. The User's Group meeting would be less expensive than having Comstow send trainers to this location for two days. No one else here has this function or this training. (Keep my skills sharp or pay for it in increased downtime when there is a massive increase in Bibliotech usage.)

Allied-Signal wants everyone to go thru quality training. This course, "The Quality Imperative: An Introduction to Total Quality Management for Information Professionals" will provide a multi-industry look at quality, providing a focus for meeting the challenges of applying a quality improvement program.

I could ask each of the over 300 vendors/exhibitors to come to Bendix and display and explain their latest products and services. I assume this would take more than the four working days the conference takes. I can see new products demonstrated; compare suppliers; research new vendors; discover what new free services are being offered; collect product samples; solve supplier and supplier problems; meet with management personnel instead of just the customer reps.

One of the most fulfilling, satisfying, and helpful feed backs from SLA is meeting other librarians from the aerospace industry as well as other industries. When I am unsure or stuck on where something can be found when someone in house wants it, I reach for my stack of SLA business cards and call someone who can help me or who might know where I should go. How many times do you do this?

Here is one email for SLA 2007 sent to my manager Tim. Notice how every course I mentioned is relevant to the company and my job in it. Do the same.

    Special Libraries Association Conference
    June 1 – 7, 2007 Denver, Colorado

    Tim,
    I would like to attend the SLA Conference in Denver to:
        Present a course entitled "Selecting Document/Records Management Software"
        Attend informative seminars and workshops
        Listen to leading information experts
        Meet with vendors to assess how their products may meet TMC's information needs
        Network and exchange ideas with my peers

Alphabetical by Color

> These are some of the courses and workshops relevant to TMC:
> Pharmaco-Vigilance: Online Resources and Strategies for Monitoring Adverse Events
> Mapping Networks and Knowledge Flows
> Knowledge Management: Best Practices from the Field
> Increasing Access to Information
> Elusive US. Private Company Information: Sources and Search Secrets Revealed
> SLA Tech Zone: So What's the Buzz About SharePoint?
> SLA Tech Zone: Creating Product Demonstrations with Adobe Captivate
> SLA Tech Zone: Best Practices – Top 10 Essentials of a Successful Web Site
>
> As of February 2007, there were over 215 companies signed up to exhibit and demonstrate products and services at SLA. This is a great opportunity to research products of use to TMC such as online databases, document delivery services, and software before having the vendors come on-site.
>
> Please let me know if you need more information. The conference website is http://www.sla.org/content/Events/conference/ac2007/index.cfm.
> Dale

I sent this email to other librarians to help them get approval to attend.

> When putting in a trip authorization to attend the Special Libraries Association Convention, this is what I write for the purpose of visit. Since this exact wording has worked for the past three years, I am sharing it with you so you can gain the benefits of attending the SLA Conference, or any other convention you decide to go to.
>
> "To learn and discuss new ideas and techniques in productivity, quality, competitor intelligence, maximizing customer satisfaction, and information gathering; to attend the business meetings of the Aerospace Librarians, Science-Technology, and Library Management Divisions to which I belong; to view over 400 exhibitors and vendor's products and services; to meet with other AlliedSignal Librarians."
>
> Just modify this using the conference brochure and your interest in

the conference. For example, change the number of exhibitors and vendors, change the names of the meetings to something specifically related to your location and its business, but keep all those buzzwords.

Of course, I'm not sharing this with anyone at this location because I don't want it to show up on everyone's trip request, especially anyone who reports to the same people I do. I'd advise you to do the same. Good Luck.

When the conference was held in Cincinnati Ohio, there was a dance being given on a riverboat. A number of us librarians jumped into a cab to go to the event. The cab driver asked what we were in town for. And when we told him, he said "You librarians are the rowdyish partiers I've ever seen in this town."

Just to make sure you don't think I only do boring things at librarian conventions, such as discuss the pros and cons of Dewey vs the Library of Congress cataloging systems, here are some postcards I sent back to friends at Bendix from an SLA conference in Denver.

(This title was on the 4 postcards.)
A story on postcards numbered 18, 19, 20, & 21 sent from Denver to folks (Keith, Shel, Pat, Dean) back east. continued from postcards 1 thru 17 and continued postcards 22 thru 37.

> Previous postcard sent to Kim K. in Vermont
> THE HUNGARIAN FLAMINGO DANCER YELLS, "FREE LITHUANIA" AND SLUGS THE REDNECK. ONE OF THE REDNECK'S FRIENDS YELLS "YO MAMA" AND CRASHES A BOTTLE OVER THE DANCER'S HEAD. SOMEONE THROWS A CHAIR AND THE BAR BREAKS OUT INTO A FREE-FOR-ALL. I GRAB THE REDHEAD AND THE BLONDE AND HEAD FOR THE DOOR. A SHOT RINGS OUT. A DOOR SLAMS.
> Next Postcard sent to Shel F.
>
> Previous postcard sent to Keith D.
> A PIRATE SHIP APPEARS ON THE HORIZON. THE BAND BREAKS INTO THE THEME FROM 'RAWHIDE'. A GRINGO STEPS IN FRONT OF ME WITH A KNIFE. I GRAB FOR A

Alphabetical by Color

SELTZER BOTTLE AND START SPRITZING HIM. THE BLONDE TOSSES A SHOT GLASS THAT BOUNCES OFF HIS HEAD AND THE REDHEAD KICKS HIM IN....
Next postcard sent to Pat C.

Previous postcard sent to Shel F.
...HIS FAMILY JEWELS. WE DODGE AROUND HIS FALLEN BODY AND OUT THE DOOR. WE RUN TO OUR CAR AND SEE THE TIRES HAVE BEEN SLASHED. THE REDHEAD YELLS "GRAB THE HORSES". WE GRAB REINS AND JUMP INTO THE SADDLES JUST AS THE HUNGARIAN FLAMINGO DANCER'S BODY CRASHES THRU THE FRONT WINDOWS.
Next postcard sent to Dean A.

Previous postcard sent to Pat C.
THE BLONDE PULLS A CARBINE FROM THE SADDLE SCABBARD AND STARTS PUMPING SHOTS INTO THE AIR. A COWBOY COMES FLYING OUT THE FRONT DOOR AND CRASHES INTO THE DANCER WHO IS JUST GETTING UP. THEY START PUNCHING EACH OTHER. I HEAR SIRENS IN THE DISTANCE. "LETS GO!", I YELL, JUST AS....
Next postcard sent to Diane K.

More humor can be found in "Email From the Librarian" at www.Lulu.com.

This is an article I wrote for the Special Library Association (SLA) New Jersey chapter newsletter.

Hints and Tips for Attending SLA Annual Conventions

I have attended SLA Annual Conventions for some years and would like to share some ideas I use to prepare for SLA.

The SLA convention happens every year in early June. Prepare your manager and your co-workers by starting to refer to it in conversations in January. "You think you might go on the cruise in April? Fine. Then that won't interfere with my being at the SLA convention in June." "Remember, boss, I'm planning to attend the SLA conference in June so let's plan to finish up the budget by the end of May. Then we can start on our relocation plans after I return." By doing this you prepare them that first; you are planning to attend a

Alphabetical by Color

conference and will be asking for the time and money to do so and second; you will be out for a week and they will have to exist without your brilliant management style.

I prepare a day/hour chart for attending which helps me to map out functions I wish to attend and shows me when and where my free time is. My chart is a piece of 8 1/2 by 11-inch paper divided into 7 columns vertically and 10 columns horizontally. The 7 columns are named for the days of the week and the 10 columns are numbered hourly, starting at 7 am. The reverse side of the chart is drawn the same but starts at 5 pm since the first side ends at 4 pm. After I receive my preliminary brochure I write when the courses and lectures are taking place. I don't worry about conflicting courses because there will be changes.

I also decide what I will be wearing the week of the conference. I know how many days I will be there, how many functions I will attend and I plan what I need. The local weather forecast I check right before I pack because that might change what I bring. Usually the local chapter will publish something in all the divisional newsletters telling what to expect weather wise, as well as touristy tips.

For Pittsburgh I decided I could exist with 2 suits, a blazer, 7 dress shirts and 2 pairs of dress shoes. I chart out what and when to wear and it comes out looking like this:

day	activity	suit	shirt	shoes
Sun.	class	blue	blue	first pair
Sun.	river cruise	blazer	white	boat shoes
Mon.	lectures	gray	white	second pair
Tues.	lectures	blue	blue	first pair
Wed.	banquet	gray	white	second pair
Thur.	class	blue	white	first pair

Before the conference I check my travel kit supplies. I use the half size containers of shampoo, toothpaste, etc. to save space. I carry two pairs of dress shoes because I like to alternate them but I could get by using one pair. I would never go anywhere without a pair of comfortable shoes for walking. Of course, I take clothes for traveling, relaxing, wandering around the city, and exercising.

No matter how I pack clothes they always end up wrinkled. After arriving at the hotel, I unpack, hang everything up and let them air out. Bringing clothes into the bathroom while you take a shower will aid in smoothing out wrinkles.

About a month before SLA, I pull out my collection of business cards. I start contacting people who may also be attending and who I would like to see. I ask if they will be at SLA and if we could meet at some time. Since the conference is so hectic, planning these meetings makes sure I have time to meet and talk with friends.

About a week before I leave, I start throwing things in a pile. A pad of paper and pens and pencils for taking notes; mailing envelopes to mail back the pounds and pounds of vendor information I always pick up; camera and film; aspirin; sunglasses; sneakers; and especially business cards from previous years. When I meet someone, I try to jot down something on their card to help me remember them. It may be about their appearance, where we met, or some subject we talked about. During the week before I leave for the conference, or on the plane traveling there, or in my hotel room, I scan cards and try to remember the person. Doing this aids my memory.

While filling out a vendor's forms to win a prize (don't we all do that?), I was commenting I never seem to have enough business cards. The vendor said one person brought return address labels and used them on the entry forms. Another person brought along a little stamp with the library's address on it. Great ideas! Next year I'll bring along the "Return to the Library" stickers the library uses on its periodicals. That way I only need to add my name to the entry forms and I'll have plenty of business cards to hand out.

I like to get into the convention city a day or two before the activities start. I spend the afternoon and evening checking into the hotel, getting registered at SLA, and strolling about the city to get a sense of direction and a feel of what the city is like. I also tip the bellhop quite generously (it goes on the company expense report) and ask about good restaurants where the locals go to eat. By doing this I get an idea of where the tourist traps are and what to avoid and what to see. You could also call or write the local chapter ahead of time to inquire about things you are interested in. As soon as you get the preliminary brochure, start asking around to see if anyone has been there. I also check local libraries to see if there are any traveler's guides to the city.

Late the first evening, after walking around town and eating supper, I relax in the hotel, the radio tuned to a local station. I compare the final conference brochure with the preliminary one to see what changes have been made. I put a mark by each class or session I wish to attend and look at the map of the conference center to see how everything is laid out. I dog ear the map page, and the page on which my first session is listed. Then go to bed to get a restful sleep-in order to face the excitement of an SLA convention.

I have noticed more people using luggage carts to carry around materials at SLA. Not a bad idea, especially when you load yourself up with vendor literature. I plan several sections of time in which to view the exhibits. At first, I just walk thru and get a sense of where everything is. The next time I start at one side and wander up and down the aisles, stopping at any vendor with which I deal or am interested in. I selectively take material, only if someone I know is interested in that vendor's products. This way, I don't load myself down with tons of paper and get "vendor overload." The next time I just continue from where I left off in the aisles. When I do my vendor shopping is about the only time, I carry the bag I receive at registration. I find my backpack is more convenient to carry items. And I certainly prefer not to be known as a tourist while walking around the city.

When SLA is being held in your city or in a city near you, please bring the non-SLA members of your staff to the convention for a day. The experience of seeing vendor displays and the activities of SLA will give them an idea of the variety of our profession. Also they might understand a bit better when you come back exhausted and full of ideas.

I used to take classes on Saturday, Sunday and Thursday and try to be back to work on Friday. Not anymore. I realize I'm missing a great chance to view a city I might not return to for several years. Now I stay over Thursday and perhaps Friday night to see more of the city and its lifestyle. Even if I must personally pay for the room and board, it is worth it.

I hope you found this collection of suggestions helpful and it aids you in some small way. See you at the next convention.

In 1994 I was at the Special Library Association Convention. I had just finished a workout in the hotel gym and stopped in the hallway to drink from the water fountain. The water fountain was next to an exterior door which led out to the pool area. After taking a drink I looked outside and saw there were several female librarians sunning themselves by the pool. I bent down to take another drink as two hotel bell hops came in through the exterior door. One of them said to the other "They sure don't look like I thought librarians would."

Why do we always see the images of librarians presented as either Elvira Gulch from "The Wizard of Oz", or Aunt Bee from Mayberry, or some nerdy looking computer operator? Why have we never seen a 'Librarians of the USA' spread in Playboy? I have never heard of or seen a calendar of sexy librarians.

SLA needs caucuses and sessions on improving our librarian images. These should include such things as personal presentation (fashion sense, makeup, colors, etc.), public speaking, hosting meetings, and travel tips. How about a course on "How Not to Be a Librarian: Improve Your Personal Self-Image and Improve Your Professional Image".

Don't wait for your professional association to put forward any sessions on improving your personal or professional image. You need to do this yourself. One of the first things I did early in my career was to spend money on very good work clothes. I went to a tailor recommended by someone who I knew dressed well. It was expensive to have suits custom tailored but they fit far better and lasted much longer than anything I could have bought off the rack.

And no matter where I have worked, I have always worn dress clothes and a tie EVERY day to package myself to appear as a KNOWLEDGEABLE PROFESSIONAL LIBRARIAN.

I was in a meeting once at Bendix and an engineer asked "Dale, why do you always dress so well and wear a tie?" My reply was "I don't want to be mistaken for an engineer." Since most of the attendees were engineers, this raised a great cry. I explained by saying "Guys, I work with you. I also work with upper-level management like Zomick and Fairchild and Kraus and Hughes. I could get called to go into a meeting and be asked do some competitive intelligence or marketing research and find some people from Morristown (where our headquarters was) there. I want everyone to see I'm a professional and serious about my work. I dress like the management people to project that professional image."

One of the engineers walked into the Bendix library one day wearing sneakers, blue jeans, a dress shirt, and a tie. "A tie?" I asked. "Yea, I've got a meeting today with a vendor." I wonder what the vendor thought of his outfit. Half-dressed? Half-relaxed?

Engineer Pat C. said you could tell when an engineer graduated by the style of his suit. He said after graduating an engineer bought 1 suit for job interviews and wore it for the rest of his life.

If you dress like a professional, you are more likely to ACT like a professional. I tell people "This is my superhero outfit I put on to go to work as a LIBRARIAN!"

**"Shall we go to your room and give pleasure to each other?"
Dale Carpenter, At multiple SLA Conventions**

Business Cards Are Essential

In this age why would someone carry paper business cards?

Because you surprise people when you hand them one with your contact information. It sets you apart from everyone else. People remember you. They will remember you again when they find it when they get home.

A paper business card can effortlessly carry far more information than can easily be entered into a smartphone. A paper business card never runs out of batteries and will never be accidentally deleted. Someone must make an active decision to throw it away.

You can write information on them. I take the time to write down more identifying information about the person I met on their card. (If they did not have one, I asked them to write their info on one of my cards.) For example, Barbara A's card received these notes: "shoulder length brown hair, unmarried, very attractive, drinks gin & tonic in tall glasses with lots of ice". Every year, before the SLA conference, I call Barbara and ask if she was going and if we could meet so I could buy her a gin & tonic in a tall glass with lot of ice. It makes a great impression.

Beth W's card says, "SLA '94 baseball game; 5' 8"; thin; brown hair; glasses; quiet; good sense of humor; intelligent; unmarried."

Carol S's says, "SLA '92; fun, lives in St. Jo; says Bendix plant blocks her valley view; shoulder length brown hair; no wedding ring; wears sensible shoes".

I write down where and when I met the person. If it was in a course, I write it down so I remember we have that in common. If they say they are interested in a subject, I write it down so if I see something in that subject, I might send it to them. If I am going to travel to their area, I call or email and ask for suggestions on what to do or see.

If the other person does not have a card, let them write their contact information on the back of one of yours. Then add your notes on that card.

If your company does not provide business cards, it is easy now to buy card stock and print your own. I carry both work related business cards and cards with my personal contact info on them. People often ask me about the note on my card.

> "Librarian, Author, Paratrooper,
> Hitchhiker, Fly Fisherman,
> & Other Things"

> **"You can never satisfy librarians.**
> **Whatever you give them is not enough."**
> **Herbert White,**
> **SLA Convention, Detroit, 1982**

Management: The Good, the Bad, & Especially the Ugly.

Having worked in both blue-collar and white-collar professions, I know management is very different in the two. It's different in various industries. For example, but not so much anymore, blue-collar managers tended to use more profanity compared to white-collar managers. Of course this is on a case-by-case basis.

Most people do not want to endanger their careers. Management, especially in academia and government, is very passive. If you want to get something done you have to appease all upper levels of management and make them happy before they approve your request. And it's always done with a "what's in it for me attitude". Management is highly regimented, compartmentalized and by committee. You must get approval from your department head, who must get approval from his department head, who must go to HR, and the hiring committees. A whole lot of people to appease.

Public library systems are a great deal like this. Especially if it is a civil service state. Everything must go up to the state level civil service people and everybody makes sure the decision won't reflect on them.

It is usually easier in academia, civil service, and any government position, to say 'no' to any request than to approve any changes. In those positions, I always went ahead and did something, and if anyone objected, begged forgiveness. My argument always was 'I saw this needed to be done so I did it and everything works better so what is the problem?'

Corporate management tends to move a lot faster. Usually if you need to get something done you go to your supervisor and they will say yes or no. Perhaps you may have to go to their manager and get approval but usually only up one or two levels. A lot of times I've just gone ahead and done something and if it was ever noticed, I said "Hey, I saw this needed to be done, so I did it."

Of course the occupation affects the management style. A couple of the worst managers I've had were librarians. We are sometimes control freaks. We like organization, we want things nice and tidy and in their proper place. But the librarians who move up into library management sometimes forget our primary aim and focus is customer service. And sometimes while serving the customers things get messy.

These librarians wanted everything to be done by a certain process and were not open-minded about possible changes or efficiencies. They had things working their way and they did not want to change. When I come along and say, "Excuse me, this other library did it this way and here's why I believe it would be better that way", they did not want to listen.

Other poor managers I've had have been teachers and human resource specialists. Teachers tend to be autocrats, handling their staff with the same amount of control with which they run a classroom. Human resource specialists tended not to understand what I was doing, but if they did not hear anything bad about me, they were happy.

What I just said was a direct quote from a manager who worked in HR. At a yearly evaluation Marilyn D. said "I really don't know what you're doing Dale, so it's hard for me to evaluate you. But I haven't heard anything bad and I have heard some good things. So that is how I'm going to evaluate you".

When reporting to the head of the Drug Safety department at a pharmaceutical company, I found Gary K. also wanted more of a 'how are you getting along and do you have any problems' type of a report. He was more concerned with relationships than data.

Sargent Smith said it precisely and best. While watching a second lieutenant walk away after displaying an extraordinary lack of knowledge about a situation, Sarge said "You can give them the bars but you can't teach them how to lead." This was a common trait in officers who had gone through the paths of either ROTC or OCS (Officer's Candidate School). Just because they had gone to college before entering the service and were selected for OCS, did not mean they had any leadership skills. And leadership can't be taught. You either have the knack for it or you don't.

Engineers I found to be decent managers. They may not have the best people skills, but I have been able to relate by providing them evidence of what I'm doing in a numerical manner. "This past month I've done these many searches, we have processed these many invoices, fulfilled these many information requests, and so on". They understand your work if presented in this manner.

For people in finance, I present the information the same way and add the dollar figures. "I did these many searches and it cost this much". I created a form to give to people with their search results. One of the questions asked is for them to estimate the time or money it would have taken them to find the same results. This data I use in my reports.

I once reported to a vice president of information technology. I gave David M., if he requested it, more detailed information about the searches, information requests, and so on in my monthly reports.

Every new position I have taken, I make it a point to have an early meeting with my manager to ask them what they want reported, how they want it reported, and how often they wanted reports. I explain I want to make their job easier by giving them the news they want and need in the form they can best use.

At times I have given managers the same information but presented in two or three different formats so they could tell me which one was most useful to them. One way might be a very detailed list showing what tasks were performed for each department. Or I might present the numbers in a bar chart, a pie chart, and some other chart.

Marketing, Competitive Development, and Intelligence department individuals have seemed to desire detailed information on work related to their activities. All other library functions could be presented numerically.

Of course any research I did for Legal, Competitive Intelligence or Human Resources was often done confidentiality and I did not report those details. If my manager asked about it, I told them to talk to the requester. This showed my manager and the requester I could keep a secret.

Many in upper-level management support the library if they receive services directly from the library. Those finance or legal or marketing individuals to whom I provided resources and research support the library. Except when budget time came.

Most management view the library as a necessary expense. They realize they need persons to do research and provide support services and the library was the place for this. However, I never found any management who invested enough in the library. They could never see the direct result of investments in library services. About the only time I ever saw it happen was when a top-level marketing person came into the library and asked me to do some research right then. It was a rush job and very important to this person. When he saw how slow the online searching was going, he immediately found the money to upgrade all the computer equipment.

Within two weeks we received a new computer, printer, a higher speed modem, and a phone line dedicated to the computer. This was in the days of dial up access to online data bases so having a dedicated phone line meant your connection was never broken by someone calling on that line.

Employees or workers tend to think of the library in a neutral way unless they use it. If they come in and read the newspapers and magazines, they are glad to have a library. But if you don't have the exact crap they want, then they perceive you as useless. Even if you try to explain they are the only person in the company who wants that exact crap and your budget does not afford the purchase of resources for only one person.

The employees or workers who love the library will support you. But you must constantly remind them to praise the library in department meetings and with their managers. Tell them all they have to say is "Yes, the library got this for me" or "The library had just what I wanted". Remind them advertising is just repeating the same thing over and over and if they will do that for you, it allows you to keep providing the resources they need.

Alphabetical by Color

Years ago before office copiers were commonplace, if someone wanted a copy of something from the library, one of the clerks would walk it down to the Reproduction Department to get it copied. This would take a minimum of 15 minutes even if the Repro could copy it right away.

So if the clerk was making $16 an hour, that was $4.00 spent to get a copy of the specification. Plus what Reproduction charged us for the cost of the copy. And if the Reproduction Department was busy and it took longer than 15 minutes, there's an added cost. And you can't forget the work the clerk could have been doing in those 15 minutes.

When I received permission to bring a copier into the library on a two-month trial basis at no cost, I kept a very accurate count of everyone who asked to use the copier, what departments they were in, what they copied and the number of copies made. At the end of our trial period, I multiplied the number of copies by our clerk's hourly salary to show time and money saved. In my report to management, this was the first and most important item shown. Having a copier in the library saved the company time and money.

Nobody really knows what you want until you tell them. You need to figure out how to tell them in such a way they realize it is something they also need, want, and can use.

If you don't ask, the answer is ALWAYS no.

Successful persuasion depends on you presenting your request in these 5 ways.

1. Believe in its value. Say "This is a good idea." Don't say "I think this is a good idea."

2. Anticipate arguments and defuse them before anyone brings them up. If you predict they will argue money, say "Yes, initial costs are high but payoff is quick." or some other way to defuse that argument.

3. Add power to your points by numbering them. "First, payoff of initial costs, Second, after that time period, only x will cost us, then Third..."

4. Focus on their needs and tell them in their language. "The system

will give all departments faster access to the specifications and standards they need to do their job. It will totally eliminate the time needed to take our Library copy down to Repro and make a copy for you."

5. Involve them in the discussion. "Now which would you rather do? Print the spec or standard off right now or sit and wait while Diane walks the spec or standard down to Repro to have a copy made?"

No manager will ever admit to being a bad manager. I have never heard of a course to train someone how to be a manager. Most people are just promoted into the position. They may have been an excellent employee, but without the native ability to manage people, they have reached their level of incompetence.

One of the best things a company ever did was when Allied-Signal, as part of a Total Quality initiative, gave the employees classes on how to run a meeting. I have attended many meetings which were a waste of time because the agenda was not kept to, or side conversations or personal complaining went on. Or the person or persons who had the decision-making authority was not there. Every company, if they want to prosper, should train all their employees on how to run a meeting. And empower every employee with the right to say "This meeting is off track. Either we move it back to the focus of the meeting or we end the meeting."

If you really have to hold a meeting, here is how to make it time efficient:
 1. Hold it right before lunch or at the end of the day.
 2. Circulate a written agenda in advance to everyone.
 3. Communicate your clear and achievable objective for the meeting.
 4. Don't serve refreshments. Not even coffee.

If you have to attend a meeting:
 1. Figure out in advance what information you have to contribute and prepare a presentation to give it using the minimum time.
 2. Have an exit strategy to get you out of the meeting. Have someone come to get you for another meeting, or a prearranged call on your cell-phone. Excuse yourself to take the call and don't go back.

Most managers, and especially upper-level managers, are unaware of, or do not understand, or don't care what the scientific and technical manufacturing groups do to get a product out the door. And most of them are also unaware of or not knowledgeable of the logistics involved. "I just give it to X and they take care of it." is their depth of knowledge. I have always tried to educate everyone involved in the library materials purchasing process. Often I have drawn flowcharts showing every step it takes to bring something into the library and pointed out they are involved in only 1 or 2 steps in that process. Sometimes it wakes them up and they endeavor to help simplify or speed up the process.

Organizational Chart

You should always obtain a company organizational chart. Ask the secretaries how you can obtain one. I said I needed it so the library could efficiently route periodicals, information requests, and purchase orders. I told them I didn't want to waste their time with phone calls to find out to whom I should send something.

Once I get an org chart, I make a copy which I call a "Who's What" chart. I mark my direct supervisors in green. For example, I report to Ed who runs Drafting, who reports to the head of Engineering, who reports to the head of Operations, who reports to the President at our location. All these people I need to keep happy. Using our phone list which shows names, phone numbers and department numbers, I write down who reports directly to of the heads of Engineering, Operations, and the President. I find them by checking department numbers. If the head of Engineering is 2706, for example, anyone in department 2706 gets added to a "be nice to these folks" list. Because they can say good or bad things directly to one of my supervisors.

Then I look for other departments in the company which have great influence, impact, or power such as Competitive Intelligence, Marketing, Finance, Human Resources, etc. If they report directly to the President at our location or have a major say in what our company does, they get marked in yellow or orange. Then I list all the people in their departments and try to think up ways in which I can market myself and the library's services to them. If I help them, I gain support for the library.

I also mark the other very important departments. Maintenance, Security, Shipping & Receiving, Cleaning, Reproduction, etc. These people can make your life easy or hard. Be very nice to them.

You can also use it to build an affinity chart. By this I mean a chart showing who talks to who across department lines. You need to find out who does what for who, who knows who, and who has power and influence. If you see several secretaries lunch together on a regular basis, write those names down because there is a power clique.

> **"Part of my problem is ignorance."**
> **Kathleen Trimble,**
> **SLA Convention, Denver, 1988**

Industries and Working in Them

I've worked in academic libraries, private and public libraries, non-profit libraries, government libraries, and corporate libraries. I worked for aerospace, defense, telecommunications, career transition or as it used to be known 'outplacement', and the pharmaceutical industries.

I found aerospace and defense very fascinating because I was interested in those industries and what the companies were doing. One company, Singer Link, made aircraft and helicopter simulators. I got to try to fly one. I crashed more often then flew. One other company, Bendix, made guidance and navigational equipment for all types of products. They made the guidance gyroscopes for the Hubble Space Telescope. People in these industries seemed, in general, to have outgoing and vocal personalities.

AT&T and Lucent, in telecommunications, was interesting because I learned a lot about the technical side of telecommunications. However, I found a great many people were personality wise, dull. They didn't seem to be enjoying life as much as the people who worked in the aerospace and defense industries. A lot I met were introspective and quiet, at least at work.

The career transition industry is a difficult one because of the emotional upheaval individuals are going through after having lost a job and while searching for one. You had to be very supportive while supplying help but you could not let yourself get emotionally involved with them. The offices used a lot of tissues. The upside of this industry was the joy and relief when someone got a job. Often individuals we helped would contact us to mention their new company was hiring or looking for specific skills.

The pharmaceutical industry was interesting because I learned a lot about pharmaceuticals, the drug development process, and the science behind it. But like the telecommunication industry, there seem to be some dull personalities working there. The sales and marketing people, like those in all other sales and marketing positions, were friendly and outgoing. A lot of people on the research side were rather low-key.

Alphabetical by Color

I went to Merck Pharmaceuticals once for a job interview. The phone interviews had gone well and I was looking forward to visiting the company. I was greeted by a Human Resources person and after filing out a few forms, was escorted up to the area for the interview. While waiting, I read several memos on their bulletin board. Oh boy. One memo reminded everyone ONLY steel push pins were to be used. NO color pins were allowed. Another memo reminded employees that ONLY photographs of family could be displayed in their cubicles.

I decided at once Merck was to up tight for me to work for them. If their management was focused on such petty issues as colored push pins and photographs in cubicles, they had to be controlling assholes and I didn't want anything to do with them.

The interview went well and the manager and I got along well. But at the end of it, I walked the manager over to the bulletin board and told him this was the reason I was not going to accept the job. "I want and need a happy, relaxed work atmosphere where the job gets done and people enjoy coming to work. At other companies I've worked at, people display in their cubicles products they have worked on to show pride in what they do. If Merck management is worried colored push pins will hurt their market share, you have idiots as management."

Back with the Human Resource person, she asked if I had any questions. I asked what percent of the employees dressed up in costume for Halloween. She looked at me like I had just grown another head. "I don't think anyone dresses up for Halloween." she said in a confused manner.

The manager who interviewed me called me the next week to try and talk me into accepting the job. I politely declined again.

I have noticed in certain industries the noise level is different. In construction, aerospace, and some others, it was not uncommon to hear laughter coming from work spaces and offices. In telecommunications and pharmaceutical companies, at least the ones I worked at, I rarely heard loud conversations and laughter. Sometimes raised in arguments or discussions but rarely in laughter.

In the aerospace and defense industries, individuals showed pride that their work was defending and protecting our country. In pharmaceutical, individuals knew they were helping to improve the healthcare the public received. I did not sense any "we are improving the world" feelings in other industries.

Most industries will push the spending decisions down to a division or department level. Their management realizes people at that level know best what is needed to do the job. Academia and government keep financial spending approval at a very high level. Right now I am waiting for approval for our periodical renewals and my professional membership dues. They are not approved by the group I report to. They are approved by an entirely separate department in another branch of state government. What the heck do these people know about the library's needs?

I believe working in multiple jobs and in multiple industries has made me a better librarian than if I had stayed in one industry. Most workers, once they settle into a position, tend to focus on specific, detailed work. Because I moved and worked in different industries, I had to learn the different processes, tools and patterns of work found in those jobs. This made me a generalist, someone not only more adaptable to a new workplace and new ways of doing things, but able to easily move from one assignment to another.

Those who are engaged in one task develop a great ability in that one task but may lose the general facility of applying their mind to the improvement of the task. If your management always tells you to do your work one way, how can you ever improve it? If you are never exposed or shown multiple ways of doing something, how can you determine the most effective or efficient?

"We're leaving the bus tour and going to drink margaritas."
The Back of the Bus Librarians,
SLA Convention, 1991, San Antonio

Solo Librarian Versus a Library Network.

Most corporate libraries I have worked in have been standalone libraries. That is a library which existed in and supported one group or division specializing in one area. The first library at Singer Link only supported the Special Projects group which did modifications on existing simulators. The Bendix Library supported the 3 aerospace divisions in Teterboro and did little for the automotive or engineered materials sectors of AlliedSignal. The library at The Medicines Company supported a pharmaceutical company. The libraries at Manchester and Right International supported those career transition offices in Northern New Jersey and the metropolitan area of New York City.

In a standalone library I do everything. From greeting people when they walk in, answering information requests, doing online searching, database management, ordering books, newspapers, and periodicals, cataloging and indexing, shelving items and shelf reading, cleaning, weeding materials, staff training and supervision, creating and presenting informational sessions, everything and anything which needs to be done in the library. Including watering the plants.

When I worked in a large library for Lucent Technologies I was pigeon-holed. I only did online research or answered reference questions. My manager Betty K, a librarian who had gone into management, did not want me to even greet customers coming in and asking for help. Betty thought they should go to the main desk and ask for help. However, she had me sit at a desk in the middle of the library. So people would come over and ask me for help. I was the first person they saw when they walked in so of course they walked over to me. What was I supposed to do, ignore them? Why not let me sit in my office? Then when I said, 'Could you go to the main desk, please?' they thought I was rude.

Also I was doing research in online databases, which charge access by the second. Every time I got interrupted, it cost money. But when I mentioned this to her, her reply was she wanted me to be seen by entering customers. No thought of how they interrupted my work or the extra cost to the search.

It probably is part of my personality and skill set, but I have always been more of a generalist instead of a specialist. I have the knowledge, skills, and ability to do all the tasks in a library. I know there are other librarians who are the happiest when doing only one or a few tasks. That is their personality. My advice is to know yourself and know what you like to do. Focus upon finding the position and the tasks which will make and keep you happy.

**"I'm not comfortable being preachy,
but more people need to start spending as much time in the library
as they do on the basketball court."
Kareem Abdul-Jabbar**

Bendix and Allied-Signal Aerospace 1987 to 1996

In early 1987 I saw an advertisement from another aerospace/defense company called Bendix in Teterboro, New Jersey. Bendix has an interesting history. Vincent Hugo Bendix was interested in automobiles and invented an electrical self-starter for cars. After Charles Lindbergh flew across the Atlantic, sparking a great interest in aviation, Bendix started developing products for aircraft. During the Second World War at the Teterboro plant, they had over 25,000 people working in three shifts around the clock to produce products. When I joined them, the 3 divisions, Flight, Guidance, and Test, had between 12,000 and 15,000 people.

The Guidance & Control Systems Division designed and built guidance and navigation equipment and systems for aircraft, missiles, spacecraft, and satellites. Their guidance systems had been on every spaceflight from the Gemini, Mercury, and Apollo missions up to the Space Shuttle and the Hubble Space Telescope.

The Guidance Division had a very large engineering library and was looking for a library manager. I applied and was hired. I reported to Ed S, who was the head of the drafting department. Ed had started out as a draftsman, back when draftsman worked on drafting boards and worked his way up to department manager. He still wasn't sure using computers and drafting software was a good idea. He kept a drafting board in his office. He was old school management, but as an engineer I could relate to him and report to him in terms he accepted and understood concerning the library.

Ed's perception of me changed greatly one day when I asked him about the drawing on his drafting board. When he looked at me curiously, I explained I had taken architectural and mechanical drafting courses in high school, made money drawing lot plans so neighbors could get building permits, and also used those skills when working construction. He then realized I came from a working background, like him.

The library consisted of technical books on mechanical and electrical engineering, aircraft, avionics, guidance systems, and related subjects. It had a collection of technical magazines going back decades and a very large paper collection of military specifications and standards on all subjects. I immediately got busy making myself acquainted with all aspects of the library.

One of the first changes I made was changing our name from "The Engineering Library" to "The Bendix Library". When Diane K, one of the clerks who had been there for years asked why I was doing this, I asked if we only provided services to the Engineering Group. She said, "Of course not, we serve the entire company". "So why not reflect that in our name?", was my question.

Bendix had been owned since 1983 by AlliedSignal, whose headquarters was in Morristown, New Jersey. They had a library, library staff, and online database researchers at their headquarters.

Periodical Subscription Process Changes

Soon after I started working for Bendix Guidance Systems, I found out all periodical and newspaper ordering was done by individual department secretaries. Seeing a chance to increase the power of the library, bring cost savings to the company which would make me look good, and increase the efficiency of the process, I resolved to bring it all into my department. Every day for 3 months I went down to the mail room and wrote down the title of every periodical and newspaper, the person and department it was addressed to, and the publisher's name. Every day for 3 months. My staff and the mail room people thought I was crazy and they told me so.

I put the information into Excel spreadsheets and wrote letters to the publishers requesting a list of every periodical they were mailing to our address. I explained I was the new corporate librarian and I wanted to help them by consolidating the ordering, shipping, invoicing, and payment process. I then made phone calls to follow up on the letters, making personal contacts and answering any questions they had.

After I received information from all the publishers, I created a complete list of periodicals and newspapers coming to our site. I sorted the information by department. During one of our monthly meetings, I asked my manager Ed S. and the Department Secretary Rose, how many periodicals the Drafting Department was receiving. The conversation went something like this.

Ed and Rose looked puzzled. Rose said "About 10 or 12, I think."
"You are getting 14. Here is a list of them and who receives them."
"Where did you get this?"
"I walked down to the mail room everyday for 3 months and wrote down the information on every magazine coming into the plant."
"Why?"
"Because I want to save you money, time and work. You get 8 Aviation Week & Space Technology (AW&ST) every week. Every year you have to handle 8 renewal notices and invoices. I can have AW&ST put all those invoices together so you will only handle 1 piece of paper. Wouldn't that be a lot easier?"
"Sure would." Said Rose.
"And you will save money."
"Eh? How?"
"How much does it cost to order a periodical? Any guess?" They looked bewildered.
"Between $225 and $250 for each periodical."
"How do you know?" (The step by step flowchart is detailed in the next chapter so I'll just skim through it here.)
"Someone puts in a request for a subscription, Rose makes sure it is correct, you approve it, Rose walks it over to Accounting, who makes up a purchase order and cuts a check, they send it back to Rose, who mails it out to the publisher. I called up Payroll, explained what I was doing and why and asked them for an hourly salary figure in the mid-range of everyone who handles the paperwork. I figured out what they make per minute. So if you took 3 minutes to decide to sign a request, that is 3 minutes of your salary. If you take 5 minutes, that is 5 minutes. I estimate how long it takes Rose to review the paperwork, walk it over to Accounting, and how long it will take her to prepare to mail the PO and check off to the publisher. So total up all those people's minutes times what they make a minute, and the low end is $225 and the high end is $250." (I put in front of them the flowchart of the periodical process so they could see how it worked.)
They looked at it for a minute.
"So now to order those 8 AW&ST it costs somewhere between $1800 and $2000. But if we put all those subscriptions on one invoice, it will only cost $225 to $250 and save both of you money and time."

Alphabetical by Color

"Are you sure you can do this?" Ed looked doubtful.

"Ed, the publisher would be happy to do this because it will save him work too. He only has to track 1 invoice a year instead of 8."

"It will be a lot of work. Are you sure you can handle this?"

"The hardest part, gathering what periodicals are coming to the plant, is already done. I've also called each publisher I could find and got from them lists of what they mail to this address. All the data gathering is finished. Now all we have to do is convince David Z (VP of Engineering, who Ed reports to), John R (VP of Finance), and David T (President at that location). And Ed, you see how this will save you and Rose money, (I ticked each off on my fingers), time and work. It will do the same for every department in the plant."

"You want to do this for the whole plant?"

I pulled out some department periodical listings and the employee phone book and pointed out several periodicals were being mailed to individuals who were no longer with the company. Someone had obtained a subscription, then either left or retired, and no one ever stopped the magazine from coming in. I said this would never happen again.

"Let me think about this a while." (That was Ed. Never one to jump to a decision.)

About 2 weeks later Ed, and I met with David Z, John R, and David T. I gave them the information on periodical subscriptions and explained what I wanted to do. After a long discussion they agreed. They also agreed all periodical purchases had to go through the library. The big selling point was the money, time and work savings. You can see why upper management quickly approved the process. Another big selling point was the time saved by looking at only one invoice for all periodicals received in one department. All the secretaries loved me for this.

John R., the VP of Finance of course focused on the extra cost the periodical jobber would charge us. I stood up, pulled 8 sheets of paper from my briefcase and put them in front of him. Each sheet had "Drafting Department Aviation Week & Space Technology purchase order" on it in large type. I pulled another sheet out and put that to the side. It had "8 copies of Aviation Week & Space Technology for Drafting Dept. purchase order" on it.

"John" I said. "These are your options. You and your staff can read, proof and sign each of these 8 purchase orders or you and your staff can read, proof and sign this 1 purchase order. Don't think about money, think about the time and work. That is what we can do, cut out a lot of unnecessary time and work for everyone." That graphic example made up his mind.

This is an example of how a decades old process was changed in several months after I gathered information and presented it to management. Such a change could never have been done in the academic or government world as quickly.

Oh, I should mention I told Diane K., the Library clerk who handled the Library subscriptions, since I was bringing all this work into the Library, I was going to do it instead of her. It took almost a full year to smooth out all the problems and issues. After that, Diane took over the process.

While I was doing online database searching, I had individuals come in to say they would like an alert service set up so weekly or monthly they would be notified on developments on certain topics. These might be strategic planning, competitive intelligence, technology updates, etc. By marketing the service I increased the online search requests 30% within two years. It would have been more, but several individuals, especially in planning and marketing, wanted to do their own online searching. I helped train them and helped improve search strategies for others.

The library contained shelves packed full of paper copies of government and military specifications and standards, going back decades. If someone needed a copy, they came to the Library and asked for one. Since this was before the days of department copiers, we would send it down to our Reproduction Department and have them make a copy for the requester. Often, once they were done with the spec or standard, they would give it back to the Library. I found we had multiple copies of many very old specs and standards. I knew Ed would never agree to throwing any away. I started coming in on weekends and weeding out duplicate copies of very old specs and standards to make space on the shelves. I took the ones I was tossing out downstairs and put them in bins in the recycling room so no one would see what I was doing.

Eventually I talked Ed into bringing in a microfilm system which had all the specs and standards. When someone asked for a copy, I would just put the roll of film into the machine and print it off for them. Much faster than walking a spec or standard down to the Reproduction Department and waiting while they made a copy.

After Ed S was forced into retirement, I gained a new manager Marilyn D. She was from Human Resources (HR). I don't know why, but no one seems to know where to have the library report to in the corporate world. Engineering, Human Resources, Marketing, Finance, Information Technology (IT) and Drug Safety, all these and more are departments to which I have reported.

Marilyn could see the benefits of bringing in-house a CD-ROM based system for the specifications and standards. We brought it in for a trial, tracked the usage, and showed it would save money and time. Another factor was the Test Division, located on the far side of this very large corporate site, had brought in their own specifications and standards CD-ROM system. They had shown the time spent by walking to our library to obtain a specification or standard made it worthwhile to bring in a system for them. This allowed us to get rid of a lot of the paper copies which were not actively being used. Ed wanted us to keep a paper copy of every spec and standard, no matter how old or outdated it was.

In 1989 Guinness brought to market their draft beer in a can. It had a widget inside which released nitrogen when the can was open, giving the beer more of a draft beer taste. Several engineers in the plant wondered how this was accomplished and one of them, John M., came up to the library and asked me what I could find out. I found the patent Guinness had filed on the process and printed it out. The engineers and I met at The Front Porch, a local hangout, and while they looked over the patent, I drank my payment of several Guinness.

The library was on the second floor in a corner location. Upper management got jealous, and decided they wanted to put their nice offices there so we were kicked downstairs. We moved from our location to an area only 31% of the former library space. We were required to get rid of all the old paper copies of the periodicals, and drastically reduce our book holdings. We still could obtain articles from the periodicals online but it was a nuisance not having the originals.

Alphabetical by Color

Of course the personnel hired to move the library were not professional library movers. When they took books off the shelf, they would start from the left-hand side and put the books into the box. And when they took the books out of the box, they put them on the left-hand side. The books originally on the left now were on the right end of the shelf. And the books originally on the right-hand end were now on the left-hand end of the shelf. I had to shelf read the entire library to make sure all the books were in the correct order.

We noticed the stock quotations were missing from our copy of the Wall Street Journal. I started positioning myself so I could watch everyone who read the paper. One day I noticed an engineer ripping out the entire page. I went ballistic on him. I grabbed his badge, wrote down his name and employee number and told him I was reporting him to his supervisor and to Security and to Human Resources for damaging corporate property. I told him other employees were pissed because they came in and they couldn't see the stock prices. I told him he was an idiot and to get out of the library and not to come back for a month. Then I did just what I said I would do, reported him in writing to Human Resources, Legal, Security, and his manager.

There was not a process in place for individuals to sign out through the library when they were leaving Bendix. I would find out someone had left when I sent out an overdue notice and it was returned with a note saying the person had left. I fought with Human Resources and Security and Accounts Payable on this issue. I pointed out we were losing company property and money because the person did not go through the library before leaving. They were not concerned. Until one individual left with over $600 of library books. I told the departments this was a felony and I was contacting the sheriff in his neighborhood and swearing out a warrant for his arrest unless the books were returned. I then sent a letter by registered mail to this individual's address.

The departments did not see the point until I asked if they would act if someone stole a computer or something else of high value. Of course they would. I said this was the same thing. They are taking company property.

The individual contacted me and said he was owed money by Bendix to reimburse him for college courses. I told him all I was concerned with was the books he had taken. I told him I would swear a warrant out for his arrest unless the books were returned. He returned the books within a week and I gave him a signed receipt. After this incident, the exit procedure was changed and the library department was added to the exit form an individual had to fill out before leaving.

This process brought about some uncomfortable moments. Occasionally Human Resources (HR) would call in the afternoon and ask me to come in a little early the next day. This was because there was going to be a layoff of employees and HR wanted a list of materials those individuals had out from the library. I would come in early, HR would send me a list of individuals and I would look up their names. If anyone had anything out, I would tell HR what it was.

However, I would also find out the time the person would be notified they were being let go. At times I saw individuals in the hallway and talked to them knowing they were going to be let go later that day. It was quite uncomfortable.

I created a simple library homepage on Bendix's intranet. It listed our contact information, a list of periodicals and newspapers we received, and a few other facts about the library. I also published several newsletters promoting services such as the online database searching and the specs and standards on CD-ROM.

Remember how I talked about ghosting and wandering around to deliver information to someone can be useful? Bendix was remodeling and replacing all the wood furniture with modular components. I was wandering one day and happen to see a cart load of wood desks being taken out of the back door by the loading docks. I asked one of the maintenance men what was going to be done with them. He said they were going to be thrown away. I hustled over to the Maintenance office and asked if I could have one of the desks. Sure, here is a scrap pass so the guard will let you take it out. Thinking quickly, I asked if I could have 2? Okay, the pass was made out for 2 desks.

I walked over to my friend Dean A. I showed him the scrap pass. I said you have a pickup truck and I have a scrap pass for 2 nice wood desks. He smiled. After work, we drove his truck into the fenced in back lot, showed the guard the scrap pass and loaded 2 desks. Dean looked at the wood office chairs and said something to the effect a desk and a chair are a pair and they go together. 2 chairs then went on the truck. Dean got a desk and a chair. Mine are sitting in my office as I write this.

While the library was still up on the second floor of the building, we had wonderful views of Route 46 and the Teterboro Airport. The building was almost underneath the approach path to one of the runways so at times it looked like an airplane was heading right for the building. And since the airport was right across the street, we got a very good view of the pilots as they came in to land.

On the second floor, there were no windows into the library so no one in the hallway could see in unless the door was open. I found out early in my career it was more efficient to come into work on a Sunday than on a Saturday. More people come in to work on Saturdays and tend to waste your time talking while you are trying to get work done. Since fewer people come in on Sundays, there are less interruptions.

Since our computers were networked to our mainframes and our print jobs were sent to a central printer, I would run overdue notices on Sunday and pick them up Monday. One Sunday I was going to go to brunch with the girl I was dating and she suggested she come into work with me. We would then go directly to brunch. While in the library, she suggested the excitement, the thrill, and the danger of having sex at work.

So we did. And on several other weekends. An adventurous lady, that one.

I worked closely with the IT department and became friends with members of that department. One day, Keith D from IT told me the band he played with was playing that weekend in a bar nearby and he was inviting a lot of the Bendix people to come and listen. I decided to attend. Now I was always dressed professionally at work with a suit and tie. There were some remarks made when I showed up in casual clothes. There were plenty more remarks made when I showed my partying side and danced the night away with all the ladies. A couple weeks later, Shel F, one of the senior members in the IT department, was walking a new employee around the plant and brought him into the Library. He introduced me this way.

"This is Dale. He is the Clark Kent of librarianship."

So that is how I got that title.

Well, maybe also influencing Shel was the fact the each Halloween, I came to work in costume. One year I had come in as Fritz, the hunchbacked lab assistant from the 1931 "Frankenstein" movie. Another year in a barbarian costume with copper metal armor, a copper helmet with horns, deerskin boots with fringe, and two swords. Okay, the swords were plastic and not real. But they looked good.

The IT department had set up a few in-house private email networks. Groups of people could email each other and know these personal jokes, insults, and messages could not be read by anyone else. On one I was invited to join, I started a "what happened on this day in history" newsletter filled with jokes, lies and misinformation. You may read some on it in my book "Email From the Librarian."

> **"I don't have any trouble with my filing system.**
> **It's my retrieval system that sucks."**
> **Joe Zaleski, Bendix co-worker, 9/5/85**

This article was sent out to and published in several SLA chapter and division newsletters.

The Cost of Ordering Materials Using a Purchase Order and Check

This is how to track the process for cutting a purchase order (PO) and a check: list the number of people involved, multiply the minutes it takes each to handle the PO by their hourly salary, add it all together and you will have a fair idea of the cost.

When managing the Bendix corporate library, a major aerospace firm, I needed facts for the argument of bringing in a subscription agency to handle all periodical orders. I tracked the process by which a purchase order traveled from the originating department, through the library, through the Finance office for approval and signature, back to the library, down to Accounting to have the check cut, and back to the library where the check and purchase order was mailed out. Estimating the hourly wage for each person who handled it (a friend in Payroll helped by giving salary ranges for job titles), it turned out each purchase order cost the company between $225 and $250.

Does the company want to order every copy of Aviation Week with a separate purchase order or shall we put all the copies on one purchase order? Put in those financial terms, it is an easy decision.

Once the VP of Finance saw what it cost to order each periodical, he helped me implement a corporate procedure requiring all periodicals be ordered through the library. As part of the subscription agency's contract, I required them to provide separate invoices for each department, as we charged back the cost of the periodicals to each department. The next year I gave the invoices to the department managers for their approval. This showed them exactly how much their department spent and they could adjust the number of periodicals to relate to their headcount. Instead of 14 copies of Aviation Week & Space Technology for 30 people, they could order 10, for example. The managers were very happy to have precise numbers for their budgets and I gained valuable support for the library.

The Ordering Process at Bendix Guidance & Control Systems

1. Employee brings in a Library Material Request Form, filled out and signed by their supervisor or manager.
2. Library staff determines if we have enough information to order item. If not, we search for the item, going back to requester if we must.
3. Library Clerk types out Purchase Order (PO) with ordering information. Library Manager signs PO.
4. Library Clerk takes PO to Engineering Finance Manager for his signature.
5. Eng. Finance Manager signs PO and returns it to Library.

If item must be Prepaid.
6. Library Staff sends portion of PO to cashiers, who double-checks math, department number, and tax status.
7. Cashier send PO on to Accounts Payable.
8. Accounts Payable cuts checks. (done only twice a month).
9. Accounts Payable sends checks to Library.
10. Library staff mails out check, and portion of PO to vendor.
11. Item is received in Library.
12. Item is check against PO and vendor's invoice.
13. Item is entered into Library database, signed out to requester.
14. Requester is called to pick up item.

If item doesn't have to be Prepaid.
6. Library staff orders item.
7. Item is received in Library.
8. Invoice is received in Library. At times with item, at times separately.
9. PO is filled out with cost of item.
10. Portion of PO is sent to cashiers, who double-checks math, department number, and tax status.
11. Cashier send PO on to Accounts Payable.
12. Accounts Payable cuts checks. (done only twice a month).
13. Accounts Payable sends checks to Library.
14. Library staff mails check, PO, and invoice back to vendor.
15. Item is entered into Library database, signed out to Requester.
16. Requester is called to pick up item.

Alphabetical by Color

This sequence leaves out, for clarity's sake, everything we do with the 3 parts of the Library Material Request Form, the 4 parts of the Purchase Order, the hand walking of forms and checks from one department to another, and all the faxing, telephoning, and so on it takes to order, receive, and pay for an item.

This is the sequence no matter what an item costs, $10 for a document, $15 for a subscription, or $500 for an organizational membership. For the last 9 years, we have done an average of 675 Purchase Orders a year. There had to be a better, faster, and cheaper way. By consolidating subscriptions together, we found it.

A newsletter sent to all departments at our Teterboro location.

The Bendix Library

Our Library's Card Catalog is available electronically if you have access to GSD2 on the VAX computer system. After you sign on with your password, type "Browse" to bring up our database. Call extension 3190 and we will send you an instruction pamphlet which will aid you in searching.

- The Library has over 200 different periodical subscriptions. If we don't receive the one you want, you can put in a request for it. If you need an article from a magazine we don't have, we can find out what other libraries in NJ receive it. If you want a list of what we receive up here, just call and ask for one. Our extensions are 3190, 3967, or 4678.

- The Library has access to DIALOG, a service which allows us to search over 380 databases containing more than 260 million records. Records can range from a directory-type listing of companies, associations, or famous people; to an in-depth financial statement for a particular company; to a citation with bibliographic information and an abstract referencing a journal, patent, conference paper, or other original source; to the complete text of a journal article. These databases cover all areas of information from agriculture, aerospace, business, medicine, metallurgy, chemistry, law, engineering, economics, current events, newspapers, social sciences, to mathematics, and more. Here is a description of one of the many databases available, the Aerospace Database:

Provider: American Institute of Aeronautics and Astronautics
Coverage: 1962 to the present
File size: 1,725,620 records (as of January 1991)
Updates: twice a month

"AEROSPACE DATABASE provides references, abstracts, and controlled vocabulary indexing of key scientific and technical documents, as well as books, reports, and conferences, covering aerospace research and development in over 40 countries, including Japan, Eastern Europe, and the Soviet Union. The database supports basic and applied research in aeronautics, astronautics, and space sciences, as well as technology development and applications in complementary and supporting fields such as chemistry, geosciences, physics, communications and electronics."

We can provide business, technical, economic, industry, and competitive information. The cost of these searches is charged back to your department. If you would like a subject researched, just come up and ask how to go about it.

- If you need an address or telephone number for a government agency, a scientific or technical association, or a business or company, we can help you find it. Or if you need to find out what agency, company, or association does work in a certain field, we can usually find it out.

- We have maps for most of the New Jersey counties, a United States road map, and a world atlas. These do NOT leave the Library. If you need to photocopy part of a map or two, we will allow that.

- We have a list of the toll free 800 numbers for all the airlines. We also have phone numbers for the tourism offices in each of the 50 states in case you want to get some travel information.

- Do you need the area code for Hondo, Texas or Eagle, Idaho? We have books which will give you the area codes or zip codes for all the cities in the United States.

- Need to spell something for the report or crossword puzzle you are working on? Come and use our unabridged dictionaries.

- Need some general information? We have the Encyclopedia

Britannica, the McGraw Hill Encyclopedia of Science & Technology, and the New Columbia Encyclopedia. Next to them are many other reference books covering other subjects.

- Need business information or information about a company? We have Standard & Poor's Register of Corporations, Directors and Executives; the Thomas Register of American Manufactures; the IHS Vendor Catalog service which shows the catalogs for many vendors; the Scientific and Technical Organization and Agencies Directory; and the Corptech Corporate Technology Directory. In all of these, you can look up a business by name, or by its CAGE (FSCM) code, or by its geographic location, or by the products it manufactures.

- We have specifications and standards available from the military, many industry organizations, and the federal government. We can usually find out who originates specifications and can order specifications and standards for you.

- Did you ever come across an acronym or an abbreviation you did not know the meaning of, such as 'SLA'? We have a dictionary which will help you. 'SLA' has 42 different possible meanings, from the Scottish Library Association, sealed lead acid, Side-looking LASER Altimeter, Showmen's League of America, Sierra Leone Airlines, Slovak League of America, square loop antenna, State Liquor Authority, stored logic array, Svenska Linne-Sallskapet Arsskrifft, synchronous line adapter, to the Special Libraries Association.

- Would you like to continue your education but do not know which colleges in the area offer the courses you want? Barron's Profiles of American Colleges gives profiles of more than 1500 accredited four-year colleges, with programs of study, tuition, financial aid, application procedures, faculty data, computer facilities, student organizations, sports, and handicapped facilities. We also have catalogs for some of the local colleges.

- Do you ever have need for a perpetual calendar, need to know the state song of Colorado ("Where the Columbines Grow") or the state bird of Maine (Chickadee), or desire to know the birth date of Zachary Taylor (Nov. 24, 1784), or where the world's longest railway tunnels are? These are just of few of the many and varied facts we have available here in the library. Come up and visit.

Alphabetical by Color

- We have started a file of general information about the local area and major cities of the United States. We are keeping information about tourist attractions, shopping centers, often-called phone numbers, restaurants, museums, parks, and other items. If we can, we obtain maps of the major cities for someone traveling there. As with our other items, these are available for photocopying.

- Our bookcase of phone books contains the books for the local counties as well as a few of the New York City phone books and are available to you anytime we are open.

- The Library. It's just not for book reports anymore. Give us a call. Extensions 3190, 3967, or 4678.

**"What did the chicken say in the library? Book, book, book."
Roger von Oech, author of "A Kick in the Seat of the Pants"
SLA Convention, Denver, 1988**

Allied-Signal Total Quality (TQ) Library Network Team

The year after I had consolidated the periodical ordering into the Bendix Library, I was attending a SLA convention. I had arranged to meet other AlliedSignal librarians for an informal working lunch. While we were discussing periodical ordering and working with periodical vendors, the fact came out there was a wide discrepancy between the discounts we were receiving. They ranged from 8% to 13%. We decided to set up a corporate wide total quality team to obtain a corporate wide agreement for discounts. Since I was the one doing the loudest bitching, I got volunteered to lead the team.

I created a survey to send to all corporate libraries. I asked for information on their subscriptions, their vendors, what discounts they were receiving, and any other pertinent information. Once all this information was gathered, consolidated, and reviewed, I then spoke with the corporate librarians to gain their agreement to approach the various vendors and ask for a corporate wide agreement and discount.

I knew this would require corporate level support so we partnered the Library Total Quality (TQ) team with corporate purchasing to obtain corporate wide agreements with our subscription services, our book jobbers, and the online services providers. Corporate purchasing was the department which worked out the contracts with the vendors. By obtaining a corporate wide agreement we gained savings of 25.6% of total expenditure for the first year. (About $289,000 I believe). That is correct. We cut the corporate wide cost of spending on periodicals by over a quarter.

This is the first of several letters and surveys the team used to start the TQ process.

> AlliedSignal's Corporate Wide Library Total Quality (TQ) Team Communications
>
> Since access to information is crucial to AlliedSignal's vision of becoming a premier company, a corporate-wide Library Total Quality (TQ) Team has been formed to study the corporation's libraries/information resources. The Team's first steps will be to:

Alphabetical by Color 87

- compile a directory of libraries/information resources, which will include locations of libraries, and department information centers.
- determine what services and products are at each of these locations.
- publicize the available resources list company wide.

The Team recognizes some sites do not have the personnel to offer information services to other locations. This TQ effort will not lead to a demand you share resources, rather it is an information gathering effort to ensure we are receiving the best possible discounts from the vendors of these various resources.

The Team will then focus on improving communication (via electronic means) among the libraries and information centers, reduction of bureaucracy and cycle times, elimination of waste and duplication of effort, and standardization of software, vendors, work processes and procedures.

The Team includes individuals from all Sectors. They are:

Mary Ann B   201-455-IIII   Business Library, Morristown, NJ
Dale C   201-393-HHHH   Guidance & Control Sys., Teterboro, NJ
Patricia C   602-469-GGGG   Controls & Accessories, Tucson, AZ
Sam D   410-964-FFFF   Microelec. & Tech. Cntr, Columbia, MD
Nina H   313-827-EEEE   Automotive, Southfield, MI
Janice H   716-827-DDDD   Buffalo Research Labs., Buffalo, NY
Anne McK   201-455-CCCC   Technical Lib., Morristown, NJ
Rosemary M   804-520-BBBB   Fibers Technical Cntr, Petersburg, VA
Mitzi R   602-893-AAAA   Aerospace Equipment Sys., Tempe, AZ

As this Team's work will benefit everyone in the corporation, please give them all the assistance possible if they contact you. If you can provide information which will help, please call any team member.

CORPORATE SITE SURVEY TO FIND RESOURCES
(survey number 1)

Since access to information is crucial to AlliedSignal's vision of becoming a premier company, a corporate-wide TQ Team has been formed to study the corporation's libraries/information resources.

Alphabetical by Color

The Team's first steps will be to:
 survey all AS sites to compile a directory of libraries/information resources.
 determine what services and products are at each of these locations.
 obtain corporate wide discounts from magazine and book publishers and library product vendors.
 publicize the available resources list company wide.

This survey is the first step in the TQ Team's effort. Please pass it on to either your site's librarian or information researcher, the person who orders magazines and books for your site, or someone else who can answer these questions. If no magazines or books are purchased at your location, or another location buys these materials for you, please provide that information and fax it to one of the people listed below.

Please answer the survey questions and mail or fax the results to:

Dale Carpenter,   AS Aerospace, Teterboro, NJ   07608-AAAA
Nina H.,   AS Automotive, Southfield, MI   48086-BBBB
Mitzi R.,   AS Aerospace Equip. Sys., Tempe, AZ   85285-CCCC
Janice H.,   AS Buffalo Research Lab, Buffalo, NY   14210-DDDD

The purpose of this corporate wide survey is to:
1. find information resource sites within AlliedSignal,
2. gather from each site information on the ordering of periodicals, books, on-line computer services, and CD-ROM's.

The information gathered will be used to:
1a. obtain, for the first time, a full overview of AlliedSignal corporate libraries and information centers, their staff, and the resources they contain,
b. share locations of resources to company employees and the Customer Access Center,
c. provide library and information center staff a network in which to share information, provide help and support to each other, and promote library/information issues.

2a. ensure all sites are receiving any corporate discounts currently available from vendors,
b. arrange for corporate discounts on purchases of books,

periodicals, online computer services, and CD-ROMs from vendors, if possible.

The Team understands some sites do not have the personnel to offer information services to other locations. This TQ effort will not lead to a demand you share resources, rather it is an information gathering effort to ensure we are receiving the best possible discounts from vendors of these various resources.

Library and Information Services TQ Survey Questions:
1. Job Classification: librarian: information specialist: library assistant: other:
What department are you in: To whom do you report:

2. Percent of time spent on library and information related work:
0 to 25%   25 to 50%   50 to 75%   75 to 100%

3. Who orders the books, periodicals, newspapers your site needs:
each department: an individual (who):   central department (what) (who):   nobody:

4. Who orders the articles and documents your site needs:
each department: an individual (who):   central department (what) (who):   nobody:

5. Who orders instructional materials (videotapes, cassettes, training programs, etc.) for your site:
each department: an individual (who):   central department (what) (who):   nobody:

6. Who orders company-paid memberships in professional societies:
each department: an individual (who):   central department (what) (who):   nobody:

7. If you order ALL the books, periodicals, etc.:
how many per year (estimated)   cost per year (estimated)
books   magazines   documents   articles   patents   CD-ROM's   online services   other
What vendor(s) do you use?

8. Who does the software ordering/upgrades/documentation, (this

Alphabetical by Color   90

may be called a Data Center, MIS Dept., IS Dept., Computer Center)
each department: an individual (who):   central department (what) (who):   nobody:

9. Does your site have reference materials collection:
are they available to the entire site: who maintains the collections?
are they specific to one department: if yes, who maintains the collections?
do not have any reference materials:

10. Does your site have collections of specifications and standards, military, commercial, or industrial:
list all and contact names:

11. Does your site have any information/services on CD-ROM's:
list them and a contact name:

12. Does your site have access to on-line services (Internet, CompuServe, Dialog, STN, etc.):
list service and contact person:

13. Does your site have any internal standards for the operation of the library/information center?

14. When you need internal company information, where do you go:
co-workers: department secretary or administrative assistant: corporate headquarters:
AlliedSignal Access Center: AlliedSignal library or information center: other library:

15. When you need external company information, where do you go:
co-workers: department secretary or administrative assistant: corporate headquarters:
AlliedSignal Access Center: AlliedSignal library or information center: other library:

16. Who is the planner for corporate strategy for your site or is it done at a sector or corporate level?

If you have a listing of all periodicals/subscriptions received at your site, please return with the survey.

Once we received results from the first survey, a more detailed survey was sent to the 47 libraries and information centers found. Here it is.

Allied-Signal Corporate Wide Library Total Quality Team

ALLIEDSIGNAL
Guidance & Control Systems
Corporate Library
Teterboro, NJ 07608-AAAA

Dear Information Provider:

As the company changes, so must we.
The company wants to:
- focus work processes on customer satisfaction
- support meaningful team projects
- eliminate waste and unnecessary work
- reduce cycle time and bureaucracy
- promote creativity
- strive for technical leadership.

We can use these guidelines to improve the company's libraries and information centers.

This survey is the first step to gather and share information, find out how the libraries and information centers function within their groups, determine what services and products we use, and provide a basis for discussion on how we can work together to increase our effectiveness and make our jobs easier.

The goal of this project is to present this information to corporate headquarters and receive their support, time, money, and people in a successful effort to:
- select and establish corporate accounts with vendors for library services
- increase effortless communication among libraries, by human and electronic means
- compile a list of corporate information resources
- increase sharing of company resources
- reduce bureaucracy and cycle time in fulfilling our customers' requests

- become more established as providers of information for corporate/division future planning efforts.

and perhaps most important of all
- recognize our own achievements as information professionals.

I appreciate your help in this effort and welcome your suggestions and comments.
Dale Carpenter
Corporate Library Manager

ALLIEDSIGNAL LIBRARY SURVEY #2
Please provide name & address including phone & fax numbers and Internet & E-Mail addresses.

How many are employed in the library?
Professional: Non-Professional:

Is any training or continuing education available to the staff? __ Yes __ No
Does the company pay for it? __ Yes __ No __ Partially
What training is there?

Are any library staff members of any professional organizations?
Does the company pay your dues? __ Yes __ No
Special Libraries Association: American Library Association:
American Society for Information Science: Others:

How large is the library? __ square feet (estimate)
Books (Number):   Periodicals (Annual subscriptions):
Documents (Standards, Specs, Reports, etc.):

Who are your customers?
How many employees at your location?

What is your location primary focus?
Aerospace: Automotive: Engineered Materials: Other:

What are your customer's specialties?
Engineering   Manufacturing   Marketing   Design   Research and Development
Sales   Administration   Maintenance   Other

Do you serve other locations? __ Yes __ No   If yes, who?

Where does the strength of your reference collection lie?
Generalities   Philosophy & Psychology   Social Science (statistics, economics, law)
Language   Mathematics   Astronomy & Allied Sciences   Physics
Chemistry & Allied Sciences   Earth Sciences (geology, hydrology, meteorology)
Life Sciences (biology, genetics, microbiology)   Engineering & Allied Operations
Management & Auxiliary Services   Manufacturing   History
Computers & Related Subjects   Other:

What cataloging system does your library use?
Dewey Decimal System: Library of Congress: Other Cataloging System:

What library software does the library use and who is the vendor?
What sort of computer system does it reside on? _ PC _ Mainframe
How satisfied are you with the software?

Is the library database accessible to the employees at your site?
__Yes __No
To off-site personnel __ Yes __ No

At your location does the library order all the books, periodicals, and documents? __Yes __No
Or does each department handle its own orders? __ Yes __ No

How are your costs paid?
Directly by the library?   Library charges back costs to the departments?
All bills sent to accounts payable?   All bills sent to departments who requested services?
Other methods:

Do you have signature authority for purchases and if so, how much?
__ Yes __No

Does the library use a book jobber and if so, which one?
How satisfied are you with the service?
Do you receive a discount from this jobber and if so, how much?

Alphabetical by Color

Does the library use a periodical order service and if so, which one?
How satisfied are you with the service?
Do you receive a discount from this jobber and if so, how much?

Does the library use a document delivery service and if so, which one?
How satisfied are you with the service?
Do you receive a discount from this service and if so, how much?

Does the library have any special discounts with any other vendors and if so, which ones and how much?

Does the library access any online database services or networks? Which ones?

Are you receiving any discounts from these vendors and if so, how much?
Dialog   Lexis/Nexis   Other

Any form of electronic mail?

Does the library have any CD-ROM services and if so, which ones? Are these services standalone or networked?

What are your biggest problems and your solutions to them?
Insufficient money   Marketing your services
Unresponsive or uncaring upper management   Dumb customers
Other:

Does your location have written procedures governing the operation of the library?
Yes   No
If so, would you please send a copy of each when you return the survey.

Besides more money and personnel, what would be the most useful acquisition the library could obtain?

Where in the corporate chart is the library positioned and whom does it report to?
Does this seem sensible to you? __ Yes __ No

Do you ever deal with other AlliedSignal libraries and for what?
Obtaining copies of articles or documents: Interlibrary loans:

Sharing services:
Other:

Does the library provide information for future planning or strategic planning at your location?
__ Yes __ No   To whom?

Are any of the library staff a part of any corporate planning committees or boards? __ Yes __No
Which ones?

Can you think of any other library areas that should be looked at?

Do you have any suggestions or comments?

I sent out this letter after all the survey results were collected and complied by me, no easy task since 47 sites responded. Some people said they only wanted the complied results, others wanted to see all the raw data. I put the information into graphs, Excel spreadsheets and text formats.

AlliedSignal
Guidance & Control Systems
Corporate Library
Teterboro, NJ
07608-DDDD

May 1994

Dear Information Provider:

Thank you for your help in providing information on the library or information center at your site.
I have complied the results and am sending them back to you and asking for more of your insights.

First, a spreadsheet of sites which responded to the survey. If you know of any others, please invite them to join us. I'll gladly mail them a copy of the survey. The 'code' is the name I used on each spreadsheet as I complied the answers, grouping related questions together. If a site did not answer a question, the chart was left blank. Ten spreadsheets are next, followed by my impressions of what the results show. If I made any errors in putting the information on the sheets, please let me know.

I have included some material related to the survey. First is a copy of a memo stating how the Corporate Library at Morristown is being reorganized. A copy of a library survey produced by Janice H at the Buffalo Research Lab, which she used to survey her library users, is next, and last is a description of the order process here at Teterboro. I have included this as an example of a process which could be TQed. I'm sure each of you could point out one or two processes at your site that need the same.

Now for the insights I mentioned. What are your suggestions and comments after viewing this? What questions does this raise in your mind about how your information center compares with others and how it fits within AlliedSignal? If we were to form a TQ Team on library services, what would be its problem statements, and goals or desired outcomes? Do any of the spreadsheets point the way to a good area for interlibrary cooperation? What other sort of information might be useful to gather?

Please jot down your thoughts and comments and mail them back. I'll compile them and revise the survey results accordingly. I'm also searching for someone at corporate headquarters to provide the muscle, money, time, people, leadership, and support to get implemented whatever we decide would be best for the libraries and the corporation. If you know of any likely candidates, please let me know.

Thank you again for your help.
Dale Carpenter

STAFFING: Seems most of us work in a one-person library. Our divisions provide for some training, mostly for computer software training. The company doesn't seem to value memberships in professional organizations. Here at Guidance & Controls (G&C) in NJ, the division pays for IEEE & AIAA memberships to get discounts on their publications, documents, and specifications.

CUSTOMERS: Most of the responses came from the Aerospace sector. Our locations seem to be focused on engineering, R&D, and administration. The 1994 Laboratory and Technology Directory provides a good overview of each location's focus and fields of R&D. If you don't have a copy, please give me a call and I'll send you one.

REFERENCE COLLECTION: Collections are focused on engineering, math, physics, chemistry, manufacturing, and computer science. Here at G&C, we have some chemistry holdings but the majority are down in our Materials Lab. We need to be aware of departmental collections as they are a rich source of information. I put down 'company' under history because we have saved company newsletters, brochures, marketing and advertising materials, and publications for many years. What are your thoughts on interlibrary loans of materials? Is this possible without losing control of materials?

SOFTWARE: Most of us have automated catalogs. INMAGIC is used by 25% of us, two locations use BiblioTech, and over half of us have our catalogs accessible on-site. Over three quarters of us have access to on-line databases and 10 of the 14 have CD-ROM services or will get them this year. Should we inquire into corporate discounts from software vendors? Should we investigate some way of accessing each other's catalogs?

SIZE: The size of the libraries varies quite a bit. Half of us use or are converting to Library of Congress cataloging system. I wonder if we could get corporate discounts on volume purchases of periodicals. How many copies of Aviation Week & Space Technology or PC Magazine or Byte does AlliedSignal buy a month? We purchase 25 copies of AW&ST for this location alone.

ORDERING: 6 of us use Corporate Book Resources as a book jobber and are satisfied with them. For periodical ordering, 3 use Faxon, 3 use Ebsco and it seems 3 of us do all the work ourselves. We use all sorts of document delivery services and 6 of us get discounts from our organizational memberships. Do we get a corporate discount of any sort from these vendors or are we receiving their standard discount? Should this be something we should investigate, going to one vendor for us all?

BUDGET/COST: Most of us do the ordering for books and periodicals at our locations and charge back the costs to the departments ordering items. 6 of us do not have ANY signature authority. I know at this location it delays our ordering/receiving cycle time by at least 30%. Please look at the description of our ordering process.

DEALING WITH OTHER LOCATIONS: Most of us share information, services, and documents with other locations. What would be the ways in which this process could be increased, sped up, and improved? E-mail access between locations, improved shipping and handling, fax machines in every library, (and of course more staff)?

REPORT: Very few of us provide information for planning purposes. Where is management getting the information they act on? Shouldn't we, as the prime information providers, be doing this function?

PROCEDURES/PROBLEMS: We seem to be saying management does not support us and does not provide adequate budgeting and staffing. Perhaps with a greater effort on marketing our services, while tracking the increase in demand, would show management concrete evidence for increasing our budgets and staffing. 9 of us need equipment (computers, CD-ROM services, audio-visual, etc.), and all of us could use more staff, space, and visibility.

On the returned surveys, people have suggested we look at:

- Industrial and military specifications and standards: control and dissemination of; how many locations have collections of specs and standards? could we consolidate collections, network them in some way, get corporate discounts from the vendors?

- Getting AlliedSignal libraries their own Internet listserv discussion group / getting AlliedSignal libraries access to Softswitch: we need our own communication system for sharing information, requesting help or ILL of items, and providing help to each other, at the very least, we all should have e-mail access through the company's computer network and fax machines.

- Formal training and suggestions on how to run a library: a good idea - one of the rewards I get from attending the SLA conference are tips and suggestions from other librarians on how they do things at their libraries - since many other areas in AlliedSignal are adopting standard procedures across divisional lines, perhaps we should look at doing the same thing.

Here is information on the financial expenditures of 12 locations, in 1994 dollars.

Item	Annual Expenditures
Books	397,622.30
CD-ROM services	299,348.70
On-line Database Searches and Sources	370,760.50
Periodicals and Subscriptions	1,155,975.30
TOTAL	2,223,706.80

The following are comments from survey responders.

"These subtotals represent estimates of what is typically ordered through the Technical Libraries on an annual basis. I am discovering many pubs/subscriptions are ordered directly through departments who do not take advantage of our vendor discounts, or through inexperienced employees dealing with individual publishers in payment and problem resolutions, etc. This results in lots of hidden personnel costs. These items managed by individual departments then become hidden from the use of other employees, resulting in duplication of purchases, and lack of corporate control of materials for which it has paid. More research is needed. I have some particular suggestions I'd like to discuss and pursue."

"At the corporate level there should be a mission statement, policies, and procedures to cover all the libraries in the organization. There should also be a formal information policy which says something like "our organization commits to the idea there must be information resources for use by the organization and these will be funded by the organization."

"You need someone in senior management, who should not be a librarian, to promote libraries, "librarianship" (by which I mean the hiring of professional librarians), and senior level management funding and sharing of information resources."

"You should obtain company information policies and statements for the library. You should have copies of all corporate documents affecting the entire corporation sent to the library. Use the rational if anyone is looking for a corporate document, the library would probably be the first place they would check."

"You should promote and have regular communications between

the libraries in different divisions and sectors. This could be done by emails or newsletters. There should be at least one yearly meeting of all librarians and if possible, library staff."

"Everyone should check on library job descriptions, titles and pay grades. Corporate headquarters must standardize across all divisions. But each division or section should promote within their own ranks."

"The library group should determine and recommend company wide resources. Each division or sector or group should decide what information resources and services they need and should fund it themselves. This will maximize customer satisfaction within each division or sector."

> **"Don't dwell on your past mistakes.**
> **Concern yourself with the ones you might make in the future."**
> **Dale to co-worker, 10/2/2013**

Attaboy Letters

February 20, 1992
Edwin S.
XX XXXX Avenue
North Haledon, NJ 07508
Tel.: 1-201-XXX-XXXX

To Whom It May Concern:
Dale Carpenter is a Senior Technical Engineering Librarian who is responsible for the overall operation of the Engineering Library in supporting the three Bendix Allied-Signal divisions located in Teterboro, New Jersey.

Dale has been with Bendix since June 1987 and has been instrumental in computerizing the various manual library operations in achieving productivity goals. The implementation of DIALOG and DTIC on-line service, and the installation of the BIBLIOTECH software package on the VAX computer have greatly enhanced the Engineering Library service to the three divisions at Teterboro.

Dale's library service has been part of the Documentation Department which supplies overall program support to the Engineering Department. As librarian he has proven himself to be very innovative, cooperative, reliable, as well as very proficient in the implementation of all phases associated with the operation of the Engineering Library.

Furthermore, Dale's personality and helpful spirit have been instrumental in transforming the Engineering Library into a technically skilled professional library, fully adept to servicing the needs of the individual employee. His skills in developing and maintaining the Engineering Library have been a great asset to the entire Teterboro operation.

In summary, Dale is highly qualified and is recommended as the person to develop, implement, and manage a cost effective and efficient professional library.

Sincerely,
E. S.
Mgr. Documentation Department
Bendix Guidance Systems Division

Attaboy Letters

Allied Signal
Date: August 28, 1992
To: David Zomick
From: R.C. Morris
Subject: Teterboro Library

Memorandum
Morristown, NJ
received by
SEP 2, 1992
David A. Zomick

During the recent Light Age vs. Allied-Signal trial, our lawyers requested the February 1985 issue of Laser Focus for use as evidence in the cross examination of John Walling. This issue contained an early press release describing Allied's intentions to begin selling alexandrite laser rods for commercial use.

However, older Laser Focus issues had been discarded from the Morristown Library. After some searching the magazine was finally located in the Teterboro Library by Dale Carpenter and supplied to our trial lawyers.

This press release in a widely read trade publication dramatically countered Walling's assertion that he had been led to believe that Light Age would somehow have a privileged position with respect to alexandrite rod availability as a part of his June 1986 license agreement. As a result of this and other factual evidence, the Light Age case lost momentum and credibility with the court and was settled on terms favorable to Allied.

We greatly appreciate the help of the Teterboro Library in locating this key piece of evidence for use in the trial.

R.C. Morris

RCM/ris
xc: L.A. Davis
L. Ditchey
M. Shand

Attaboy Letters

AlliedSignal Aerospace
Date: 3/30/94
To: David Zomick
From: David Fairchild
Subject: Reward & Recognition candidate

Memorandum
Guidance & Control Systems
Teterboro, New Jersey
cc: C. Bernhardt
K. Bogdan

GCS is fortunate to have a very skilled and industrious librarian. Most of us have benefited on one or more occasions from services or efforts that went well beyond the routine.

Dale Carpenter has assisted me on numerous occasions when no advanced notice was possible, schedules were very demanding and the sensitive nature of the material precluded special accolades. He has never complained about the tasks or the lack of recognition for extra effort.

Over the past couple of years, we have developed and refined an on-line search approach which is yielding very valuable competitive data. Must of the credit is due to Dale's thorough finished understanding of the DIALOG file formats and professional search techniques.

Recently I found it necessary to call Dale back into work after normal working hours. It was not convenient for Dale, because of previous plans, but he returned in good spirits and worked diligently for about six hours. This is not the first time that extraordinary events have required long hours and personal sacrifice from Dale. Each time he has given all that was required in the spirit of teamwork. Please extend my personal thanks for his "can do" attitude and pleasant demeanor.

Non-Disclosure and Outside Work Letters

This is an example of the outside interest letters I send to employers before I start working for them. Copies are sent by certified mail, return receipt requested, to Human Resources and Legal departments and a copy goes to my manager. When I have been questioned on this, my answer is "What does your company have to do with hitchhiking or librarianship or science-fiction? That is what I write about and since your company is not doing anything in those fields, it's my work and I own it." Of course, I assure them I won't publicize any company processes or secrets or do work on company time.

TO: The Medicines Company:
FROM: Dale Carpenter
DATE: June 1, 2004
SUBJECT: Personal Outside Interests

To establish a fair and honest business relationship between The Medicines Company and myself, I wish to advise you of my interests in the library profession and my personal writing and publishing business. Regarding the Invention and Non-Disclosure Agreement and the Non-Competition and Non-Solicitation Agreement: I write, publish, and give educational and entertainment oral presentations, articles, and books. As these writings are created on my own time and with my own facilities, The Medicines Company does not have a current claim and shall not have any future claim to these or any of my other non-company individual employment activities.

Regarding the Non-Competition and Non-Solicitation Agreement: I am the owner of a non-profit publishing company, Lies Told Press, LTD. As there are no points of conflict with my ownership of Lies Told Press, LTD and employment by The Medicines Company, The Medicines Company does not have any claim to any work performed by me for Lies Told Press, LTD, any publications of Lies Told Press, LTD, or any compensation paid to me by Lies Told Press, LTD.

This letter will be attached to the copies of the offer of employment and the Non-Competition and Non-Solicitation Agreement I sign.

Sincerely
Dale Carpenter

Also, in the acceptance letter I send to any company when accepting their offer of employment, I include this section: "My only legal signature is one which is written on paper. No electronic facsimile or any reproduction of my signature is legal."

If this is questioned, I ask them if a photograph of a 5 dollar bill is worth the same as a 5 dollar bill. When they say 'of course not', I tell them that is the same difference between my signature and a copy of my signature. I do not allow any reproductions of my signature to be used. In this manner if someone claims I signed a document, I just demand to see the original. If they can not produce an original, they are lying.

My Ideas and Work Belong to Me.

Some people might say all the work you do for a company belongs to that company. I certainly agree if I produce something specifically for the company as an employee of the company. However, if I bring an idea or work into the company, the idea and work is mine.

For example, I have been a collecting books my whole life. When people came to visit and saw my books, sometimes they would find something they were interested in and ask to borrow it. Since I could not remember who I had loaned books to I was losing them. I went to an office supply store and bought heavy weight 5" x 8" bright yellow file cards. From then on, when someone wanted to borrow a book, I grabbed a card, wrote the book's title, wrote the person's name, and wrote the date on the card. I then had the person sign the card. I stuck the card on the shelf where the book had been and gave the book to the person. Of course they asked why I was doing this. I told them I could not remember every book I loaned so this was my process to remember you borrowed this specific book on this date and I will be asking for it back in a month.

When I become a librarian, I used this process. I have the company buy big sign out cards of heavy cardboard. I write down the document or manual's name or number, and the person's name, and the date, and put it on the shelf. How can any company say it is their process when I was using it years before I joined the company?

I've written this process up as a standard operating procedure (SOP) for several libraries. Yes, that specific procedure as written, belongs to the company. But the whole idea and process belongs to me.

On every occasion when a company wants me to sign a confidentiality agreement, or a non-disclosure agreement, I modify it. I scan it, do optical character recognition, and modify sentences which refer to ownership of ideas and work. I re-write them to state I own any idea I come up with and any original work I do. I do this to make sure I own my original ideas and work I do on my own time. Of course, I will never disclose proprietary company information. If you think this is wrong, remember a contract is an agreement between two parties on all points in the contract. I just re-wrote the contract to what I think is fair and agreeable. If the legal people did not re-read the contract I signed and sent to them, it is not my fault.

Model Release Forms

Sometime in the 1980s, I saw a marketing and publicity campaign for some national company whose name I can't remember. Each ad showed a company employee and described their contribution to the company's success. I later read a business magazine article about the campaign and it mentioned none of those employees were compensated for appearing in the ads.

"What? You want to use my name and image in a national advertising campaign and not pay me? No way!"

Since then I have told every employer, in writing, I have signed a model release with another company and they did not have the right to use my name or image in any way. This has never been questioned. But if they ask, I tell them I signed with Lies Told Press, LTD., which is my company.

A friend of mine came to me with a problem. They had gone to a vendor's event, had been photographed and their picture was posted on the vendor website and on the WWW. They asked what they should do. I told them to tell their manager and CEO the other company was using them to advertise the other vendor's products without permission and/or compensation. Their CEO should call or email the vendor and tell them this was not acceptable. But if their CEO brushed off this incident, any time in the future they were invited to a vendor event, make sure to tell the vendor when you accept the invite, no photos of you are allowed. And if you see anyone point a camera at you, tell them they do not have permission to take your picture, as they or the vendor have not signed a model release with you.

> **"Information professionals are specialists like everyone else. It is crazy to have people doing their own research, badly, when information professionals have spent their lives learning to do it very well."**
> **Dave Pollard,**
> **SLA Convention, 2007, Denver**

Library Marketing and Publicity

These are some ideas for marketing and publicizing the library. Remember, while you are doing this you are also marketing your professional skills and services.

Marketing is making people AWARE of your product, your service or yourself. Public relations is making people THINK about your product or service or yourself. Selling is making people BUY your product or your service. I have found the best way to do all 3 of these is to "Walk Around and Be Seen". Let everyone in the company know you are their librarian and you are there to help them.

– Stay open during lunch time because co-workers often use this time to come to the Library. I always brought in my lunch and made sure the company knew I was available during this time. I let other Library staff go to lunch but I stay in the Library. Unless a group wanted me to have lunch with them.

-- Make friends with secretaries, maintenance, the reproduction department, security, mail room, etc. Departments which serve everyone know how to get things done easily, quickly, and cheaply and they know when something new is coming. A lot of times these people may not use the library themselves, but they will recommend the library as a resource if somebody asked them something. (And they are a great source for company news and gossip.)

-- Newsletters and postings on internal company bulletin boards, either paper or electronic. Include staff pictures and a short biography. If someone complains about not being aware of what is happening, tell then you did your part to inform everyone.

-- New employee tours, orientations, and brochures.

-- Have local maps and phone books in the library because they really get used.

-- Chase's Annual Calendar of Events tells what events are happening when and where. Not many people know about this great resource.

-- Invite top management to breakfast in the library, especially right after you have introduced a new service or product. Have coffee, juice, Danish, muffins, and a chance to talk before the day begins. But make sure you cut the food into halves or quarters or some pig will grab a whole one and someone else won't get a bite.

-- Offer to do bibliographic sketches of individuals (visitors, speakers, vendors, and so on) visiting the company.

-- Put stickers or markings on and in everything which goes out of the library. People might cover-up the mark on the outside but miss the mark on the inside.

-- Offer in-house service to other departments to help organize their files. If they don't want you touching their files, offer to look at how they organize, then give suggestions based on your skills & experience.

--Ask to sit in on department meetings to gain a better sense of what they do and are working towards.

-- Ask employees to write reviews of books they are reading and include them on your website and in your newsletters.

-- Write an annual report on what the library did during the past year and come up with a topic for each letter of the alphabet, from a to z.

– Research and create a list or list of World Wide Web bookmarks related to your industry and place it on your website.

-- Ask electronically or send letters to local colleges and universities asking for their current catalogs and the list of their periodical holdings. This helps in your reference and weeding.

When you do marketing and public relations, use language a nine-year-old person can understand. Leave out jargon, buzzwords, and acronyms in your speaking and writing. But if you write something only for a specific group or department, you can use their jargon.

Once again, every piece of paper going out of your library must have the library's name, phone number, and usually the address on it. And nowadays, the library email and website address.

If you have a library handout, brochure, or newsletter, it should fit into a standard number 10 size envelope. It should have the library's name, mailing or physical address, where you are if you're in a big building, phone and fax number with area code, a website if you have one, and your hours of operation. If you describe a service the library provides, make sure the description is in very clear language.

Bookmarks with the library's name and address on it are useful to have available.

You know how to find the answers others can't find by themselves. When others at Bendix started doing their own on-line research, I offered to look at their search strategies and suggest ways to increase their effectiveness.

Your competition is the people who think the World Wide Web can provide all the information they need. Let them know you paid to have access to databases and information EVERY search engine can NOT find.

What others say about your product or service, is at least a 1,000 times more convincing than what you can say. Ask EVERY satisfied customer to tell their co-workers and managers about you.

> "When I read about the way in which
> library funds are being cut and cut,
> I can only think that American society has found
> one more way to destroy itself."
> **Isaac Asimov**

Making Changes

Do whatever you can get away with. Management expects sharp, intelligent people not to ask about things, but to do things. You get credit for innovation. Usually you don't get credit for the things you were hired to do. Innovation and marketing are always essential but especially during a tight financial crisis.

The most important question always is: 'What are you doing for your users?'

Changes I've done which gained me status and respect.
– Developing and presenting training sessions at all companies.
– Periodical bundling and using a periodical vendor at Bendix.
– Leading a company wide library group while at Allied-Signal.
– Writing a library newsletter for Whippany wide distribution at Lucent.
– Moving file cabinets and putting up shelves at the Fire Academy.

You should gather endorsements from your customers whenever you can. If someone thanks you for doing a good job, asked them to put it in writing and forward it to their manager and your manager, with a copy to you. Keep all the copies in a folder. And copies at home. That is where all the 'Attaboy' letters in this book came from. The copies I kept at home.

When someone asked for a database search I would sit with them and brainstorm search terms. Often, I would suggest terms they had not thought of which added value to their search. Or I would suggest another avenue of research which might result in more information.

I always kept copies of the online database searches I did, because often the requester would come back and ask for an expanded search. Or they would ask months later if there was anything new on the subject. Having kept the old search, it was easy to run the search again.

Often the requester was quite surprised when I walked their search results to their office or work area. They often said the previous librarian had never done that. I just said it was part of the service and I also wanted to see where they worked. (And be seen by others in their work area.) Most of the other library staff were surprised I was taking the information to the patron, instead of having them come to the library.

When I talked to friends at Bendix after I left, they told me the replacement librarian never left the library and never delivered materials to customers. Not very good customer service.

You must educate your patrons as to the cost, time, and the effort it takes to get any item or piece of information. I use this information in reports to management as proof the money invested in the Library is benefiting the company. This is called "Return on Investment" or "ROI". This form asks employees to show or guess how much time the Library saved them and how valuable the information we provided to them was.

WHIPPANY CORPORATE LIBRARY
Return on Investment Performance Report

Name   Date
Department   Phone

Research Request Question:

Please give us your assessment of the value of the information you received and return it to the Library.

Are you fully satisfied with the information?

How will the information contribute to achieving your department's goals?

How much time do you estimate was saved by having the Library obtain this information rather than you doing the research?

What monetary value can you put on having this information?

Here are the responsibilities and tasks I did while at Manchester. I wrote this up to aid in marketing myself within Manchester, at professional meetings, and for use in job hunting.

Alphabetical by Color

Regional Research Director Responsibilities:

Provide business research support, both on-site and remotely, to Manchester's job candidates and to sales and marketing staff, using a range of print and electronic resources.

Market Manchester's research capabilities to prospective clients through demonstrations, presentations, sales calls, and other events.

Conduct group orientations for job candidates in several offices on a regular basis, covering research strategies, in-house resources, and Internet resources, with individual follow-up for high-level candidates as needed.

Develop instructional materials as needed.

Maintain, review, and make purchasing recommendations for office library collections to support business plan and candidates' needs. Together with Office Managers and Regional Market Leader, monitor research budgets for each office.

Consult with client companies to recommend appropriate materials for short-term, on-site career centers.

Function as backup to other regional researchers as needed for vacations, etc.

A good way to structure your desire for change is PAS: Problem, Agitate, and Solve. You state what the problem is, you get the other individual or individuals emotionally involved or agitated about the problem, and then you produce a solution.

> **"If you want to get laid, go to college.**
> **If you want an education, go to the library."**
> **Frank Zappa**

Marketing Write-Ups

Here are some marketing write-ups to use as examples when you write up your own. I've sent these out as library brochures and posted them on bulletin boards in the plants I've worked in. This brings attention to the Library from departments which may have never used us. The blue collar guys down on the factory floor might never come into the Library but now they know, after seeing this on their bulletin board, we have stuff they might find useful.

Bendix Guidance and Control System Library Resources

You are invited to use the Information Resources of the Library. Contact us by visit, telephone or use your computer. We're here to assist you from 8 am to 4:30 pm daily.

LIBRARY RESOURCES

Books and Journals
Specifications and Standards
Research Reports
Company Information
Gale's Business Directory
Jane's Yearbooks
Standard & Poor's Register of Corporations
CD-ROM Files
Federal Acquisition Register
US. Patents
Learning Tapes
Telephone Books
Thomas Register of Manufacturers
Maps

LIBRARY SERVICES

Acquisitions
Reference
Online Computer Searching
Circulation (Books, Journals)
Current Awareness Service
Copier

RETRIEVAL

Need information in a hurry? Your job runs smoothly if you regularly tap into the information resources of the Library.

TOPICS

Business
Chemistry
Commerce
Finance
Government
Industries
Patents
Pricing
Production

Alphabetical by Color

Computer Science	Government Regs.	Research
Corporations	Management	Safety
Country Profiles	Marketing	Standards & Specs
Current Events	Materials Science	Statistics
Data Processing	New Products	Technology
Engineering	Environment	

SEARCH BEFORE RESEARCH

Before starting a project, request a literature search and briefly describe the subject with a few 'key words. We will comb the world literature via online databases and provide a timely briefing on the published literature in that field.

COMPETITIVE INTELLIGENCE

Finding current and accurate information about the competition is necessary for business survival and growth. The various resources of the Library can provide practical approaches to learning and using competitive information.

CD-ROMs

Our collection is not limited to paper. It also resides on media such as CD-ROM, microfilm, and computers, which facilitate retrieval of information.

Department of Defense Specs & Standards	Maps
Industry Specs & Standards	Telephone Books
Vendor Catalogs	Quality Standards
CAGE Codes	Integrated Circuits Product Selection

We're here to help you!

For assistance call (201) 393-AAAA   or   (201) 393-BBBB
            fax   (202) 393-CCCC

WHO YA GONNA CALL?

If your problem is not ghosts or demons, but a lack of knowledge or information, you usually call your friends. When they can't come up with an answer, someone always suggests the Library.

We can, using our reference resources, provide you with information on many subjects. Give us a call at 3190 or 3967 or stop in with your questions.

The Library provides services to all Teterboro employees and any other AlliedSignal locations who ask for help, as best as the staff's time allows. We usually mail or fax items to about 25 other AS sites during a year.

Our collection of books and documents is oriented toward scientific and technical areas and business-related interests, ranging from computer software, mathematics, various engineering sciences, management studies, quality, optics, marketing, electronics, lasers, and so on. Books can be borrowed for 1 month and renewed if no one else has asked for the book.

We have over 100 magazine subscriptions ranging from Aerospace America to Working Woman and they cover such areas as personal computers and computing (BYTE, Online Access); software (Inside Microsoft Access, PC Magazine); GPS (GPS, Navigation); aerospace (Aviation Week & Space Technology, Air & Space); business (Forbes, Fortune, Business Week); design (Design News, Machine Design); electronics (Electronics Now); and science (Scientific American, American Heritage of Invention and Technology). Magazines are loaned for 2 weeks.

You can order a book or a magazine subscription and keep it for reference purposes until you leave the company. Your department will be charged for any books or magazines you order. All books and periodicals for this location must be ordered through the Library.

The Library recently obtained a PC with a CD-ROM drive and now has several reference works on CD-ROM. The Encarta Bookshelf contains The Columbia Encyclopedia, Roget's Thesaurus, the American Heritage Dictionary, the World Almanac and Book of Facts and the Columbia Dictionary of Quotations. We have CD-ROM road maps of the US to help you plan your travels and CD-ROM phone directories for business and residential phone numbers.

Outside of the Library, available 24 hours a day, are a collection of CD-ROMs with military specifications and standards, various industry specifications, many vendor catalogs, and an IC/Discrete database. Stop by and we will show you how it works.

We have most of the phone books for New Jersey cities, and several directories of 1-800 numbers. We have maps of most of the New Jersey counties, and atlases of the United States and the world. These can be very useful and are some of the most often used references in the Library.

We also have catalogs from most of the area's colleges, Consumer Reports Magazine, encyclopedias and dictionaries, business directories to help you find information about companies, a dictionary of acronyms and abbreviations, and zip and area code directories.

We have a freebie bin where we put extra copies of magazines, old books, or materials we receive and don't want to keep. We let employees to bring in their magazines from home after reading them and put them in our freebie bin. Or if you are cleaning out your library at home and don't want to throw away those books, bring them in and share them with other people. We'll take almost anything.

We're a bit crowded for space, and always busy, but we're glad to take the time to answer your questions or to point you towards other sources of information. That is our function in this company and we're proud to do it.

A Short Note on New Services from the Bendix Library

We have received more industry standards and specifications on CD-ROM. We now have most of these organization's standards:
AIA/NAS   SAE   ASTM   IEEE   EIA   UL   DIN
ASHRAE   ANSI   IPC   ISHM   ARINC   AIAA
as well as military specifications and standards, and many vendor catalogs. If you need training on the CD-ROM systems, please give us a call (3190 or 3967) and we'll let you know when the training sessions will be held.

We have a new service called 'CAPS' on CD-ROM. This helps you find information on electronic components such as integrated circuits and semiconductors. You can search by part numbers to find the status of parts, data sheets, replacement parts, upgrades and downgrades, related parts, and related generics.

Need phone numbers? We have phone books from most of the New Jersey counties. We also have 'PhoneDisc' on CD-ROM which covers the entire US. PhoneDisc has both business and residential numbers. You can even search by category to find, for example, all the golf courses or all the pizza parlors in NJ.

Need a map? We have maps for most of the counties in NJ. We also have 'StreetAtlas USA' on CD-ROM for the entire US which can take you down to street level in cities and towns. 'Global Explorer' and 'World Atlas' on CD-ROMs cover the world, but in not as much detail. If you need information on another country, the CIA produces 'The World Factbook' every year and we have it on CD-ROM. If you need specific information, we have the 'Microsoft Bookshelf 94' on CD-ROM which contains:
– The Concise Columbia Encyclopedia
– The American Heritage Dictionary
– The Original Roget's Thesaurus
– The Columbia Dictionary of Quotations
– Hammond Intermediate World Atlas
– The People's Chronology
– The World Almanac and Book of Facts 1994.

We also have the index to 'Electronic Design' magazine from 1989 to 1993 on CD-ROM. We plan to get more magazine and subject indexes on CD-ROM to make your information searching easier.

We have a 'freebie bin' where we put duplicate copies of magazines, old materials we are discarding and things we get in the mail. You're welcome to bring in books or magazines and give them away in our 'freebie bin'.

Speaking of books and magazines, remember all books and subscriptions for this site must be ordered thru the library. Using our corporate accounts with publishers, we can usually get very good discounts.

If you want to suggest services the Library should get, please call me at 3190. We are always looking for ways to serve you better.

Alphabetical by Color

AlliedSignal
Guidance & Control Systems
Corporate Library
Teterboro, New Jersey
07608

Our Corporate Library is an information system used to support business decision making. Our mission is to provide information to individuals and departments to aid in their goals of developing new products and improve profitability.

In supplying the information needs of scientists, technicians, and managers in 1994, we dealt with over 70 different departments at:

Teterboro, NJ	Morristown, NJ	Montrose, PA
South Bend, IN	Buffalo, NY	Montreal, Canada
Boyne City, MI	Columbia, MD	Cheshire, CT
Tempe, AZ	Mishawaka, IN	Torrance, CA
Huntsville, AL	Ft. Lauderdale, FL	

In fulfilling these needs, we searched for (just to list a few)
- competitor intelligence: addresses, corporate officers, product information, company financial reports, regional newspaper articles on their actions
- contract announcements and requirements
- material & alloy properties, resistance to fungus, radiation, ozone degradation, welding, and brazing information
- ice detection on aircraft surfaces & helicopter rotor blades
- market forecasts
- productivity and bench marking measurements
- program information: JDAMS, IAM, AIWS, FISTV, Warbreaker
- patent & copyright searches
- project management software
- government documents, laws, specifications, standards, reports
- Federal Acquisition Regulations

We generated 629 purchase orders last year for 662 books, 247 periodical subscriptions (new or renewals), 385 standards, specs., patents, and other articles.

Alphabetical by Color   120

This is just what we have records of. We were too busy to keep track of the items requested which didn't need a purchase order or the number of copies made of items already on our shelves. (Our estimate puts it around 2000 copies.)

Our customers in 1994 were mostly the engineering and engineering support departments, the management/administration departments, and the marketing departments.

The Medicine Company Library Department Services Summary

We provide a full range of reference and information services, from directional assistance to online searching and research. We have access to DIALOG, a service of almost 1200 different databases covering all scientific, technical, and business areas. Examples of the type of requests we handle range from the number of deaths each year in the US caused by resistant gram-positive bacteria; biographical information on the board members of possible partners; to the requirements for running a clinical trial in Columbia.

We also provide support for all submissions to health authorities and support for all regulatory filings by compiling references, providing citations, and creating Table of Contents (TOC).

We maintain an electronic library of over 18500 journal articles, medical meeting abstracts/posters and slides. The electronic library also houses all current company Policies and SOPs. There are over 250 POLs, SOPs, and Work Instructions and over 200 templates for them.

We create and maintain bibliographies for all MDCO products. These bibliographies contain hyperlinks to the complete articles housed in our electronic library.

We operate in Parsippany a secure storage library for all MDCO regulatory submissions, clinical trial materials, DDMAC materials, original Policies, Standard Operating Procedures and Work Instructions.

The department is responsible for archiving and retrieving company materials at secure off-site storage facilities (Iron Mountain). Company materials include clinical trial documents and studies, regulatory submissions, legal documents, manufacturing documents, etc.

We create, establish, and maintain working TeamSpace collaborative sites to support all teams (START, ENGAGE, TRANSACT, SUPPORT, R&D, Legal, HS, IT, Finance, Communications, Library). We aid with site set up, site rearrangement, and we create and update site access groups. We also maintain a calendar of all relevant medical meetings and conferences with workspaces and conference documents when appropriate or available.

We fulfill all company requests for journal articles, book and book chapters, and conference proceeding materials. We also manage journal subscriptions.

We issue the Weekly News Briefs which gathers and summarizes all information on our products with a synopsis of clinical updates, peer-reviewed journal articles, and info on competitive companies, info on competitor trials, and relevant industry information.

We provide individual and /or group training (new and remedial). We call them "Lunch and Learns".

We fulfill all requests for copyright clearance and we research answers to any questions on Copyright compliance. We also make sure the company contracts are renewed annually.

Surveys on Ways to Improve Services

Here is a company wide survey done at Bendix in 1999 to find ways in which we could improve our services. I spent my own money to purchase five $20 gift certificates to a local bookstore to increase returns. It worked!!

ALL SURVEYS RETURNED WITH A NAME WILL BE PLACED IN A DRAWING FOR A $20.00 GIFT CERTIFICATE

GSC LIBRARY SURVEY 1999

PURPOSE: The information world has changed greatly during the past decade. To evaluate the library in terms of its services, who uses it, what your needs are, and how we can best meet these needs with the resources available, please complete this questionnaire and return it to the Library by August 31, 1999. One of the most important aspects of this survey is your comments - please be candid and state what we are doing or not doing, areas for improvement, or areas not needed. Thank you.

1. Name (optional)
Occupation (e.g., chemist, technician, secretary)
Are you currently on any distribution lists from the Library?
YES _____ No _____

2. How often do you use the library services?
Daily   Weekly   Often   Seldom   Never

If seldom or never, please check all that apply:
My work does not require the use of a library.
Information I need is not available from the library.
I am not aware of the services the library provides.
Library services are too slow.
The library staff is not helpful.
Organization of materials is confusing.
I use other sources of information (explain).
Other (explain)

3. When using the library, how do you contact the staff? (Check all that apply)
Telephone   Visit   Mail   Combination

4a. How often do you use the following library services? Please use the following scale: D = Daily, W = Weekly, M = Monthly, Y = Yearly. You may also indicate other usage frequencies, for example 3x/month, etc. Also, in the space provided, please rate the importance of the service from 1 - not very important to 3 - very important.

         Amount of Use   Importance

Online Literature Searching
Journals
Book Collection
Patent Information & Documentation
Maps or Phone Books
Technical Reports
Government Documents & Standards
Electronic Library Catalog
Reference Materials

4b. Now please rate your satisfaction with the same library services, with (1) least satisfactory service and (5) most satisfactory service.

        Not Satisfied   Very Satisfied

Online Literature Searching
Journals
Rook Collection
Patent Information & Documentation
Maps or Phone Books
Technical Reports
Government Documentation & Standards
Electronic Library Catalog
Reference Materials

5. If you have had a literature search done by the library in the past year, please answer the following questions:

a. Was your request interpreted accurately?
YES ____ No ____ Partially ____
b. Did you discuss your request with library staff before beginning the search?
Always Sometimes Often Never
c. How helpful was the library staff when discussing your question before and after the search?
Poor Fair Satisfactory Good Excellent
d. Was the response (printout) received in a timely fashion?
YES ____ No ____

e. Do you think it would be more efficient and cost effective to do your own literature searching? YES ____ No ____

f. How much time would you estimate your LAST online computerized search saved you?

Hours of manual searching   Days of manual searching

Could not have been done manually (resources not available or exist only online)

g. How much money would you estimate your last online search saved the company?

6. How important is the library as a source of information related to your work?

Crucial	Nice	to	Have	Not Important to Me
5	4	3	2	1 0

7. If you receive routed materials, journals, or current awareness information, please answer the following:

a. With regards to its quality and timeliness, how would you rate our service?

Poor   Fair   Satisfactory   Good   Excellent

b. Would you prefer to receive a table of contents as a replacement to the current routing system?

c. If you are not on any distribution lists, why not?

8. Please select five aspects of library service you find most important and/or useful, then rank them from "1"(least important) to "5"(most important).

Ability to Offer Helpful Suggestions
Ability to Retrieve Information from Outside Sources
Attention to Details
Guidance in Finding Things for Myself
Immediate Access to Materials
Keeping "Red Tape" to a Minimum
Keeping the User Informed of Progress
Knowledgeable Library Personnel
Quality of Research
Quick Response to Requests
Speedy Turnaround
Willingness of Library Staff to Meet Deadlines
Other (Please Explain)

9. Future planning so you can access information immediately will involve the following services. Please indicate whether you think each service is important or not important by checking the

appropriate box.

Crucial / Nice to Have / Not Important to Me
5   4   3   2   1   0

a. Microfilming of old journals
b. Information on CD-ROMs
c. Online databases training
d. Computer software training

10. Our library catalog can be browsed using the VAX computer system on Node BGCS2. If you browse the catalog, please answer these questions. If you are unfamiliar with this service, please contact us and we will show you how to access it.
a. How helpful is browsing the catalog: [ ] Good [ ] Satisfactory [ ] Fair [ ] Poor
b. Is the catalog easy to use?   [ ]Good [ ]Satisfactory [ ]Fair [ ]Poor

11. What services would you like the library to provide that it does not already provide?

12. What services does the library provide now that you feel are NOT necessary?

13. Other comments and suggestion.

Thank you for completing this survey. Your feedback will help us to improve our services and plan for future needs.

SUGGESTIONS GIVEN DURING LIBRARY SURVEY
NOVEMBER 1995
sorted by question number

1. if you do not use the Library, why not?
   - library focused on technical material and my needs tend toward market, economic, & general business materials
   - little need for most references, do use computer references and magazines
   - always need assistance to find things
   - would like more info about software manuals the library has available
   - library does not have latest technical publications in my field

2. literature/patent searching
   - online services should be available on-line for anyone to do

(within financial limits)

3. other comments
- publish a guide to the library services. include bios of staff, list of services, 'how-to' access those services, list of journal subscriptions, diagram of library layout, etc.
- concise awareness memo to Teterboro public letting us know what services you offer
- I would prefer memos detailing new acquisitions, features available now, new features, & special events.
- survey very helpful - please make all aware of library services
- probably you need better PR for where you are located and what GREAT things you can do for all of us who barely have time to know our own names but must try to keep current of the latest trends in are areas.
- electronic listing of what is available in library
- some sort of newsletter listing what is available in the library. specs, ASTM, documents, etc.
- a category listing of books, magazines, etc. distributed to administrators/secretaries
- a listing of journals subscribed to so that people will see what the library has to offer.
- a listing of books, articles, etc. that would apply to the quality department.
- I have found the staff to be very helpful in any assistance requested of them.
- thank you for opening during lunchtime hours
- I have used many of your textbooks for everyday job and graduate classes.
- The library staff is always friendly & efficient. It is the most pleasant department in this facility to deal with. They are never too busy to help when you need them.
- staff has always been very helpful.
- people should be discouraged from talking loudly in the library so others can concentrate.
- be more pro-active in getting ideas for new textbooks & periodicals.
- distribution of routed materials frequently gets stopped at one or more individual's desks making material old by time they arrive.
- just having the library there for my use when I need it is the greatest service.
- this is a well-run library. you get the feeling when you come in here that you will be helped.
- I personally think keeping Teterboro's 'history' is also important.

- Dale Carpenter is always customer focused.
- I feel the library does a very good job on the whole for the amount of people they handle.

4: planning for future improvements: increasing scope of CD-ROM collection how?
- optics
- optics & statistical quality topics
- vendor data sheets
- vendor catalogs, military drawings
- better index for commercial products would help
- cover all industry standards (VESA, MPEG, video)
- more depth in mil sections
- various parts guides
- electronic component catalog
- NASA, MSFC, JSC, ASQC
- industry standards, IPC, NHB
- same day government spec retrieval.
- DTIC indexes and access to data would be valuable
- access to electronic catalogs/databases on integrated circuits
- electronic access to military specs and industry standards from various points in the plant, plus being able to print documents
- CD-ROM based mil specs/dwgs., Bendix dwgs, and vendor data sheets remotely accessible from PC via networks with printouts available at any laser printer.
- terminal access to commercial catalog information and to current mil-specs and QPL information
- more terminals and higher speed printers
- Microsoft Developer's networked CD's
- all info currently available in hard copy should be in soft as well to provide multi-user access
- software users manuals
- databases & computing
- PC computing & business journals
- displays technology (US & foreign)
- CCD technology
- general references
- research aids
- management & other skills training
- finance
- engineering
- journals, standards
- information technology
- closer to my desk

5. What new services would you like the Library to provide?
   - enlarge the size of the library.
   - more space to read
   - facility expansion suggested. need for more workspace separate from library staff.
   - more PCs to use CD-ROM references
   - be loaner of all software packages used in Engineering, etc.
   - provide more manuals & materials (mags & other literature) on software products in use around the plant
   - provide software on CD-ROM rather than discs
   - continue acquisition of updated computer manuals & training videos, CD's, etc.
   - more training in the use of PC & VAX software
   - interactive computer
   - online D&B service
   - easily accessible on-line access from my desk to the relevant databases in displays technology
   - a connection to the Internet and CompuServe like any 'world class' library should have
   - provide summary of databases available to potential users
   - some possible access into university machines (Internet).
   - provide services on VAX to others
   - anything that increases computer accessing of information.
   - browsing for Readers Guide to Technical Periodicals
   - would be great to access the library over the network
   - movie rentals
   - video tapes
   - training materials
   - more recent books on engineering subjects
   - DTIC indexes and reports
   - trade journals in accounting & finance areas
   - updated books and an easy way to find them without asking
   - outside of industry topics, none
   - GCS & Allied organizational structure
   - benchmarking information across many different process areas in many industries
   - multiple copies of popular periodicals (Computer Shopper)
   - a larger selection of reference & journal material
   - interlibrary loan service (not only among company's libraries).
   - archive program technical reports.
   - increase copies of well-read magazines and books.
   - expand book collection/expand video tape collection (educational, various topics)/continue expansion of software services &

literature
  - broader base of inf. (in addition to engineering) such as chemistry, materials science, corrosion, analytical instrumentation
  - more discipline journals (IE. techpubs, electronic publishing)
  - availability of latest issues of technical textbooks so that employees can have access to state of the art in their designs, processes, etc.
  - open when the staff arrives and don't close until the staff leaves

Here is another survey done while at Lucent. It was sent out with the information an employee requested so it was focused specifically on an individual's or department's needs.

PLEASE RETURN TO: Dale Carpenter WH 5E-FFF

1. Are you satisfied with the products and services you are receiving from the Information Services Network (Library)? Are there any changes you would suggest or products you would like to see us offer?

2. How much literature (books, journals, internal or external standards, manufacturer catalogs) does your department purchase for itself? Approximate number of copies purchased per title? Why? Would it help to have copies available in the library? Would your department purchase these titles anyway if the library did have copies? What sources, other than The Information Services Network, do you use to answer your information needs?

3. Please discuss your literature/information needs as related to your work. How do you share information within your group?

4. Into which of the following areas would you categorize your information needs?
  - Quick reference (addresses, telephone numbers, definitions, molecular wt., formulas)
  - Literature searching (in depth searching for external information in the journal literature, annual reports, competitor information, internal AT&T information such as TMs, IMs, archives)
  - Browsing and/or borrowing materials
  - Utilize ITDS (obtaining or supplying documents)
  - Access or contact us (electronically, phone, visit, mail, coverdoc, LINUS) Other? Please explain.

5. What projects are you working on and will these continue into 1998? Do you foresee any changes in your department soon which could affect your literature/information needs?

6. Could you suggest someone in your department we could contact from time to time to get clarification on subject/information interest?

I posted this promotional sign in the hallway window of the Bendix Library in January and February 1999.

In 1998, to serve you, we spent in the Library:

$97,752.00 on military and industrial specs and standards & vendor catalogs on CD-ROMs

$12,404.96 on books

$5,234.30 on periodicals

$3,357.08 on documents

$1,469.00 on CD-ROMs

$572.08 on training videos

$186.30 on language tapes

$1,409.18 on online research

Plus lots of cash on a computer, a copier, a fax machine, and other office supplies. (The plants, snacks, coffee, and tea, we paid for ourselves.)

AT&T and Lucent Technologies 1996 to 1998

By the mid-1990s I could see the AlliedSignal Teterboro location was having economic problems. We were down to less than 3000 people and the three divisions had been combined into one. I decided it was time to move on. I passed the word around at professional networking meetings I was looking for a new position.

A librarian at AT&T called me at work and asked if I was still looking. AT&T was spinning off their telecommunications equipment manufacturing businesses from their phone service businesses. My friend said several people were retiring from the library network of AT&T and the new companies would be hiring. She said if I sent her my resume, she would give it to the hiring committee.

I sent my resume and was hired by AT&T in August 1996. I was part of the group which became Lucent Technologies. From aerospace and defense I moved into telecommunications. Unfortunately, Lucent Technologies management had the mindset they were still the invincible force Bell Labs had been and consequently over hired. Lucent also in 1997 entered a joint venture with Royal Phillips Electronics in the mobile phone market. They didn't gain enough market share and ended the project in late 1998. In just over 2 years I was let go from Lucent Technologies. Last hired, first fired, as the saying goes.

I started working as the librarian for the Wireless Network Division at the Whippany, New Jersey location. I did online database searching for engineers and scientists and managed the library. Using circulation figures and user surveys, I eliminated low use periodicals from the library and in 1997 saved the company over $93,000. I designed and produced library newsletters, chaired library focus groups, and held instructional programs to market the library and the Library Network services. For a Lucent partnership in India, I created a bibliography of reference books on wireless technology.

Here is an explanation for one of the Library newsletters about what I did while at Whippany:

As the Information Reference Specialist at the Whippany site, I perform 4 main functions, and other tasks as required.

1. Provide information research, analysis, and reference services to customers throughout Lucent but primarily those at the Whippany location, by interviewing clients to determine specific parameters of their requests, designing and executing a search strategy using a variety of online retrieval systems, printed sources, and verbal contacts, and then delivering the information request in any format requested. I also provide a quick ready-reference service to walk-in or phone-in customers.

2. I review and select books, journals, conference proceedings and other materials including CD-ROMs and online services to support Lucent's overall and Whippany's specific interest areas. I identify problems, weaknesses, or demand patterns in the Library's collection and address any gaps in its coverage.

3. I design and implement a variety of programs to keep customers informed of the latest products and services from the Library Network. I make recommendations to customers on the use of Library Network products and services to solve business problems. I conduct and/or sponsor workshops, demos, and presentations of internal and external information services provided by the Network.

4. I participate on committees and teams to improve processes, review products and aid in coordinating information flows within the Library Network and Lucent.

The Library Network supports all Lucent Libraries worldwide by providing cost-effective in-depth services.
If a customer or group brings me an information request that would monopolize my time and effort for several days or longer and prevent me from providing service to other customers, I send them to the Business & Information Resources Service. These experts can devote the long-term, in-depth effort it will take to support this customer or group. The Library Network also has a group which will set up and track issues, technologies, or companies for Lucent groups or individuals who need this sort of data.

After I select materials Whippany should own, I request the Materials, Acquisition & Processing Group to get them for us. This group orders, tracks, and delivers the materials and by providing one contact point to vendors for the Library Network, develops personal contacts, obtains corporate discounts because of Lucent's volume purchasing, and reduces internal paperwork/invoices while saving money. After items are received, the Cataloguing section checks them in, catalogs them, attaches barcodes used for circulation purposes, puts spine labels on them and ships them to the Library which ordered them.

I could not track the purchasing, invoicing, and renewals for the almost 600 periodicals we receive at Whippany. The support groups in the Library Network can by bundling all the Library subscriptions together and dealing with the vendors.
I could not support our virtual library, InfoView, and make it available to all Lucent employees. The Library Network does.
I could not handle and track the ordering of documents for our customers, the Document Supply Service does.

So by concentrating functions which support many groups, as Lucent does with Human Resources, payroll, legal, and computer support, the Library Network puts experts to work saving the company money, resources, and time.

In 1998 I was transferred down to Lucent's Murray Hill location where I worked as an information reference specialist, doing only online database research for engineers and scientists. Not having the day-to-day contact with users was very frustrating. The Library Network had set up reference contacts who took information requests and passed them to us online searchers. They did not do informational interviews, they just took down the requests. I often found myself contacting requesters directly to find out specifically what they wanted and what they were going to use the information for. I did this so I could provide the best results for them. The Library Network management did not like me doing this. The individuals requesting the search loved it.

For example, I received a notice a person wanted to know what fiber optic cables existed in the Caribbean. I looked at this request and wonder why they wanted to know. I called the guy and asked what he was going to do with the information. He said he was part of a group who was looking into entering the Caribbean market, either with cables or with wireless. I told him he might also want, besides what cables existed, who owned them, how old they were, where they started and stopped, and what other networks with which they were linked. And, perhaps, what wireless networks existed in the area, along with any other related information. And perhaps, if any of Lucent's competitors had mentioned recently they were planning to expand in the Caribbean.

The guy was delighted I took the initiative to call and expand the search request to include all this extra essential information. After I did the search and sent them the information, they wrote a nice note to the manager of the Library Network praising my work. I got in trouble for not following the proper procedure of going back through the person who took the request and having them ask those questions.

My response was since the reference contacts did not conduct a proper reference interview to find out specifically what and why the requester wanted, I saved them time and several more reference requests by doing it myself. I even offered to coach the reference contacts.

Bell Labs and specifically the buildings at Murray Hill where we worked were designed to facilitate communications and interactions among disciplines. People with different specialties and talents, theoretical physicist, experimentalists, material scientists, engineers, etc., were mixed to encourage creativity. And here Nancy M, the director of the Library Network, was actively working against open communication. I mentioned in the "A New Broom.." chapter that the Library Network had 3 signs compared to 45 signs with the other department's name on hallway office doors. Another example of not communicating and marketing the Library Network.

I had issues with the management of the Library Network. Many have commented once a departmental group gets above a certain size, creativity, entrepreneurship, and the willingness and spark to take chances disappears. The Library Network reported to Nancy M, a person with no background or experience in librarianship. She seemed to let Betty K, a manager of one of the library groups, run the entire department. Betty would boss people in other groups, interrupt speakers in meetings and Nancy M never interfered or put Betty K in her proper place.

Libraries are a unique service provider in companies and they need to be managed as such. We act as a purchaser of materials like a supply department, we provide services like a payroll department and we communicate information like an HR department. We contain, offer, and use many different skills sets and it can be difficult to manage all these services.

For example, the newsletters I wrote contained library related jokes and humor. This is a way of relating our human side of librarianship to our users. The Library Network management did not see it that way. They thought everything relating to the library should be serious. I always put a disclaimer on the newsletters stating they were written by me and I was the one responsible for the materials. Many of the other librarians in the network loved the newsletters and requested copies.

Nancy M, the head of Lucent's Library Network, never caught on to the idea of library newsletters. I once asked her if everyone knows about Honda cars and McDonald hamburgers, why did Honda and McDonald keep advertising. Her blank look told me she had no idea of what I was talking about. Constant marketing and publicity keeps reminding people of your products, services, and anything new you are introducing.

Another factor was Betty K. While driving me to various Lucent sites to introduce me to other members of the Library Network, she started asking questions about my personal life such as 'Do you have a girlfriend?'

I told Betty K because I was working 2 jobs, Lucent and my writing and publishing company, and I was involved in several volunteer organizations, I did not have any time for a social life. I also stated my practice was never to date or socialize with any co-workers because I kept my personal and professional lives separate.

Betty K's manners towards me cooled greatly as I maintained a professional relationship with all staff, especially her, and rarely did she have a kind word to say about me or my work. She actively worked against every I suggestion I made. This is also the same manager who was so far removed from the day-to-day work in the library she could not work the library software to sign out a book. She was at the desk, a patron came up to sign out a book, and she had to go in the back room to bring out a clerk to do it.

I was taught a manager should know how to do every job done by everyone who reports to them. The manager does not have to be an expert but should know how to do it. Otherwise, how can the manager provide an evaluation of their direct reports if they do not understand what that person is supposed to do?

> **"For business reasons,
> I must preserve the outward signs of sanity."
> Mark Twain**

Here are examples of the newsletters. What are your opinions of them?

First is a letter to other members of the Library Network explaining the newsletters. Following the newsletter are several examples of emails I received from other employees at the Whippany location and an email from Ruby, a Lucent corporate librarian at another location. I forwarded all these emails to my manager and the Library Network director. Neither acknowledged them.

>Whippany Library
>October 27, 1997
>
>Hello All,
>
>As some of us talked during last week's Global Library Network (GLN) Annual Meeting about ways in which we market or publicize our Libraries, I was reminded I had not sent copies of my Library Newsletter to you all. So, with apologies, here are copies of my first 3 Library Newsletters.
>
>They are published irregularly, whenever I find enough material to write about. (4 ideas which came from the GLN Meeting are the care and handling of books with CD-ROMs in them when the borrower returns them to the Library through interplant mail; the services we will provide to sections of Lucent sold to other companies; the new Wireless Mobility Gateway website; and the EMEA Libraries and the services they are providing to our fast-growing overseas locations.)
>
>Nothing is duller than most department newsletters so I write mine in a very informal manner so people will read it. After the first one was sent out, I received a phone call from a person here who said it was the first company newsletter he had ever read all the way through. I even saw one posted up on a department's bulletin board. So it does get people's attention. But as you will see, I put in a notice these are my thoughts and opinions, not Lucent's, not the GLN, or even the other staff at Whippany.
>
>The newsletter is printed and delivered to everyone's desk at Whippany. Being available in paper, they can read it immediately, put it aside to be read later, or even file it for reference. Derek

mentioned a test of a library announcement sent electronically in which it was found 75% of all recipients deleted the message without reading it. I don't doubt it. I read email with one finger on the 'delete' button. Paper catches the eyes and requires a bit more thought and effort before someone discards it.

You are welcome to use any items from my newsletters in your efforts to publicize your Library. If you want to discuss writing newsletters, please give me a call or email. I will continue to send you further editions as they come out. Please send me a copy of yours.

Dale Carpenter
Whippany Library
library!dc or dc@lucent.com

PS. These are reprints done on a copier with a dirty glass screen, not first edition prints.
PPS. The GLN Meeting was not long enough for all the conversation and exchange of ideas I feel are needed. I regret not talking with you more.

THE WHIPPANY LIBRARY
CONTAINING MORE THAN YOU KNOW (newsletter #1)

You may know we have a Library here at Whippany. You may even use it. But how much do you know about what we contain?

How many periodical subscriptions do we receive?
A: more than you
B: 500 to 600

How many books does the Whippany Library contain? We're counting unique books, not multiple copies.
A: lots but not the one you need
B: 30,001 to 40,000
C: less than the Library of Congress

How can you search for these books and magazines?
A: randomly wandering about
B: alphabetically by author
C: by the color of the book cover
D: using our computer card catalog
E: asking a friend to do it for you

How many videotapes does the Whippany Library have available for you?
A: the 'I Dream of Genie' series in Beta format
B: 6 Discovery tapes on 'The Life of the Flamingo'
C: 350 + and more being ordered each month

How many audio tapes does the Whippany Library have for your pleasure listening?
A: 27 scratchy country and western music tapes in 8-track format
B: over 100 on various subjects
C: many of dull management 'pep' talks

How many copiers do we have available in the Whippany Library?
A: 1 old mimeograph machine
B: 2
C: one we don't want you using

How many videotape players do we have for you to use?
A: 2 Beta format machines
B: 3, with plans to get more

Alphabetical by Color

C: 1 with which we watch movies at lunch time

How many study carrels are here for your use?
A: 6 which we rent by the hour
8: 14
C: what's a 'carrel'?

How many different newspapers do we get each day and what are they?
A: 4 supermarket tabloids so we can track Elvis
B: 5 local and regional newspapers
C: only the Racing Form

'The man who doesn't read good books has no advantage over the man who can't read them.
Mark Twain

Yes, it's a trick quiz but you figured that out very quickly. This is just a fun way to remind you our Library contains many more things than books and magazines and using the Library Network can provide you with access to the resources you need to do your job.

The Network has 17 libraries and staff members are constantly looking for, reviewing, and ordering material to keep you current with new and changing technologies. I can tell you we have almost 150,000 books and 2,470 magazine subscriptions and we are constantly adding to our collection.

Did you know we have 2 copiers in the Library for copying materials? They get a lot of use, as do the 2 videotape players in our media room. We are looking into adding more tape players because there is often a waiting line to use them. We'll let you know when we do.

A carrel is a desk or table, usually partitioned or enclosed, and used for individual study. We have 14 of them by our windows where you may work but we ask you not to bring food or drink into the Library because of the danger of damage to books and magazines.

Each morning (well, almost every morning) we receive 2 copies of The New York Times, 2 copies of The Star Ledger, and 1 copy of the Daily-Record. Our 2 copies of The Wall Street Journal arrive in the morning mail, and a copy of USA Today arrives in the afternoon.

Newspapers are for use only in the Library.

"There is no sin greater than ignorance." Rudyard Kipling

It is hard to track periodical usage. Many may get read in the Library but if they don't get checked out how can we tell they get used? Of the almost 600 subscriptions the Whippany Library receives, there are 105 MAGAZINES WHICH WERE NOT CHECKED OUT AT ALL in the last 2 years. So to make sure we keep magazines useful to you, we are going to start a LOW USE ITEM tracking period. Bright colored tags will be placed behind the low use items on the periodical shelves saying this magazine may not be renewed because of low usage and the ONLY way it will be kept is if every person who reads it tells the Library staff, they want it renewed.

In April we will be putting on a lunch time show in the cafeteria demonstrating Info View, the Library Network's Virtual Library, offering World Wide Web access to scientific, technical, business, and proprietary information. Watch for it.

The Library is staffed from 8 am to 5 pm Monday through Friday. Stop in and visit. We're at SE-233 or call:
386-XXXX   386-XXXX   386-DDDD (that's me)

Dale Carpenter
Reference Librarian
Whippany Library
Lucent Technologies

I write this newsletter in a very lighthearted manner so people will read it. All silliness and opinions are my own and not those of Lucent, the Library Network or even the other Library staff members here at Whippany.

THE WHIPPANY LIBRARY
CONTAINING MORE THAN YOU KNOW   (Newsletter #2)

You Can Do It Here

Do you need a laboratory notebook in which to keep records of all your work to insure patent protection? Lucent Lab notebooks are available in the Library. We record your name, department number, the date, and the number of the notebook. You fill out a registration card, have your supervisor sign it, and mail the card to Internal Technical Document Services in Holmdel so the notebook can be registered.

The Whippany Library now receives Consumer Reports. This is a reference item and will not be loaned out.

Yes, you may borrow the Library's periodicals and take them out to read. This fact might not be widely known as I've had eight people in the last two weeks show surprise when I mentioned magazines could be taken out of the Library. Magazines go out for 1 week, books for 2 weeks and you may renew them if no one else requested them.

Wondering if we have a journal? Our journals database shows if a Lucent Library gets it and the issues held by that Library. However, there are journal titles listed for document ordering purposes no Library receives so don't be surprised if an item is shown but no Library receives it.

Looking for an article from a periodical, book, or conference proceedings? We can find out if any Lucent Library has it or order it for you. If a book is held by a Lucent Library, you may request it by using the "req" command in the Books catalog database. The database will ask for your Social Security number (and will accept your badge number) and your last name. This enters an electronic request for the book which, if not out on loan, is pulled from the shelf by the Library's staff, checked out in your name and mailed via interoffice mail to your office. You may drop the book off at the Whippany Library when you are finished and we will return it for you.

Some books and conference proceedings have their table of contents entered in the Books catalog database and you can view them by using the "toc" command. If there are no table of contents

Alphabetical by Color 143

entered, the system will tell you.

Need a New Jersey state or county map? We have them. We also have other state maps, a US road atlas, and world atlases. Need a phone number? We have local phone books, plus residential and business phone numbers for the entire US on CDs.

"Be careful about reading health books. You could die of a misprint." Mark Twain

If you need to find information about a product or service, we have several resources which can help you. The big green 33 volume Thomas Register of American Manufacturers is one, listing over 148,000 companies, and indexing products and services in over 56,000 headings. Our Vendor Directory on CD-ROM lists over 17,000 vendors, over 160,000 brand/trade names and over half a million product terms. In both sources, you can find vendor names, addresses, contact numbers (telephone, fax, email addresses), and sales office/distributor locations.

If you need information about integrated circuits or discrete semi-conductor devices, go to CAPS on CD-ROM. Computer Aided Product Selection gives textual information about more than 675,000 components from more than 500 manufacturers and over 600,000 pages of datasheets. You can search generically, by specific part number, by function and value, or by keyword.

Specifications and standards are available in several forms. Some are on our Worldwide Standards Service CD-ROM service, others are in file cabinets, and others are listed in the Standard's database on our OPACs. Search the CD-ROMs first and print it out if it is available. If we do not have it there, ask one of the people at the desk to see if we have a paper copy in our files. If we don't have it, we can order it.

As part of the breakup agreement, the Lucent Library Network agreed to split their library materials so AT&T could create libraries of their own. Teams of staff members have been going through our books and selecting materials to ship to AT&T. We've finished doing this at Whippany and have shipped dozens of boxes of books to Basking Ridge where a new AT&T library is being created. So if you come to the Library for a book you KNOW we have, and you can't find it, now you know what happened. But don't worry, we made certain at least 1 copy of the book is kept somewhere in

Lucent's Library Network. You should be able to borrow it from another library. Ask any of us for help.

"You see, I don't believe that libraries should be drab places where people sit in silence, and that's been the main reason for our policy of employing wild animals as librarians." Monty Python's Flying Circus

The Library is staffed from 8 am to 5 pm Monday through Friday. Stop in and visit. We're at SE-233 or call 386-DDDD {that's me).
Dale Carpenter
Reference Librarian
"Whippany Library
Lucent Technologies

I write this newsletter in a very light-hearted manner so people will read it. All silliness and opinions are my own and not those of Lucent, the Library Network or even the other Library staff members here at Whippany.

THE WHIPPANY LIBRARY
CONTAINING MORE THAN YOU KNOW   (Newsletter #3)

We didn't ask Martha Stewart for advice. We renovated our video room ourselves to provide more service to you. It had 2 video tape player/monitors Whippany employees used for watching training tapes and being in great demand, many times people found both machines already in use when they arrived. So we ordered 2 more machines and put divider panels down the center of the room to make more viewing stations. All the new machines have head-phone jacks so several people may use the room without disturbing each other. Of course, there may be times when the place gets crowded and noisy so we ask for your understanding and cooperation in using the headphones and keeping the noise level down. Come by and use our video room. Just don't expect it to make the cover of Better Homes and Gardens.

Have I told you about our 'Free Magazines' basket? When we get extra magazines or catalogs, we put them in our 'Free Magazines' basket for anyone to take. The Library staff sometimes brings in personal magazines from home and adds them to the basket so you never know what you might find. You are welcome to bring in your personal subscriptions to place in the basket. Sharing your magazines is better than throwing them away. You may also bring in any books you are no longer using.

You may notice some new signs hanging from the Library ceiling. We are trying to make it easier for you to find things such as our book return slot which is directly under our "Book Drop" sign.

Did I mention the Library carries the Graduate Record Examinations (GRE) and the Graduate Management Admission Test (GMAT) information and registration bulletins? These bulletins give you the test dates and locations, fees, registration forms and sample questions from the tests.

Have you looked at the Wireless Mobility InfoView Gateway at <http://infoview.lucent.com/wireless> for information about the wireless, mobility and cellular industries and the companies, products, and trends in them? The Global Library Network is planning to set up sites like this for Lucent's core businesses so we really need your feedback to ensure we are providing the resources our employees need.

Alphabetical by Color

Speaking of InfoView, Lucent's Virtual Library, you may now view it in our Library and have access to technical, scientific, business, and proprietary resources both inside and outside Lucent. There is far too much for me to list in this newsletter (database searching in over 100 databases, for example) so stop by and browse on your own or ask any of us here for help. I'll set up some bookmarks to interesting places for you.

Occasionally Bellcore sends out messages about learning and training courses they have available for purchase. I am sure you have seen them but have been discouraged by the cost. I would like to purchase some for the Library but I want to make sure they get used. If you would like to look through the Bellcore catalog and make recommendations for purchase, please call or email me and I will send you the electronic file or a paper copy of the catalog. I will buy a course if 5 or more people request it.

I need your help. Part of my job is finding new books and materials for your use. I know I can't review all the literature in our industry and I sometimes don't have the engineering or technical skills to recognize when an item would be helpful, so if you see a book, periodical, or resource which would be helpful, please let me know about it. (mail stop 5E-233, <dc@library.lucent.com>, or phone 62DDD) This way we can get those resources your tight-fisted manager won't buy for you. (But I'll warn you in advance, my manager is way too sharp for me to slip "Golfing the Ben Hogan Way" or "Yachting in the British Virgin Islands" onto our shelves.)

The Whippany Library has a collection of CD-ROMs you may find useful. Using Moody's or Dun's you can find business and financial data on various companies. CAPSXpert provides information on semiconductors and components. The Vendor Directory lists manufacturers of different products, while the Worldwide Standards Service gives the full text of many standards. Searching through periodicals may be done with Compendex or Wilsondisc. Commerce Business Daily announces products and services wanted or offered by the US government as well as federal procurement and contract information. Patent Abstracts, Selectphone and College Source do just what their names imply, help you search for patents, phone numbers, and college information. The computers, readers and printers are to the left as you walk into the Library and anyone at our front desk will help you with the quirks in the CD-ROM software.

Alphabetical by Color

"One must cultivate vigor of body to maintain vigor of mind."
Vauvenargues, French essayist, 1746.

While we are waiting for a health center to be built in Whippany, let me tell you about the Parsippany Health Fitness Center, located close by in the Parsippany Lucent building, on Woodhollow Road. It is open Monday through Thursday 6:15 am to 9 pm, and Friday 6:15 am to 6 pm. It contains treadmills, stationary bikes, stair climbers, NordicTrack, rowers, a full line of Cybex selective resistance equipment, and an assorted variety of free weights. There are men and women locker rooms with showers, sinks, toilets, lockers, and hair drying facilities at the site.

The entry procedure is easy. A new participant is required to fill out a health history questionnaire and turn it into the fitness center staff for review. A blood pressure reading is taken at this time. The new participant can now schedule a fitness evaluation or an exercise orientation. The fitness evaluation is designed to measure a person's base line fitness level and consists of 6 tests: height and weight measurements, body composition, cardiovascular and muscular endurance, muscular strength, and flexibility test. The tests take only about 20 minutes. The exercise orientation assures all new members are knowledgeable in both the proper and safe use of the equipment. It is also an opportunity for the staff to help you design an individualized workout program. Give them a call at 973-581-XXXX for more information or go over to look. It's a great way to work off frustrations after a day of work, it's less than 10 minutes' drive from here and it's FREE to Lucent employees. I hope to see you there.

The Library is staffed from 8 am to 5 pm Monday through Friday. Stop in and visit. We're at SE-233 or call:
386-XXXX   386-XXXX   386-DDDD (that's me)

Dale Carpenter,
Reference Librarian
Whippany Library, Lucent Technologies

I write this newsletter in a very light-hearted manner so people will read it. All silliness and opinions are my own and not those of Lucent, the Library Network or even the other Library staff members here at Whippany.

Okay, those were the 3 newsletters. Here are some of the responses I received and forwarded to the Library Network management.

> From nxxxx@lucent.com Wed Oct 29 15:21:04 1997
> Date: Wed, 29 Oct 1997 15:19:00 -0500
> From: "Neelu Sxxxx WH 2D-204 (973) XXX-XXXX" <nxxxx@lucent.com>
> Organization: JC51E2300
> Subject: The WH Lib Newsletter
> Hi,
> I just wanted to thank you for the excellent WH Library newsletter we have been receiving. Please continue to keep us informed about our Library. It is fun reading this newsletter and being informed at the same time. Thanks and keep those newsletters coming!!!
> Neelu Sxxxx

> From: Shayna Axxxxxxx <saxxxxxxx@whpost.wh.lucent.com>
> Subject: Library newsletter
> Date: Thu, 30 Oct 1997 15:05:45 -0500
> Dear Dale -
> I just wanted to let you know that I always thoroughly enjoy reading the library newsletter. It is consistently full of useful information I wouldn't have known otherwise and entertaining as well. Thanks for providing a little levity in the midst of all the "serious" documents that float around here. You have a gift for writing and I hope you will continue to brighten our day with the library newsletter. THANKS ! ! !
> Shayna Axxxxxxx

> From pwgxxxxx@lucent.com Wed Nov 12 11:28:06 1997
> From: "Phil Gxxxxx" <pwgxxxxx@lucent.com>
> Subject: Nice job!
> Date: Wed, 12 Nov 1997 11:24:58 -0500
> Dale,
> I just read your newsletter, and I have to tell you that it is one of the best things to appear in my mailbox in quite some time. Short enough to read through quickly, nicely organized, and full of information that is not only interesting, but that I plan to act on very soon. I thoroughly agree with your light-hearted approach. You are right on the money. Thank you for the extra effort in writing the

newsletter. I indeed find it valuable. Congratulations on a job well done!
Phil Gxxxxx
Bell Labs/Lucent Technologies
Rm 2E234A
67 Whippany Rd, Whippany NJ, 07981 973-XXX-XXXX
PS. I cc'ed Audrey Hxxxxx on the assumption that she is your manager (I got this from post). If this is not the case, please forward this to your boss.

From vxxxxx@lucent.com Fri Nov 7 14:44:32 1997
From: "Vartan Axxxxxxxx" <vxxxxx@lucent.com>
Original-To: <dcarpenter@lucent.com>
Subject: Newsletter
Date: Fri, 7 Nov 1997 14:40:56 -0500
Hi,
First of all, let me tell you that it is the first time that I read the newsletter. It was really informative and fun to read. Excellent job, keep up the good work.
Can you please provide directions to the Parsippany Health Fitness Center? I tried calling them several times, but no response and I cannot find the street on the map.
Vartan Axxxxxxxxx
CDMA PCS Performance Analysis Group
Tel: (973) XXX-XXXX
Fax: (973) XXX-XXXX

From jxxx@nwmail.wh.lucent.com Thu Nov 13 09:56:32 1997
To: dcarpenter@lucent.com
Date: Thu, 13 Nov 97 09:54:22 EST
From: jsxxx@lucent.com (Jxxx C. Sxxx, 973-XXX-XXXX)
Subject: Bellcore training tapes
Hi Dale:
I enjoyed reading your Whippany Library news. It's entertaining and very informative. Keep up the good work.
Thanks,
Jill Sxxx

Alphabetical by Color

A Lucent corporate librarian from the Indian Hill Library sent me a copy of their open house brochure and said this in an attached note:

> Dale,
> Thank you so much for the Newsletters. They are creative, funny & even so clever! This is exactly what our customers need at IH. They are funny, light-hearted. They wear jeans & shorts...very informal around here. Can I copy your ideas? Looking forward to your next issue.
> Regards, Ruby

Attaboy Letters

Lucent Technologies
Subject: Recognition
D. Carpenter:

Date: October 20, 1997

From: C. M. Carvalho
BL077512H
WH 6E-139
(201) XXX-XXXX

This memorandum is to express our gratitude for your assistance in providing information to us related to the 1991 Library Services Department (77471E). Your efforts enabled us to recover all $489,448 of the overhead dollars questioned, which has an actual government impact of $25,810.

Thank you for your assistance, it was greatly appreciated.

C. M. Carvalho
Audit Liaison, Associate

D. T. Ovitt
Manager, Audit Liaison

Copy to:
W. J. Hepp
M. Young

Reporting Your Worth

When you present information, arrange it so users can assign their own value to it. Or as my friend Geoff says "I don't care how many women are in this bar. What's important is finding the one that will go home and have sex with me."

For Geoff, it is not quantity, but a quality, which is important. Anyway, you see what Geoff puts value on. But for our friend Danny, who loves to dance, it is finding great dance partners. And the more the merrier for him. Because he will dance all evening with one woman after another.

Years ago I read in the Binghamton Press & Sun-Bulletin an article about the total number of drinking establishments in the Triple Cities area of New York. But the way they reported the raw data, as just the total number of establishments, had very little value to most people. The article did not provide information as to how many of these drinking establishments were restaurants where you can obtain a good meal and how many were just places in which people could drink.

I assume some people after reading this article complained about the great number of drinking establishments in the area. But if they had given some thought to how many restaurants or diners they frequented which served alcohol, they might have realized the data was just numbers and was meaningless without another specific value added to it.

Let us ask how many of these drinking "establishments" are:

A bar whose **main** focus is serving alcohol?

Restaurants or diners, whose **main** business is serving food?

Bowling alleys, golf courses and others whose **main** business is something other than serving alcohol?

Social or fraternal organizations such as the American Legion, Elks, Moose, VFW, etc., who **only** serve their members and not the public?

And what about the sports complex, where during sporting events and cultural events you can buy a beer? But not during the high school graduation ceremonies.

You must learn what your manager values and present your information to show that value. Ask how your manager wishes to have productivity reports provided to them. Do they want raw numbers, statistics, bar charts, pie charts, or do they want some other format? Make it easy for them to see what you are doing effectively and successfully.

You need to learn how to, first, measure and, second, report the productivity of your department. Productivity can be measured in several ways.

You can measure the number of outputs per unit effort. 'Yesterday we answered 47 requests for information or help from library patrons.'

Or you can measure the variety of output per unit's effort. 'This week we provided 13 copies of specifications and standards, we did 6 online database searches, we did 3 orders for interlibrary loans of books and periodicals, and we logged in 14 new books and periodicals as well as circulating 35 other books and periodicals.'

You could measure the speed of outputs per unit effort. 'David F came to me with a rush request for information on a competitor and I provided it to him in an hour and a half, sooner than he requested'.

Track as many different types of metrics and measurements as you can. Here are some ways to track and to report what you are doing. I usually track what I do in multiple ways.

Workload: You measure the things done, like the number of books, periodicals, or articles you order and catalog. This shows the quantity, not the quality of your work.

Time: If you do a function which has to meet a certain timeline, you measure how often you achieve it. This shows if you're meeting those deadlines.

Targets: You count the number of projects you complete. Again, this only shows the quantity, not the quality. Unless these are highly valued projects within the corporation.

Datatypes: Count the number of resources used by each department, project, individual, or division. Or you count the resource used by activity, such as how many research requests, periodicals circulated, database use, etc.

Usage change: You measure the change before and after something has been changed. If you'd adapt a new service or resource, how often is it used in the first day, week or month. If your budget changes, count what it affects. If you market your resources or services, count the increases in requests.

Use reports to report your accomplishments but, most importantly, report your problems because solving those problems is the essence of management. Managers must know about things which went wrong to protect themselves. Problems or failures need to be reported, especially those which are not your fault.

Reports can be structured in this manner.

- One: State in 1 or 2 sentences the most important points. This is your executive summary. Assume most people won't read or will either skim the rest of the report.
- Two: List the resolved problems. These are reported for the last time and are not mentioned again.
- Three: State the continuing problems.
- Four: State any new problems which have arisen.
- Five: Statistics should be plotted to your best image. Show a quantifiable measure of progress compared to what either happened before or what is planned. Statistics can't be boring. They must be designed to make your point and are best presented in a graphic form.

Report only what needs to be reported. Written reports are not a good way to present new ideas to management. They're good for budgets, documentation, and staff reports. Most annual reports are a summing up of historical materials.

Reports must be consistent in format and must be brief. The higher the management level, the less they read so use graphs or charts. Report accomplishments so you and more importantly, your manager can do a little bragging and take credit. Report problems so something can be done about them. If you don't report any problems, people assume you are overstaffed or lying. If it isn't worth reporting, don't report it.

And remember to use the same format when presenting all your data. I recently saw a presentation which said the population of an area grew over 19% in several years and was expected to grow over 100,000 people in the next span of years. Wait a minute!! Those 2 numbers don't relate or mean anything when compared because you don't have any base number to compare against. It would have been better if both figures were given either in numbers or percentages.

The only way to get more money in your job is to increase the value you bring to the company and your customers. You need to market these aspects of your worth:

 - Skill: what you do
 - Expert Status and Expertise: what you are known to know
 - Reputation: what others know about you
 - Productivity: what you get done
 - Efficiency and Effectiveness: how well and quickly you get done what you do
 - Celebrity Status: how well you are known by your customers
 - Reputation: what others know about you
 - Relationships: who you know
 - Influence: what you can get others to do
 - Vision: what you see that others do not

"Use and time are the only certain tests of the value of a library."
Joseph Green Cogswell

Money

You don't talk about money with management, you talk about ideas and services. But they will always bring the conversation back around to how much the library costs and is spending. And if they're asking you to cut your budget, or they are refusing to provide the money for added services, you must make the idea of rejection painful.

Tell management if they like the services and programs you are offering, they must pay for it or else tell you what services and programs to cut. Do not offer to cut anything, ask them what you should cut.

If you do not get the budget you request, what do you do? Do you cut the items which will be least noticed or the item which will be most noticed? Make sure whatever you cut comes from the services to your user groups. What is the project or the service everyone cares about? If you are not sure what the impact will be, maximize it. Whatever you do, your decision will get both the credit and the blame.

When cutting a budget, you can minimize the impact so no one notices the cuts in your service. (But don't do that.) If you do this, management will say 'You can get along without the money'. Or you can maximize the impact so everyone will notice it.

In my career I have never understood the concept of overhead costs being applied to specific departments. When Finance told me what my overhead cost were, and I'm speaking of such things as heating, electricity, cleaning, and maintenance of the building, I always asked them to explain specifically what I was being charged for. Then I asked them to install an electric meter in the library so everyone would know exactly what the library was spending on electricity. They looked at me like I was crazy. When I asked why not, they said each department was charged by the number of employees in the department. Then I said, so when any of my staff goes on vacation, my overhead cost should go down, because the library is using less electricity, correct? Again, they looked at me like I was crazy.

After I found out what Finance was charging me for overhead services, I added those figures to my budget so I would not lose money.

What you really spend is usually unknown to most management. Libraries are caught between the money they're given, which has no relation to the cost of user services, and between the expectations of the library users which has no relation to the money you are given.

When you are selling services to users or management, let them know precisely what they will get and what they will lose if you don't get the money. You will be told, and this has no relation to reality, times are tight and they don't have any extra money for the library. Your reply must be **"My function in this organization is to provide certain functions and services and not to spend a specific amount of money"**.

Keep telling management the library deals in ideas, information, and knowledge. You and management must first talk about those ideas, information, and knowledge and then deal with the financial numbers later.

Right after I started working in AT&T's Whippany corporate library, I decided to look at the periodical circulation figures. They seemed far too low to support the several hundred subscriptions we were getting. I made signs stating we were looking at periodical circulations to gather information to support our budget figures. I requested each time an employee look at a magazine, they place a mark on the sheet taped to the shelf by the magazine. This immediately started a flow of concerned employees to my office. I assured them we would not stop any magazines right away. Many of them told me they never took out magazines, which would have shown in our circulation figures, but they came to the library and looked at several issues at one time. I told them wonderful, this is the information we need to gather. I asked them to mark down how many issues they looked at. You may have to do something similar to gather complete statistics.

When the economy or the organization's sales or income is bad, your manager will say there is no money. When the economy or the organization is doing average, your manager will say there is no money. When things are going great, your manager will say there is no money.

Your reply should always be **"My job is to run a good library and provide great services to the company's employees. That takes money."**

Do not become a "dedicated" employee. All that means is you are overworked and underpaid.

Library schools, at least the one I attended and schools other librarians talked about, have never done their part to teach librarians necessary business skills such as budgeting, cost analysis, negotiating contracts and vendor services, marketing library services, and most important, how to blow your own horn to make sure you get credit for the services and information you provide.

In most of the organizations I worked, the library never charged for the services they provided. I always tried to change that. If I did an online search for an employee, I would charge back the cost of the search and the cost of my time to the department. When the department managers screamed about this, I said "Your department is using the information you requested. If you want the information, you must pay for it. The cost for online searching does not come out of the library budget. And if management says we must pay for it, the library can't afford it and all online services will stop."

I always kept and required each of my staff to keep a daily spreadsheet upon which we recorded the task we did, who we did it for, and how long it took. This gave us daily, weekly, and monthly tracking of our time (labor costs) and what resources were being used. This is vital information you must have when dealing with management.

Book and periodical over dues were always run monthly. My policy was if a book was overdue for a year, or a magazine was overdue for 3 months, the borrower's department paid for a replacement copy.

Most people seem to concentrate on the technology by which they obtain information or services. They do not concentrate on and appreciate us individuals who obtain, manage, and at times, add value to the information or services they request.

Keep telling management there are information requests which need to be filled. I once said in a budget meeting "The engineers keep coming to me with requests for information and for articles. Shall I tell them I can't provide that anymore because you are not going to pay our bills?" Finance replied, "Of course not." I replied "Then don't tell me to stop spending money. Tell the engineers to stop requesting stuff." That shut them up for a while.

"I probably spend the equivalent of the Gross National Product of Vermont on books and records each year. I have been told that is a disease but I am not looking for a cure."
Dale Carpenter

Budgets

There are different types of budgets. Determine the type your organization is using.

Line-item budget: Different expenditures go onto different lines or against different charges. This makes it easy to compare different expenditures for different years.

Lump sum budget: All the expenditures are lumped together and are not separate.

Formula budget: Money is allocated according to a formula. This is usually related to the number of people served by your department. This determines how much you get and how it is spent.

Program budget: The budget is divided between projects or programs and then allocated by a line-item budget within the project or program.

Performance or function budgeting: The budget is divided between the tasks performed by the library. So much is spent on acquisitions, so much on periodicals, so much on copying, and so on.

Zero based budgeting: This is money allocated into various activities which are described and qualified.

Now to justify and defend your budget you should keep these types of statistics:

Activities: How many requests or orders are received and fulfilled? I have a chart with 31 columns for the days of the month and these rows: 'Reference walk in'; 'Reference call'; 'Reference email'; 'Book loaned'; 'DVD or video loaned'; 'Other loaned'; 'Interlibrary loan'; 'Other'. Each day I put quick check marks to count the different tasks and write out on a pad of paper the details.

Production: How many items were created, copied, or reproduced, etc.?

Collection: How many items do you have? What is the increase or decrease over a period? How old and relevant are the materials in your collection?

Stopwatch: How long does it take you to do specific task?

Problems: How many do you have? What type? How many did you solve? Etc.

When I was doing online research for Bendix, the electrical engineers in one group wanted to do their own database searching. They talked their manager into allowing this by saying they could get faster results than by having me do the searches. After the first month, when the Department manager received a bill for over $22,000, their searching was stopped. The electrical engineers had good intentions, but poor online searching skills. For example, sometimes they would find an interesting article and read it online which cost much more than if they had printed the article. I used this incident to tell the department their information requests would always be given top priority by me.

Go through the library's resources to determine the yearly, bi-yearly, and tri-yearly purchases the library makes. Asking for help from a long-time staff member is the best way to find this information. This will take some time as you learn the needs of your user groups. The information in most resources does not change from year to year. An encyclopedia could be purchased every 3 to 5 years, whereas The World Almanac should be a yearly purchase. Ask your staff because they will know when something was purchased and how much it gets used. Someone will always be asking what you are going to do with the old reference book. Never throw items away. Keep them for a backup reference in case the new one disappears. Or use it as a prize in a library contest.

When a budget cut comes along, work with the system. This shows you are willing to do your part. But the most important thing, cut the items the users will bitch and complain about. When the users complain about the loss of products or services, point them down the hall to the person who made the decision to cut your budget. Tell them to complain to that person.

When discussing your budget with anyone, explain any budget cuts in the terms of "our users will not have this service available" or "our users will lose this much library time". Be honest and show what you are cutting out. Give an impact statement. Try to come up with creative solutions which will meet your managers and the company goals. And always insist, if you are not given the budget you cannot provide the products or services the users request and need.

When you are defending budget problems and challenges, try to be positive, and try avoiding gripe sessions.

-- Give an impact statement. "This is what we will cut and this is how it will affect our patrons".
-- "If you don't give me the budget, I can't do the service". Make it very clear to everyone.
-- Do not be too quick to cut services. Make it a long, drawn out painful affair. If anyone asked about it or complains, point them to the decision maker and tell them to complain to them. Keep a list of persons who complained or asked about the reduction in services and use the list for budget defense.
-- Write your corporate policy to say if an item is not kept in the Library, the Library cannot be charged for the purchase of the item.

If you are asked to make out the library budget, inflate it by 50% to 75% because management is sure to ask you to cut it.

> "I must say I find television very educational.
> The minute somebody turns it on,
> I go to the library
> and read a good book."
> **Groucho Marx**

Communication

One major purpose of communicating in organizations is to control information. A lot of people communicate not to obtain information but to obtain approval for themselves or what they're doing.

The only real objectives management has for you are 'don't go over the budget' and 'have no one complain about you or the library'. The library is not important enough to really have any enemies. But you are also not important enough, most times, to have many friends. Most people are neutral about the library. Libraries are not self-evidently good. No one cares about you and the library. They only care about the impact to the organization and to library users. This is what you must focus on and discuss in any situation.

If you're going to communicate with management, you must communicate with something useful or trivia will fill the conversation. Plan for those chance meetings with management. Most upper management doesn't really know exactly what you are supposed to be doing and therefore are not sure what you are supposed to communicate to them.

I always tried to have a fact to relate when asked how I or the library was doing. "David F is keeping me busy doing competitive intelligence." or "The whole library staff is working on the digitization of our company documents."

The organization will monitor very closely any department, group, or process directly concerned with getting a product out the door. Most libraries do not fall within that category. Fight against this mindset by saying **"The library gives our employees knowledge which they use to improve our products and create new products. The company sells those products for money. That money pays your salary. So the library helps create products which create money."**

You need to get management talking about ideas. Focus on the library's impact to the organization and the users. If management rejects an idea, a proposal, or a project, you must make the rejection painful. Stress how it will affect the users. They will often use the statement "You should do something because it is good for the organization'. Reply 'Closing the library and laying off the library staff is good for the organization because it will save money. But doing so, in both the short term and long term, doesn't make sense'.

Always remember those who do not support you and the library oppose you by supporting something else.

Some people will go out of their way not to answer questions. One way they do this is by creating obstacles by saying 'yes, but'. Most people can always come up with a 'yes, but'.

Many people do not want to hear information because it will cause problems for them. They do not want to talk to you because either they believe it is not important to them or they know what you want and they do not want to give it to you. They are making value judgments and they will only make time for the things important to them.

Some people create unnecessary tasks they need to perform or create problems just so they can avoid making decisions on the issues you raise.

Many people are very good at answering questions which are not asked. You need to get them focusing on the questions you ask. Many managers avoid making decisions because that is their nature. They believe it is better to make no decision then to make a possible bad one.

Your manager may avoid communicating with you by making you and your library and your work seen trivial compared to all the other problems they have.

In my career it has seemed nothing has ever been accomplished at a staff meeting. They might be good at communicating information downward, but they are not good for communicating information upward to management. Most of the time it seems the participants are just showing off for everyone else. Good management communication happens one on one.

Most meetings run on until they hit a barrier. Two of the barriers are lunchtime and the end of the day. If you want a long meeting, start at 9 AM. If you want a short, effective meeting, start it at 11 AM or 4 PM.

Financial Planning for Librarians

You need to do financial planning for retirement. No one else will do it for you, and you can't expect the companies you work for to aid you in your retirement. Not only did I never get a gold watch or a severance agreement when I left a company, the only real good benefit was a set of cheap steak knives after working for 5 years at Bendix.

I was laid off by The Medicines Company after working there 8 years and 11 months. They said it was for financial reasons. But when looking at the 65 people who were laid off, it seems many of us were getting near the 10 years of service when we would have been fully vested in their retirement plans. Maybe it was for good financial reasons. Theirs.

Consider, for the first and usually the last 20 years of your life, you are consuming but not producing any income. Only during the middle years of your life, you're producing income for those later years, and income for your retirement.

What can you do now to work towards a successful retirement? **Save As Much as Possible Now.** Consider doubling what you are now saving. The easiest way is to increase the percentage taken out of your paycheck and put into your pension plan. All your investments should be safe and long-term, such as an index fund from a low-cost company.

I always tried to have 20% or 25% of my pretax income taken out and put into a company's pension plan or 401(K) or whatever savings plan they had. Oh yes, it greatly reduced my take home pay. But I was willing to do it then to have money when I retire.

I always joined and used credit unions rather than banks because their fees were usually lower and they gave better service because they were not as interested in making money. Ask your human resources department or financial department if the employees can become a member of a local credit union.

You also need to think about the employment positions you consider. As I became well known in the library profession, recruiters called me offering jobs. Many offers were for positions in Manhattan. After discussing the position details, I would always ask about salary. When the recruiters said the salary was about what I was currently making, the conversation would go like this.

"So you and this company want to pay me for 8 hours but have me work 10 hours or more."
"What do you mean?"
"I would spend an hour or more commuting to work, work 8 hours, and commute another hour or so back home."
"Your commuting time doesn't count."
"My time is valuable to me and the company must pay for it along with the cost of commuting."
"You could move into the city." (They always said this.)
"Okay, I rent a 2 bedroom apartment, with a balcony and have off-street parking. So I need to get paid enough to rent the same in Manhattan. How much will that be?"
"This is a very good position with a very prestigious company."
"I don't care about prestige. I care about money and my time. You are asking me to either not get paid for my time commuting or to lower my living standard and more into a more expensive area. Neither option works in my favor. But I will give you the names of a couple of people I know who might consider this position." (I always offered to pass on job openings when contacted by recruiters.)

Manchester International & Right Management 1998 to 2003

After leaving Lucent I quickly obtained a Research Director position with Manchester International, a career transition and career consulting firm. This used to be called "outplacement" services. When a large company has a layoff, they hire a career transition firm to help those laid-off individuals find jobs. They provide everything from emotional support, resume writing and review services, industry and company research, and information resources training.

Here is the introductory note I and the company put together and sent out to all Manchester employees:

> Dale Carpenter
> Research Director
>
> Dale Carpenter brings to Manchester a combination of unique skills and experiences gained as a manager, trainer, marketer, author, and creative design consultant in such diverse industries as construction, retail sales, communication, aerospace, and entertainment media. Aware of the need to manage change, Dale has championed process improvement, project management and staff development wherever he worked.
>
> Dale assists Manchester candidates in their job searches by teaching and providing online research and the use of the library's resources. These are used to provide the candidates with company background information, industry and product studies, biographical information, and market research.
>
> His wide-ranging knowledge of all phases of the library sciences has been gained in over eighteen years as an academic, public, and corporate librarian. Dale started his library career in the State University of New York library system and moved on to create, manage, and modernize corporate libraries for such Fortune 500 firms as Singer-Link, AlliedSignal, and Lucent Technologies.
>
> Dale holds a Master's Degree in Library and Information Science and continues his education. He has published articles in library and consumer journals and is the author of several books.

Alphabetical by Color 168

A former US. Army paratrooper, Dale's curiosity, and interest in providing individuals with solutions to their information needs led him into the library and information field and to Manchester.

Wow, I sound great don't I?

I was specifically hired to create and conduct training programs and workshops. I taught everything from how to use the World Wide Web to research industries and companies, how to look for jobs online, and how to apply to those positions. I often did in-depth research for individuals who wanted a list of companies in a specific industry in a specific geographical area.

Here are descriptions of the 2 main seminars I gave while at Manchester, "Database Usage" (on the 4 databases available to candidates) and "Internet Usage".

Candidate Training Seminar: Database Usage

Introductions:
   Instructor Introduction: name, title, job function, background,
   Quick overview of what the session will entail
   Class Introductions: name, profession, industry,

How to find the databases:
   Manchester's webpage
   Resource Center and what it holds
   Databases: Overview of each database, what it contains, and how it is useful to candidate's job search

JobMatch -
   JobMatch contains jobs sent to us by companies or recruiters, length of posting, etc.
      How JobMatch is set up and view of a typical job posting
      How to use the filter function to search for positions
      Searching by state, using keywords, limiting by date, etc.

CareerSearch -
CareerSearch contains useful of lists of companies in industries and recruiters working in your specific areas

Alphabetical by Color

Industries: How to select industries, and select by number of employees or annual sales figures

Locations: How to select locations, either by region, state, county, or city, or by zip code radius

Keywords: Using keywords to focus your search

Working with Results:
    What company information is provided
    Get Data Now button
    Usefulness of Search Criteria Report, Summary List, Full Report,
    Downloading Full Report and creating a mail merge

Recruiters:
    Going into Industries and creating a list of recruiters
    Selecting Industries and Specialties
    Difference between Retain and Contingency
    Salary Level
    Getting Data same as above

InSite2 -

InSite2 contains information for creating targeted lists and preparing for an interview

Company: How to search for companies, expand basic information, and look at articles

Industries: How to search for industries, and view results, and Using SIC codes to gather targeted lists

Power Search: Using Words Anywhere to ensure a complete search

Prospecting: How to create a targeted search using different criteria: industry, state, sales figures, etc.

D&B Million Dollar Directory -

D&B contains very detailed company information and ways of creating a targeted search

Search Options 1 through 4

Searching by company name, industry, location, executive name, SIC code and using these criteria together

Candidate Training Seminar: Internet Usage

This seminar is never taught the same way twice because of the various levels of knowledge and experience the candidates bring and the questions they ask and the time available. I always ask them what they want to know and focus the presentation on the sites most useful to their professions and industries.

But a general outline would include:

Overview and history of the Internet and the World Wide Web
Bookmarks available on the candidate computers - handout given to attendees
Useful sites:
    Business information gathering
    Industry or profession specific job posting sites
    News sites, general and industry or profession specific
    Search engines: how they work and how to use them
Searching a job site, such as Monster.com or Career Mosaic
Posting a resume on a job site
Answers to specific questions

A great number of the individuals we worked with had no computer experience at all. Remember, this was back in 1999 and the World Wide Web had only existed since 1994. I did a lot of explaining and training on computer usage. One of my training sessions focused specifically on how to paste a resume on a recruiter's or a company's website or how to email it to someone.

I kept hearing from various Manchester staff members about the different ways recruiters wanted to hear from candidates. Since no one could provide me with definite facts, I decided to do a survey of recruiters. From one of our online databases, I gathered email addresses of recruiters or recruiting companies. I requested their help and offered to share the results of the survey with them. 416 responded to the survey. I consolidated the results, shared it with our management, and with all the recruiters.

Our corporate management sent a press release to the Wall Street Journal and the results were published in July 2000. Dow Jones, owner of The Wall Street Journal, contacted me personally and wanted the specific results of the survey. But when I wanted authorship credit and for them to pay every time they sold the article in the future from their database, they refused.

Sure, I do the work, you want to pay me one small lump sum, and then charge over and over for other people to view my work in your database. Great deal for you but terrible for me.

Anyway, recruiters want to be contacted by email. But they do not like attachments because of the fear of viruses. They prefer you paste your resume into the main body of your email. They also want more specific information in the header line besides your name and resume. See the chapter in the appendix for details.

Another project I completed while at Manchester was to create a bibliography of over 500 websites for professional development and industry research. It was grouped into industry categories so someone experienced in telecommunications could have one place to find websites for professional organizations, recruiters specializing in telecommunications, and the websites of major companies. This bibliography was placed on Manchester's website so all candidates could access it. My training guides for all the resources available through Manchester were also made available digitally.

I managed 3 separate libraries for Manchester. I ordered acquisitions, managed the budget, did collection development, purchasing, and managed vendor contracts. I traveled between 4 libraries weekly to give training sessions. Look at a map of New Jersey and find Parsippany, Saddlebrook, Princeton and Manhattan, New York. Those were the 4 cities I was traveling to each week.

From: Carpenter, Dale
Sent: Tuesday, September 24, 2002 3:24 PM
To: K, Linda; W, Alice; G, Kathleen; R, Kimberly; W, Pat
Cc: MAN Resource Managers
Subject: Dale's Hectic October Schedule

My schedule for October:

Every Wednesday I am in Princeton
Every Thursday I am in Manhattan
Every other Monday I am at Saddlebrook
Every Tuesday and Friday I am at Parsippany

Sept 30	Online Resource Instruction – Beginning	9 am
Oct 3	Research Resources on the WWW Manhattan	10:30 am
Oct 7	Online Resource Instruction – Beginning	9 am
Oct 7	Research Resources on the WWW Saddlebrook	1 pm
Oct 8	Research Resources on the WWW Parsippany	9 am
Oct 9	Research Resources on the WWW Princeton	9 am
Oct 14	Online Resource Instruction – Beginning	9 am
Oct 14	Online Resource Instruction – Advanced	11 am
Oct 17	Electronic Resumes: Creation and Usage Manhattan	10:30 am
Oct 21	Online Resource Instruction – Beginning	9 am
Oct 21	Electronic Resumes: Creation and Usage Saddlebrook	1 pm
Oct 22	Electronic Resumes: Creation and Usage Parsippany	9 am
Oct 23	Electronic Resumes: Creation and Usage Princeton	9 am
Oct 28	Online Resource Instruction – Beginning	9 am
Oct 31	Research Resources on the WWW Manhattan	10:30 am

Gee, whatever happened to the theory that presenting courses using WebEx would cut down on the time I spend teaching?

From: Carpenter, Dale
Sent: Friday, October 11, 2002 4:13 PM
To: McH, Peggy
Cc: W, Alice; K, Linda; MAN Resource Managers
Subject: Tasks Done In 2002

Everyone,
   Peggy asked me to quickly put together a list of tasks I have performed in 2002. Below, to the best of my ability and memory, is the list. Since we researchers add concrete value to the services Manchester provides our candidates, we all should keep lists of our efforts. Eventually I would not be surprised if we would be recording

in MCP any meetings we have with Exalts or LITs, as a way of showing their companies precisely what we are doing for them.

Please pardon the roughness of the report, as this was put together this Friday afternoon. If any of you researchers remember any other task we do, please let me know so I may add it to this list. I hope you have a good weekend.

Dale Carpenter

Partial List of Tasks Performed in 2002

	In House Seminars	WebEx Training Seminars
January	8	4
February	8	4
March	6	3
April	7	4
May	8	4
June	6	4
July	10	5
August	8	6
September	8	5
October (so far)	3	2
TOTAL	72	41

182 research requests forms found. Sometimes a candidate will come in to ask a question about how to do a search and I will demonstrate how to do it then download the search for them. I might not remember to fill out a request form. I am sure the total number of searches is over 200. (I need to keep better records.)

23 requests filled for the business developers (best estimated number). These may range from gathering news articles about a company to finding the senior VP of sales for the Fortune 500 companies.

Other tasks done throughout the year:
 Present research updates to the administration and business development staff at several offices,
  Help train new researchers,
  Update bookmark list for website,
  Team member for creation of training materials,
 Manage 4 Libraries: vendor contact person, order items, update periodicals, budgeting, etc.,

Meet with shoppers (did not keep good enough records to estimate how many),

Move computers, fax machines, and other company equipment between offices with personal car,

Copy pertinent articles from newspapers and magazines and post on office bulletin boards,

Preview information resources for possible inclusion on website (to replace other database) or into Library,

Answer hundreds of emails from candidates on procedures, Internet resources, and career transition questions.

Here is a list of the functions I performed, along with my goals for the next year. This was put together for a semi-annual evaluation meeting with my supervisor, Linda K. I also listed what I felt were deficiencies affecting my and the other Research Directors work.

Added responsibilities and duties of 2 Researcher positions to those I was hired to perform. Perform the functions of 3 Researcher positions while being paid salary for 1 position.

Provide research to candidates in a timely, accurate, and efficient in 4 widely scattered offices.

Conduct in-house and online training seminars on a regular basis in 4 offices.

Provide Sales and Marketing staff with research support.

Train staff and new researchers.

Stay current with professional trends, technology, and strategies.

Responded to interview research requests ASAP, all others within 1 week from data of request.

Company needs improved in-house and online resources for business and industry research by candidates and staff.

I need to attend professional meetings and conferences and take technical training to maintain professional skills.

I want to become the Director of Information Services., reporting to the CEO of MPS Group.

Manchester needs to create, support, and provide funding and authority to a corporate level position with the responsibility and authority to oversee the acquisition, distribution, and control of the resources needed to provide for the information and research needs of the entire MPS Group.

We served all levels at Manchester. Companies would provide different lengths of service depending upon someone's rank in an organization. Secretaries and clerks, if they got anything at all, might get 1 training session on how to search for jobs on the web. Mid-level managers might get several months. Upper-level managers might get 6 months or a year. It was not unusual in my introductory training session on Manchester's services to have administrative staff sitting next to mid-level or upper-level executives.

Often, I went beyond the level of service a person was provided. As I have been taught, I treat everyone the same. I don't care who they are, what job level they had, I treat them all professionally and respectfully. I understood what they were going through having been laid off myself more than once.

Manchester International did have an informal library network because it had offices around the United States. Us 'Research Directors', which is what we were called, reported into the general managers of the offices where we were based and not to someone in corporate headquarters. We did share and communicate with each other the training guides and materials we independently developed. Since several industries are geographically centered, such as oil and gas in the Southwest, and pharmaceuticals in the Northeast, some of us focused more on specific industries then others. If a candidate wanted to relocate, we would notify a Manchester office in the area they were planning to move to and asked them to help the candidate.

On May 5, 2000 the "ILoveYou" virus spread around the world. It infected computers when the owner clicked on an email attachment, and forwarded itself to every email address in that computer, if the owner had not taken any security precautions. Since I was aware of security concerns, I never opened the attachment and so my computer was not infected. Even if it had been I always send my email and attachments as plain text, so the virus would not have spread from me. Everyone in Manchester was infected and some people were bragging about how many times the virus was sent to their computer and forwarded.

The next year in February 2001, the "Anna Kournikova" virus did the same thing, infected computers around the world as people supposedly clicked on an image of the athlete. Again, I did not click on the image and my computer was not infected. Because there was no central IT security department and no computer security training for the employees, we had massive computer problems which took time to solve.

In 1999 Modus purchased Manchester International. They incorporated Manchester's headquarters staff from Philadelphia, with the Modus staff in Jacksonville Florida. Manchester had a director of research position at the corporate level. Modus did not have such a corporate level position so they abolished it.

Manchester's director of research did competitive intelligence as part of their job. They researched what competitors existed, their executives, their lines of business, strengths and weaknesses, reputation, and market share. This information was shared throughout Manchester, along with news events which affected our business.

In 2002 Modus's corporate finance and business development department sent out an email to over 200 people requesting them to perform competitive intelligence about Modus's competition.

I worked up a cost benefit ratio comparing hiring a corporate level director research to perform competitive intelligence against asking over 200 people to perform this job. Here it is in a nutshell.

Rough estimate of each person's salary $100,000
They are working 2080 hours per year, each being paid $48.08 per hour
If they researched two hours per week for 50 weeks that is $4808
200 people times $4808 equals $961,600.

You could easily hire a librarian and pay them to set up alerts on each competitor for far less.

In early 2000 the Saddlebrook office was closed with no notice. Candidates were told to use other offices. Not hearing of any plans to clean the office, I and a lady friend went to Saddlebrook after work one night and took all the supplies we could use in Parsippany. And used the opportunity to fool around.

In the early 2000's the career transition industry was consolidating and Manchester International was acquired by Right Management in early 2003. I was not retained by Right Management but was hired for a one-year contract position to work in a career center for the individuals affected by the Pfizer and Pharmacia merger.

Right Management rented space and created a career center in the Bedminster Bridgewater area of New Jersey. For a year I drove from northern New Jersey to central New Jersey and did basically the same thing I did for Manchester international. I taught individuals how to use the resources, how to do online job searching, do company, business, and industry research, and help them any way I could. I also worked with recruiters who contacted us and said they were looking for certain skill sets. I would send the recruiters the resumes of individuals with those skills.

Gary D., the vice president of human resources for a Massachusetts-based company, The Medicines Company (TMC), contacted me. TMC was a small pharmaceutical company relocating from Massachusetts to New Jersey because New Jersey has a much larger pharmaceutical industry and therefore a larger pool of candidates to draw upon. I made arrangements for Gary to come in and speak to the candidates, publicized the talk, and provided Gary with several CD-ROMs loaded with resumes of people with certain skills.

-----Original Message-----
From: Carpenter, Dale
Sent: Wednesday, July 18, 2001 4:17 PM
To: Catherine P/Manchester/US@Manchester, Regina N/Manchester/US@Manchester, Peggy McH/Manchester/US@Manchester, Kristie P/Manchester/US@Manchester, Kathleen P/NAmerica/MPS@MPS, Linda K/NAmerica/MPS@MPS, Lisa R/NAmerica/MPS@MPS, Janice U/NAmerica/MPS@MPS, Lillian C/Manchester/US@Manchester, Jeanne G/Manchester/US@Manchester, Rebekah S/Manchester/US@Manchester, Julie St/Manchester/US@Manchester
cc: Alice W/Manchester/US@Manchester, Ann F/NAmerica/MPS@MPS, Leslie G/Manchester/US@Manchester, Tracy R/NAmerica/MPS@MPS
Subject: Updated Research Request Forms

Friends,
  Attached are the forms used when candidates request help in finding a listing of companies, a list of recruiters, or information to prepare for an interview. They have been updated to reflect changes in CareerSearch's listings of industries. Since I get asked for regional searches a lot, I have added a checkbox for the metropolitan New York City area. It should be easy to edit to show whatever the metro area most useful to you.
  Please pass these on to anyone doing research for candidates and let me know of your suggestions to improve these forms.
    Dale

<< File: request form- Employer or Industry.doc >>
<< File: request form- Executive Recruiter.doc >>
<< File: request form- Interview Research.doc >>

From: Linda K/NAmerica/MPS@MPS
Sent: Wednesday, July 25, 2001 3:12 PM
To: Dale Carpenter/Manchester/US@Manchester
Subject: Research Forms

Your research forms are the best I've seen anywhere. Can you bring those along or base a presentation on the forms you use so we can make them the "Manchester Company Standard"?

If you can do a presentation regarding your forms and then have them emailed or a disk available along with a copy of your presentation, I would like to make your papers mandatory the day the "researchers" leave Philly.

Your thoughts?

I was asked by one of the sales directors what I covered in my 'Electronic Resume Seminar'. Here is the email I sent.

From: Carpenter, Dale
Sent: Thursday, August 29, 2002 3:10 PM
To: MAN Resource Managers
Subject: Electronic Resume Session Overview

Dear Everyone,
   Joan C asked what I covered in my Electronic Resume training session so here is an overview. The main idea is to inform the candidates why they need an electronic resume, how to create one, how to send it to recruiters, and how to post it on job boards and company websites.

   I start by showing them a humorous fake resume of mine. It is in Word and I've attached it to show you what it looks like. This gets their attention. I point out the most important part of the resume is the 'content' contained in the resume. It does not matter how it looks, as long as your resume gets pulled up when someone searches a database.

   Next, I show them how to save a Word document as a plain text file. Opening the plain text file, I point out the content is all still there.

   I next open Outlook and draft an email to a recruiter. I stress the subject line is very important and should contain their profession and level of expertise and perhaps a specialty if they have one. Ex: "VP Marketing Retail Industry". If they are emailing a recruiter using a networking name, the name should be in the subject line. Example: "Betty Judd suggested I talk with you."

   In the body of the email I draft a quick cover letter containing a candidate's profession, level of expertise, company, and industry. I mention if their skills are transferable to multiple industries, they may want to say they are open to working in any industry. I also put in their compensation as a range. Ex: "In the last three years my compensation has been between $72,000 and $77,000." This is so the recruiter can place them at a salary level.

Below this cover letter, I paste the plain text resume. Why? So the recruiter sees it at once and does not have to open an attachment. This also removes any worries about viruses. They can still download it into their database and when they want a pretty Word version to send to a company, they will call and ask for one.

At this point someone may ask if this is what to do when applying for a specific position. Yes, I say, but a bit different. It should have the position title and job number in the subject line. In the email body should be what position you are applying for and how specifically you match the skills and experience asked for. Again, getting the content to them is the important point. You can always offer to mail them a resume when you are doing a phone interview and always carry copies into an interview

Next, I pull up the WWW and ask if anyone has posted their resume on a job board and ask which job boards. I go to a job board and walk through the steps needed to register and post a resume. I don't really finish the posting so my fake resume never gets on the site but I show how to paste it. I tell them most job boards are like this but mention Monster is very different requiring about 45 minutes to an hour to fill out multiple boxes. I have read this was done so companies and recruiters can easily compare resumes printed from Monster.

Now the next subject is which job boards to use. For this I pull up the Riley Guide and tell them this is the one site they NEED to remember. I go into Job Listings and show them how to find sites specific to their professions and/or industries. I also show the wonderful Index and the section on Interviewing and Negotiating a Job Offer.

Then I mention how companies are leaving job boards to work with Direct Employers, a non-profit association of companies. I go to that site and run several searches showing how easy it is to use, how it takes you to a company website where the job is posted and how you can apply for the job.

I also might mention how many people are adding a paragraph of keywords to the end of their resume to help it get found in database searches. When a candidate asks if there is a dictionary of keywords or phrases, I say I am unaware of one but they could create their own by searching job boards for positions in their industry and writing down the phrases which keep re-occurring in the jobs.

Sorry I took so long to respond to the question but I wanted to give you enough details so you have a good idea of how I cover the subject. If anyone have any thoughts about what I could add or improve, please let me know.

Dale

Attaboy Letters

From: David H B [dbetof@home.com]
Sent: Wednesday, September 05, 2001 10:28 AM
To: jb@manchesterus.com
Cc: Dale Carpenter
Subject: Follow up to our mtg / seminar / & recognition

Jim:
   I want to thank you again for making your company's resources available to me, your advice, and contacts from our meeting on August 16th.
   I also want to take this opportunity to bring to your attention the very helpful follow up one-on-one assistance that Dale Carpenter provided me this morning by phone. Dale was kind enough to give me an hour of his time to walk me through a focused personal set of searches from your web site that will be of great value to me. As I also told you when we met for lunch that day, I thought Dale made an excellent presentation.
   Although I thanked Dale for all his help, I thought this message to you was warranted since upper management should get positive feedback on valued employees representing themselves and your company in such a positive manner.
   I will keep you updated on my progress as well, and thanks again.

   Dave B

Attaboy Letters

To: Linda K
Cc: Dale Carpenter, John G, Tom F
From: Marjorie A. M
Re: Recognition of a Job Well Done – Dale Carpenter
November 7, 2001

Since this is a time that we, as a company, are focusing on individual performance achievement, I would like to recognize Dale Carpenter.

Dale was a key contributor in our successful launch of the Parsippany Career FastTrack Center – a center that serviced 700+ candidates with revenues in excess of $4 million. Dale jumped in and provided initial and on-going learning for our consultants on the Manchester databases and website. He arranged and prepared numerous special sessions for the CFT team, so that we could deliver quality service supported by our Webpage capability. He also enabled us to learn research methods and tools so that we could uncover Industry, function, and geographical opportunities for our candidates.

When new consultants were hired, Dale was there for training and individual coaching. Often when the server was down, and consultants had scheduled candidate sessions on e-sourcing, recruiting, researching, Dale was there providing guidance and direction.

I know that Dale would find it uncomfortable to "sing his own praises", so I am doing it for him! The CFT Team considers Dale invaluable to their individual success with candidates.

I would personally like to thank Dale for being a wonderful business partner!

**"The greatest sin a teacher can commit is to bore his students."
Watson B. Duncan III**

The Medicines Company 2004 to 2013

In February 2004 the one-year position with Right Management ended and I looked for another job. Lo and behold, I saw The Medicines Company (TMC) was advertising for a librarian. I sent a cover letter and resume directly to Gary D. and reminded him what I had done. I was interviewed, hired, and started in June 2004 as TMC's first professional librarian.

TMC had rented office space in a corporate park and was renovating an area for the library. The library had been designed by David M, the vice president of IT who was to be my manager. It was a well-designed space with secure limited access, and movable shelves. The shelves slid on tracks so you could open or close various aisles. However it was designed for the storage of materials and not for the use of them. There was not a table where people could look at documents, nor a computer to do inventory or to sign in and sign out materials.

The first-floor space wasn't finished so while waiting for it to be completed, I had a cubicle up on the second floor. And since more people were being hired people were moved around so departments could be grouped together. Being a department of 1, I moved 4 times in the first 4 months before the first-floor offices were finished and we moved downstairs.

The Friday we moved, one of the salespeople found a bottle of wine he had been given as a gift so he opened it for a small celebration. This started a weekly practice of people bringing in wine for late Friday afternoons. This was shortly joined by cheese, crackers and other delights. This went on for a month and a half until management found out and put a halt to it.

David M. asked me to find software for managing and tracking the company's documents which would be kept in the library. You can read about this in my book "Computer Software Evaluation: Balancing User's Needs and Wants". While doing this project, I met with every department head and upper-level corporate management person. The first thing I asked them was **"What can the library do to provide you the most value?"** See the appendix for other questions I asked.

After each meeting, I wrote up my notes from the interview and sent them to the person. I would ask if I missed anything we talked about or wrote something down incorrectly. This is a great policy because I could always refer back to those meeting notes.

Once the physical library was ready, I drove a U-Haul rental truck from Parsippany, New Jersey to the Waltham, Massachusetts offices to bring down company documents. 145 boxes of regulatory documents, 25 boxes of marketing materials, and 6 full-size metal shelves. This way we could say there was always a company employee in possession of the documents. The people in Waltham were not happy at all to see the documents being moved. 3 other times during my employment with TMC, I drove vehicles to other locations to bring documents and materials to our Parsippany location. 55 boxes one trip, 58 boxes on another trip.

Once the documents from Waltham arrived in the library I unpacked, sorted, and shelved them. Then using Microsoft Word and Excel I did a complete inventory. There was a lot of extra materials I put in various areas of the library, and later inventoried and archived. Once the secure library was working, other departments had sensitive material they wanted stored and locked. This had not been planned for so we retrofitted some of the shelves with sliding metal doors. They slid down from the top like a garage door and could be locked. Legal, HR and Finance brought in documents they secured in those locking units.

While this was going on, I wrote library policies and standard operating procedures for the use, lending, archiving, and eventual destruction of library materials. These were passed around for comment and eventually standardized and approved. You can see generic versions of these in an appendix.

TMC purchased another pharmaceutical company named Targanta with offices in Indianapolis and Boston. I went to both of those places to help pack up information and ship it back to New Jersey. I was told all their documentation had been packed and was ready to be shipped. What a laugh. When I walked around the Indianapolis office, I found hundreds and hundreds of documents, computer discs and flash drives laying out in the open on desks, shelves, and tables. When I started opening desk drawers, I found lots more. I grabbed everything I found, packed it, and shipped it to New Jersey. Of course there were many duplicates, but a lot of items I packed were originals not matching anything they had packed. I also packed up items with Targanta' s name on it, like coffee cups, placemats, signs, etc., to save their company history. All of this was inventoried and placed into TMC's archives.

I was given the task of the corporate archivist and Karen W, the office manager, was glad to give it to me. This entailed requesting and receiving materials from off-site archiving, delivering materials to the requester, receiving returning materials back, and arranging for the return to off-site archiving. Eventually I did a complete inventory of the archives to provide highly detailed lists to each department of their holdings.

I presented management with my recommendations on what document management software TMC should purchase. David M chose a different software package, Smeadlink. His rational was that company had an office in New Jersey whereas my company of choice did not. The main problem turned out to be Smeadlink was only the retailer of the software. The company which owned it was in California and was mainly an office supply company. They had developed Smeadlink just to have an inventory product to sell and did not really support it at all. The company I selected called me more times in the next year than Smeadlink did, just to ask how things were working out. That shows the support they offered.

Once software for the library had been selected and brought in-house, I filled it with the inventory of the library materials. Once other departments had seen it, they requested it for their use. I developed custom document databases for Finance, Legal, Manufacturing, Quality Assurance, and the medical writing groups. As one example, we scanned in all the company contracts so Finance and Legal could review them at any time. I offered to, in my spare time, scan in their materials so they would be always up to date. But Finance and Legal got lazy and decided not to use the database or scan in any new contracts. A year and a half after I did all this work, they gave money to an outside firm to re-scan in all the materials and provide access.

I also did online database research for TMC. This consisted of business, scientific, medical, and technical research. There was an outside company researching for any mention of our drugs in the scientific literature. I successfully convinced management this could be done in-house for less money and with better, faster results. The research was brought in and given to me. This of course ticked off the people who had hired this outside research firm. Drug Safety, who helped me set up the alerting searches, was greatly impressed with the improved results.

Others really saw the value of my online research services. As one example, an investment company was coming in to meet with TMC. I was asked to do research on the individuals coming to the meeting. I found one of them had gone to the same college 1 of our finance directors had attended. I passed this specific information onto him along with the fact the other person had belonged to a certain fraternity.

Our finance director used this actionable intelligence to make an immediate connection with the other individual. After the meeting, the director told me the other individual was not aware our director had attended the same college. Score one for me and my research.

I made up this explanation and description of my position at TMC for use during any training seminar or presentation I gave just in case someone new was in the meeting. And to remind co-workers I did more than find materials for them.

MDCO Library Resources

Dale Carpenter Information Professional
Using the Internet to perform research since 1979
(And the World Wide Web after it went online in 1991)
Joined MDCO June 1, 2004

What has Dale recently done for The Medicines Company?

Premier Healthcare alliance research – briefing package for Clive M (our CEO) and senior management before MDCO and Premier meeting - Premier healthcare alliance is more than 2,100 US.

hospitals and 54,000-plus other healthcare sites working together to improve healthcare quality and affordability - corporate and legal structure - senior management bios and pictures - 2008 annual report - code of conduct - guide for suppliers - financial statements - news articles - details of alliance programs

Risk-sharing contracting (also called value-based contracting) – John R - gather and analyze articles on risk-sharing agreements in pharmaceutical and other industries in the US and other countries - provide both news articles and academic research papers on the subject

Brand launch investment research – Jennifer W – How companies invested their money during the launch of a new brand. In pre-launch stage, at initial launch stage, or after – Tactics companies used to launch a new brand

Find leading medical journals in foreign countries – Drug Safety - To perform complete adverse event safety searches, Drug Safety needs to know the leading medical journals in foreign countries where MDCO drugs are available - An ongoing effort - We contact foreign MDCO associates and ask what the leading medical journals are in their country, and try to find a resource which allows for online searching of those journals

   So Dale
Makes information available to the desktop
Provides competitive intelligence
Conducts research on the user's behalf
Manages a physical library

Eventually the digitization of the company documents was started. The Food and Drug Administration (FDA) was still accepting paper submissions but had stated they were going to go totally electronic. We knew we eventually had to take everything electronic. For security reasons, we scanned the documents as TIF files, not PDF files. A TIF file cannot be changed but a PDF file can with the proper software. The scanner we had purchased from the outside company, as I detail in my book, was running extremely slowly. And while the outside vendor and IT were arguing over whose fault it was, I went through the software settings and found out they had been set to the lowest possible scan rate.

A little modification by me and scanning increased dramatically.

I scanned in over a million pages of our original FDA filings and materials from various clinical trials. While doing this I discovered several cd-roms had begun to separate and it was difficult to copy the old files from them. They were less than 10 years old.

TMC had the practice of every yearly quarter holding a town hall meeting. I think this is a wonderful practice and more companies should do this. At the meeting upper management and managers from various projects and programs reviewed the past quarter, detailed milestones they had hit and the ones they missed. They gave information on any major activity which affected the entire company. And then reviewed the milestones for the next quarter. Also, all new employees were introduced. This practice of quarterly meetings kept all our employees well informed on how the company was performing as well as building a strong sense of community and commitment. It also helped cut down rumors.

At one town hall meeting, it was announced some individuals were coming aboard and negotiating different vacation levels so it was decided everyone in the company would automatically have 4 weeks of vacation a year. That got a standing ovation. However most people really worked too hard to take 4 weeks of vacation. I was within the first 125 people hired and when I was let go there was several thousand people worldwide.

TMC had grown so much in 6 years after relocating to New Jersey, we had outgrown our space in our building. We had the complete ground floor, individuals sitting on 2 other floors of the building and there was no other space to expand into. TMC negotiated the complete renovation of another building in the corporate park and moved there.

I was invited by the TMC group and the architectural firm to give some input about the layout of the new library. Most of my suggestions were ignored. For example, we had different teams working on different drugs in development. I suggested separate secure rooms for those documents. This way it would be easy to ensure only team members had access to their documents. Nope.

The library move did not go well. I packed up all the documents, crews came in and dismantled the shelves, and took them to the other building. It was found the tracks in the new library had been installed at the wrong width. The tracks had to be taken up and reinstalled.

I sat alone in our offices in the old building for 2 weeks while this work was being done. The lady I was currently seeing, a different one from my Bendix days, was also adventurous. A couple times she visited me at lunchtime and we had fun.

So this is another library I had sex in. Jealous?

After the move to the new building I discovered the installers had drilled screws through the end support panels into the shelving. Those shelves could not be adjusted up or down to fit the height of books. I dismantled and fixed them myself because I was not waiting for the movers to come back.

But this library had more space so my desk was inside the library. We had tables to spread documents out and work on them, and bookcases for reference books and periodicals. It was on the first floor in the same hallway as several conference and training rooms. Individuals meeting there were always coming to the library for supplies, to use the phone, or to informally meet in the library.

One day Chris S., a co-worker, came to me asking for help. His son was scheduled to have a surgical procedure and there were several different variations on the way it could be performed. Chris asked if I could find out if there was any studies done on the effectiveness of the various procedures. I said I could try. He brought to me copies of the literature the doctors had given him. I studied what he had given me, drafted up a search strategy and began searching. I found several comparison studies had been performed, downloaded them and gave them to Chris. He thanked me greatly. A few months later he brought in a letter his wife had written to me thanking me for my help and telling me their son was doing great.

Alphabetical by Color

About 2 years later IT decided to review their archive holdings. They ran backup tapes every day and weekly and stored them offsite. When TMC was just starting out, the tapes were stored in bank safety deposit boxes but now we had taken all the available space in the bank. Since the Library was the only room in the building which could be secured nightly, it was used for the inventory. All the tapes were brought to the library, sorted into numerical order, and repacked. The newest guy in IT and I did the job. We inventoried and repacked 82 bins into 51 bins.

Now that I had space for some projects, I did a detailed inventory of all archived materials. I found 6 copies of the original Articles of Confederation for TMC. This was common, finding multiple copies of materials because several people archived the same thing. We did not need 6 copies. I archived 1 set under the Legal department heading, 1 set in the company historical materials section, and 1 copy under the corporate department heading. Reviewing the archives, I reduced 320 1/2 ft. cubic feet to 214 ft. cubic feet saving over $120 a month while providing a more detailed, comprehensive inventory of archived materials.

Archives Cleanup Results

When viewing the Iron Mountain inventory of materials archived, I found many boxes had minimal inventory descriptions and many documents/reports were listed as being in multiple boxes. This fall I undertook an updating of our Iron Mountain inventory.

Materials were viewed, sorted, duplicates eliminated, damaged folders or binders replaced with un-damaged ones, and repacked while a much more comprehensive inventory was created.

148 boxes archived dating from 1998 through 2003 consisting of 320.5 cubic feet were repacked into 95 boxes of 114 cubic feet.

Our storage costs will go from $160.25 per month to $57.00 per month. (Iron Mountain currently charges $.50 cents per cubic foot to store materials.)

This effort has provided these benefits:
   1. Monthly savings of over $100 in storage costs.

2. A more comprehensive inventory of off-site MDCO materials.

3. Future savings when these boxes are requested. If boxes are stored outside of New Jersey, Iron Mountain uses another freight service to send the boxes to us and adds their charge to the bill. If the boxes come from Massachusetts, we get taxed for doing business in Massachusetts. The boxes formerly stored in Massachusetts are now stored in New Jersey so we will not have these charges in the future.

Below are several specific examples of what I found.

Six copies of our 2000 initial stock offering prospectus were sent to Iron Mountain on June 6, 2001. Three copies were kept for a historical record and the rest were recycled.
Box Number: 146980415   IPO PROSPECTUS
Box Number: 146980416   IPO PROSPECTUS
Box Number: 146980417   IPO PROSPECTUS

Example of old inventory of one box:
Box Number: 63720426   Box Description: P-1 OLD PRESENTATIONS

Example of new inventory of the same box:
Box Number: 641788964   Box Description: Hirulog-02

Biogen and TMC Correspondence Files 1988 thru 1990s time frame: 7/18/90 Strategy Meeting; Hirulog presentation data and graphics folder; Hirulog-thrombin presentation; Hirulog 1991 & 1992 budget folders; Hirulog 1992 PMS folder; misc. Hirulog communication folder; Hirulog slides and presentations; Thrombosis slides; presentations from 1/26/1993 Hirulog off-site meeting; Hirulog Strategy Team meeting 2/4/93; Argus Research Lab correspondence folder; Preclinical Studies report 4/20/93; dog emesis study folder; "Needs Assessment: Opportunity for a Novel Antithrombotic Agent in Selected Thrombotic Diseases" Wilkerson Group 5/25/90; "Opportunity for SERP-1 in Reducing the Restenosis Rate Following Coronary Angioplasty" Wilkerson Group 6/7/96; Hirulog toxicology testing folder; Sitek Research Labs folder; CBP sheep study; 1992 tabulated summaries forms.

Since TMC was in the pharmaceutical industry, we were subject to the Health Insurance Portability and Accountability Act (HIPAA) laws. These laws mandate the privacy of an individual's medical records. When an individual participated in a clinical trial of a drug, all their personal information must be blacked out before their records can be shared with any other individual or company. Often it did not happen. I would receive documents from a hospital, or a doctor, or another participating partner in one of our clinical trials, open a box and see names, birth dates, addresses, Social Security numbers and other data.

When this happened, I would IMMEDIATELY phone the person in our company who was in-charge of the trial and tell them what I found. Then I would IMMEDIATELY call our legal department and tell them. "Cover Our Asses" was my top priority. Then I would tape the box back shut again and wait. The people I phoned would show up, I would show them the documents, we would check a couple other boxes to see if this was just a small problem or a big mess.

They would go off to raise hell with whoever sent the records. I would type out a quick note saying when the boxes were opened, who in TMC had looked at them, tape up the boxes and lock them up. The note was to prove we had checked the boxes, what we had found and they had been resealed and locked up.

Oh yes, I was also a member of the audit team who was to provide information and support if we ever got audited by the FDA or some other official agency. Having had a high-level security clearance and having gone through some audits, this did not bother or worry me as much as some other people on the team. I was also the Fire Marshal for that portion of our building, responsible for ensuring every one left when the fire alarm sounded.

After almost 9 years at THC, I got a phone call one morning to come up to a conference room to meet with one of the Legal people. This was common when a confidential information request was made, since they do not want people overhearing a phone conversation or have information being sent through email. We would meet in a closed room, I would receive information on what they wanted researched, I would research it and then give it to them, usually on a flash drive to contain the spread of the information.

That didn't happen that morning. A Legal and a HR representative told me I was being laid off. They said it was strictly for money reasons.

After a few seconds, I offered to come in and help train whoever they hired to replace me so that person could quickly assume the duties of the librarian. They blinked and looked surprised. The next week I saw the HR representative in the hallway. She said she had been shocked when I said what I said. She said it was the first time she had ever heard of someone who had just gotten laid off offer to train their replacement.

They laid off 65 people. Some were so upset they stormed out and came back after work hours to load up their personal possessions. We were told a month before our final date so we could get our affairs in order. As I always do every 3 or 4 months, I copied everything I thought would be worthwhile and took it home with me.

This has been a long-standing policy of mine. Every 3 or 4 months, I make a copy of everything I created, or worked upon and take it home. I have seen and heard of too many people who were laid off and did not have any copies of the work they did to show in any future job interviews. By taking copies home, I could always show my reports, policies and standard operating principles, newsletters, and marketing and publicity materials.

I also make project folders for my email. I sort email into these folders and then about once or twice a year, try to copy all those emails and take them home. Especially if the project was one in which I had done most of the work. For example, all the emails and attachments from my software selection project were a great help when I wrote "Computer Software Evaluation: Balancing User's Needs & Wants".

**"You don't sharpen a knife you don't use.
But you sure do need to sharpen the knife you do use."
Doug Hay, co-worker at The Medicines Company**

Position Descriptions

Position descriptions are usually not accurate or relevant. I'm holding one from The Medicines Company dated June 2006. In my email to my manager commenting on this, I made these points. I suggest you do the same every time you have a review so your position description includes everything you are doing.

> Description says nothing about maintaining a corporate library, implementing a library document management and imaging system, and cataloging and scanning the documents into the system, or transferring documents from other sites and locations.
>
> The description says I should provide a full range of reference and information services using multiple databases, online services, and print publications. TMC does not have multiple databases, online services or print publications.
>
> States one responsibility is to find print and electronic information resources to enhance existing collection of resources. We do not have an existing collection of resources nor a place to store them for employees.
>
> Qualifications say BS degree preferably in library science. Shouldn't that be a Master's degree requirement?
>
> The position description does not include these tasks I'm currently doing:
>
> Corporate archivist: Inventory, pack and ship corporate documents to secure off-site storage and retrieve documents when requested. Maintain archive records.
>
> Conduct lunchtime learning seminars on library document management system and World Wide Web research skills.
>
> Create, publish, and maintain corporate standard operating procedures for library functions.

The description below is from Manchester. When asked if this fit what I did, I added my comments in parentheses.

JOB DESCRIPTION

POSITION: Research Manager (The position I was hired for is Research Director. How does this position differ? Where is the description for Research Director?)

POSITION OBJECTIVES: Manage business research and provide support and training to candidates, research coordinators (What is a research coordinator and how does it differ from a research manager?) and business developers. (What are business developers? If this is the sales and marketing staff, why not say so?)

EFFECTIVE DATE: July 1, 2001

ESSENTIAL FUNCTIONS: (There are 4 service areas and the functions should be broken out to show this.)

Candidate Services
- Provide business research support to Manchester candidates using a range of print and non-print resources, including electronic databases and Internet resources
- Conduct regular group orientations for candidates to cover research strategies, using in-house and Internet resources, with one-on-one follow-up, as needed, for all candidates.
- Be prepared to demonstrate the use of various databases, as part of scheduled orientations to candidates. (Isn't this the same as the previous function?)
- Ensure presentation and distribution of information for candidates when upgrades/enhancements and additions/deletions to databases are made.
- Provide all requests for research in a timely, accurate and efficient manner.
- Develop instructional materials as needed.

Sales and Marketing
- Facilitate business development in the enterprise using proposals and presentations (How? If this means to provide sales and marketing staff with information, just say so.)
- Market Manchester's research capabilities to prospective clients through demonstrations, presentations, sales calls, meetings, etc.
- Participates in the "Shopper" process demonstrating Manchester's

Alphabetical by Color

research capabilities.
- Provide the Sales and Marketing team with research requests in a timely and accurate manner.
- Attend marketing events within the region upon request.

Client Companies
- Consult with client companies to recommend appropriate materials pertaining to project or career centers.
- Support career centers with training sessions, if required.

Administration
- Standardize research products and materials throughout the region.
- Manage, review, and make purchasing recommendations for office library inventories to support business plan and candidate's needs.
- Liaise with Research Coordinators and Office Managers to develop and monitor annual library budgets for offices.
- Track accurate inventories throughout offices in the assigned region.
- Develop and maintain corporate-wide purchasing policy (What corporate wide purchasing policy? I've never seen one for the Libraries. Please send me a copy.) for databases, reference materials, magazines, etc.
- Develop / use consistent procedures and forms company wide.

According to your job description, Research Managers do not do any purchasing. If not, who does and is it centralized for all of Manchester?

This list of "Essential Functions" is not intended to be limiting. The Company reserves the right to revise this job description as needed to comply with actual job requirements. (The old 'other tasks as required' clause.)

ADDITIONAL FUNCTIONS:

- Training of Research Coordinators (If we are doing all the above, what are the Research Coordinators doing?)
- Developing training manuals for various databases (Already covered under Candidate Services)
- Liaise with fellow Research Managers to maintain consistency throughout organization. (Already covered under Administration)

PERFORMANCE STANDARDS:
- Annually developed jointly by Research Managers and their managers.
- Describes how well short-term work responsibilities are to be completed in a specific, achievable, measurable manner.

MACHINES/EQUIPMENT/TOOLS USED:
- Computer/Printer/Calculator/Fax/Telephone/Scanner/LCD Projector/Copier

QUALIFICATIONS:
- Completed or working towards Masters in Library Science Degree (If the company wants a professional in this position, require this degree.)
- Strong computer/word processing skills, familiarity with databases and Internet that will allow research of companies, industries, market research and search firm data.
- Strong service orientation, enthusiasm for working one-on-one with executive-level candidates and consultants.
- Demonstrated willingness to work as part of a team.
- Teaching experience helpful

WORKING ENVIRONMENT:
- Indoor
- Conference Room / classroom
- Office / secretarial workstation
- Some traveling to other offices (Oh really? I'm traveling to 4 'other offices' right now.)
- May require some heavy lifting of computer equipment or books

REPORTING RELATIONSHIP:
- Reports to _____ (Yes, just where does this position fit in and how does it compare/relate to Research Directors and Research Coordinators?)

[OPTIONAL] I have read and understand this job description and hereby certify that I am qualified to perform this job and can perform the essential functions of this job, with or without a reasonable accommodation. (Please list any requested accommodation(s) below if an accommodation is necessary to perform the essential functions of this job). (What is this for? The interview process determines if a candidate is qualified to perform the job functions or can be quickly trained to perform them.)

Alphabetical by Color

Name (Please Print)
Signature
Date

Accommodation(s) requested (if applicable):

You do this every time you are given a position description or an evaluation. Rewrite the description making sure it includes the tasks you are doing which are not in the description. And edit the listed tasks so they describe precisely what you are doing.

"Dale, how do you move all these books?"

"Paper shopping bags. Boxes filled with books sometimes are too heavy. First, sort all your books by size, putting the same size books together. You put 2 shopping bags together into a double bag and fill it with books of the same size. Any extra room on top, you fill with paperbacks. You turn another paper bag upside down and side it down over the double bag. Most people can carry one of these bags filled with hardcover books and most guys can carry 2 filled with paperbacks. I moved 86 bags of books the last time I moved and that was after weeding my collection and donating books to the local library."

Library Planning

When you develop a plan for your library, also develop a 'what if' plan. Your plan should show what you are doing now, where you are going, and how you are getting to those goals. In your plan, if you have set out objectives and they are not being met, why not? What went wrong? You need contemplative and thinking time for planning. Your 'what if' plan should anticipate crises, opportunities, and those thunderbolts from the blue which occasionally strike.

Libraries are focused on 3 things:
- the service you provide,
- the technology you use,
- the way you manage the service and the technology.

Libraries have 4 issues:
- The people using the information,
- the organization of the information,
- the access to the information, and
- the production, distribution, and consumption of the information.

Start by listing everything in the above lists. What precisely are the services and the technology you use? Can the technology be improved? If so, how and how much will it cost? What services could be added and what will that cost? Even if you think there is a snowballs chance in hell this would ever happen, you must have this information at hand in case someone asks how the library could be improved. (And to show you are an innovative, forward thinking company employee.)

In planning ask, who are your customers? What do they say they want? (But what are they really asking for?) What do they really need? What are their expectations of the library, of you, and the library staff? What are the products and services you are offering them?

Are your products and services at the highest level they could be? Are they dependable and reliable? Do they satisfy the function your customers require? What is their cost to value ratio? What is their image?

When I first brought a CD-ROM information service into the Bendix library and was displaying it at a department meeting, I marketed it by pulling up a list of all the golf courses in New Jersey. I asked the group if they were aware of these and printed out the list. I marketed to their interests.

In my career I've seen libraries get treated worse than other departments. Most people believe we don't have to justify what we do because we are "self-evidently good".

When someone says 'you or the library has their full support', this is what you tell them. **"Thank you, but what I really want from you is your time, your money, and your people."** Tell them honestly and plainly you want more than good words from them. You want them to spend the time to learn about the library's services and capabilities; you want them to spend money to keep upgrading current services and spend money to add needed ones; and you want the people in their department to do the same, learn and use the library's resources.

We put the names and department information of all employees, managers, directors, and senior management into our circulation and borrower records database. Why? So our numbers of 'who we serve' would be much higher than 'who uses our service'.

> **"No teacher will go to an institute without a good library."**
> **Professor J. Kephart**

Consultation Work and Other Jobs
1985 and still ongoing

After being let go from TMC, I didn't find another librarian job right away so I went back into consulting, rather I continued consulting. I've always done consulting on the side even when I have full-time jobs. Usually this is doing research for individuals but I also do resume review, resume writing and help people with job hunting.

When my family and friends found out I was working for Manchester International and was helping with resumes and teaching about job searching, they asked me for help. I was glad to offer suggestions about improving their resumes. When others started asking for help, I started asking for a little cash. Usually it would not take me long, so I would only ask for $20.00 or $25.00. If they were unemployed, I told them to pay me after they landed a job.

I also inventoried a music record collection of cassettes, CDs, tapes and vinyl records. Using voice recognition software, I made a list of all the music, the artist, and the date for a collector. He was so happy with the results, he had me inventory some other collections. I will only say he was wealthy and spent plenty of money on what he collected.

A friend manages an art and package design department. She asked me to create a better means of tracking her department finances. I created a simple Excel workbook into which she could enter billing, expenditures, and invoices. Once she was satisfied with the design, I entered in 5 years of her department finances. And noticed an interesting item. One photo lab was adding state sales tax to their bills and another photo lab was not. I pointed this out to her and suggested she ask her finance group about this. It seems if the photo lab sent digital photographs, no state tax was due on them. The company was able to regain over $6000.00 which they had paid in state sales tax.

She said she was going to give me credit for seeing this. I told her it would not help me. But it would help her reputation in the company if she took the credit for pointing this out to finance.

Some of the consulting work I've done may not be talked about for reasons of privacy and security concerns. One example is the work I did for a group of "preppers" in Pennsylvania. "Preppers" refer to a person or a group of people who prepare for adverse conditions. This might be an economic depression, climate change, social unrest, or nuclear war. They store food and materials in a location or area where they can get away from or avoid other people. Of course a group like this does not want their intentions or identities made public so I agreed to never divulge any information about them or what I did.

I inventoried what this group had collected in several locations so they could have a complete inventory of their supplies. I found companies and manufacturers from which they could purchase other supplies.

As I have written and published a dozen books, I offer to aspiring writers advice on how to write and publish books or magazine articles. I also offer advice to artists and writers on how to market and publicize their works. I do not offer to critique or evaluate their work, explaining I do not feel qualified to judge any work by my own.

I am still doing consulting work as I write this book.

"Librarians are the professors of professors."
Bashirat Husan Mirza,
SUNY Geneseo Library Science Graduate School, 1979

Woodbourne Correctional Facility 2016 to 2018

I consulted for a while, cash on the barrel only. And worked several part-time jobs. I investigated the Civil Service requirements for librarians and informational professionals in several states and took several tests. I did very well on the New York State tests and started receiving open job notices. I applied for and got a position with the New York State Department of Corrections as a librarian in a medium security prison.

And was lied to both by Luis F, the prison director and Linda K, the head librarian in Albany.

During my initial interview and tour I found out the computer and computer software were over 10 years old. The software company was not supporting the software anymore. This was a standalone system in the library. So if the system crashed, everything would be lost. They do not allow flash drives or CD-ROM burners in prison so backups can't be made of the computer information. I was told by both the prison administration, Luis F, and the library administrator in Albany, Linda K, new computers and new software had been approved and purchased and would be installed in the next year.

That didn't happen. We were still using the old software and computers when I left for a more challenging position after 2 years.

Also, after working in the position for 3 months, I had a list of questions about the position and the library network. I emailed the questions to Linda K and she never responded. She had told me during the phone interview she would come down for a visit during my first year. She never did.

The staff of the library, consisting of prisoners, were very helpful. They could tell me what was popular and circulated and what was being requested. I instituted a system of tracking so we could have data to support purchase decisions. I made up a simple form listing periodical and newspaper titles, with days of the week in columns. The person handing out periodicals and newspapers would simply put a check in the column for that day and periodical. I counted them up at the end of the week so we could see what was being read. Or rather what was being read the most. Using this I bought more subscriptions in popular subject areas.

I also did this in book circulation so we could show certain areas were very popular and other subjects were not popular and we could buy according to the data. We also ran circulation statistics and weeded out materials which had not been loaned in 10 years. These we donated to a local nonprofit bookstore which supported local literacy programs.

We purchased DVDs and each Friday afternoon we would show a movie. Since the seating was restricted, we counted people and stopped when the library was full. I would stand up before each movie and explain what movie it was, who was in it and some background trivia of the movie as an educational lead in. This was very popular.

I had no problems at all with the prisoners. Once they found out I had been an Army paratrooper, I gained a lot of respect. I treated them as human beings, not as animals like some of the guards did. Once, one of the library workers pointed out a new inmate and asked me if I knew what he had done. I replied I didn't know and didn't care. I told him I had access and could look up any inmate's records but what mattered was how we treated each other now, not what someone had done in the past.

"We are not human. We are Librarians."
Heard at 2010 SLA Convention in New Orleans

New York State Academy of Fire Science 2018 to 2021

In the New York State civil service system, you can be put on lists of job openings in your profession. I was getting a lot of notices of job openings in prisons but I did not want any of them. One day a notice came for the New York State Academy of Fire Science located in the Finger Lakes region. The Academy trains and certifies the first responders in New York: fire fighters, emergency medical technicians (EMT), arson investigators, canine accelerant detectors and so on. I interviewed for the Senior Librarian position and was hired.

The Library was started shortly after the Fire Academy was created in 1970. It is in one large, big room on the north end of the first floor of the Academy. We get indirect sunlight all day through the large north facing windows. There is room for multiple tables so classes can come in and do research. I don't have an office, just an open cubicle area.

I started the position in August 2018 and spent the first few months exploring the resources. I used the software to print out a full shelf listing of materials and started an inventory. Over 12.5% of our holdings were missing. I updated the catalog records to display what was missing. The former librarian, for some reason, had put a single book record in the catalog even if we had multiple copies of the book. I had to enter in the copies and mark them 1, 2, and so on. I also wrote the unique catalog number of each copy in the back of each book.

Part of the library ceiling had leaked at one time and the shelves had been moved from their original position against a wall. To a better spot I think, because you don't have to walk back up the aisle to go to the next one. But whoever moved them did not erect all the shelving. Books were piled on window ledges, on top of filing cabinets and in glass fronted cabinets at floor level.

I found the rest of the shelf units parts in a storage room and in several closets in classrooms. One Sunday I came in with work clothes (not my dress clothes and a tie), and moved all the shelf units back into the Library. I spent the entire day putting together a row and a half, 18 feet, of shelves, and erecting them where I wanted them. I also had noticed when the shelves were moved, all the connecting bolts were not all installed making the shelves noticeably shaky. I found a collection of bolts and nuts and installed as many of those as possible.

The next week was spent moving periodicals and books back on the shelves. I had by this time noticed some periodicals were of limited use as they were old and we had only a years' worth of holdings. I checked in OCLC and WorldCat and saw several other lending libraries had better collections so I discarded some periodicals into recycling.

The 10 filing cabinets in the Library were in several locations. This made it in-efficient when looking for resources so on another Sunday I came in and moved all the filing cabinets against one wall. You know what that entails don't you? Take out every drawer from every filing cabinet. Some are too heavy to move so you must take some materials out of the drawer. Put it somewhere. Move the filing cabinet to where you want it. Pick up every drawer and put it back into the cabinet. Replace the materials back into the drawer if you took something out. Drink lots of water, take some aspirin, go home and collapse.

Those individuals who used the Library did double-takes after each weekend when I moved things in the Library. "What happened?" was the most often question. "I'm making the Library a more efficient place to work." was my usual response.

Students come from all over New York State to take classes at the Academy. They often will go out to local restaurants to eat rather than eating in the Academy cafeteria. The former librarian had created a 3-ring binder with menus from local restaurants but it was at least 3 years out of date. I went to all the local restaurants, gave them my business card and asked them for a copy of their current menu, explaining what I was doing. I updated the binder and also put new menus on the bulletin boards by the cafeteria. I told the cafeteria staff and the office staff about this so they could refer students to the menus if anyone asked about local food. A good byproduct from this effort was I was often recognized when I went out for lunch or dinner and received very good service for marketing the restaurant.

Alphabetical by Color

The Fire Academy has been giving training courses since 1970 but fire training has been going on for much longer. In our archives are kept lesson plans, student manuals and student workbooks, and other related training materials, from the 1940s to the present. These are kept in an archive room on the ground floor in 14 filing cabinets and 2 large storage cabinets. In the first year of my job, a fireman emailed us from Virginia. He had relocated there after retiring from a job in New York but wanted to volunteer with a local fire company and wanted copies of the knowledge taught in the courses he had taken. I found those materials, scanned them, and sent him the information.

This made me wonder of what would happen if a water pipe broke or something else damaged those historical materials. I am now organizing, scanning, and saving digital copies of old training materials.

Here are some issues. The former librarian kept multiple copies of the same item. Do we really need 4 copies of a student manual from a class taught in the 1980s? NO. I keep 2 and recycle the other 2.

Also, the former librarian stored the materials alphabetical by course title. "Basic Fire Fighter Training" is stored in the 'Bs', "Intermediate Fire Fighter Training" is stored in the 'Is", and "Advanced Fire Fighter Training" is stored in the 'As". What the heck? Do I leave them where they are or gather everything together in one filing cabinet and list it under "Fire Fighter Training"?

Another issue is when every new politician comes into office, they have all the training materials re-published with their name on the cover. So a manual might have a publication date of 2002, but the politicians listed on the cover came into office on January 1, 2007. Since you can't publish something before you were born, I mark the date of issue as 2007.

I have just finished scanning all archived training materials. In this way the COVID-19 pandemic was a bit of a blessing because since all the training classes were canceled, I could focus on just this task. 1,009 files in 121 folders. 7.14 GB (7,668,850,688 bytes). All kept in a shared folder on a shared network drive so all the instructors have access. They are also copied onto multiple flashdrives kept in the Library and in the Archives.

The New York county Arson Control Plans also have been scanned for easier access and archival purposes. 72 files, 185 MB (194,306,048 bytes). These were written by each county back in the 1980's to show how they were going to fight the rising crime of arson in their county.

Also, since all the classes were canceled, I had no trouble bringing in the lady I was seeing and showing her the Library, if you know what I mean.

One big problem I had with the Academy was with security concerns. Every room in the same wing with the Library uses the same door key. I tried to convince my management to change the Library key so only the librarian, security, maintenance, and the cleaning staff could enter the Library. I told them this was the reason we were missing over 12.5% of our holdings but they did not see my logic.

The Library also had no way of enforcing overdue notices. We had individuals who signed out over $500.00 worth of materials and we could not ask law enforcement to arrest them.

"I think you have the most boring job in this plant. Doing that would drive me crazy."
"Well, I have a very good fantasy life to make up for it."
Co-worker Chappy's statement to me and my response, while working at Singer-Link

Job Skills You Need

In the Army, I was a paratrooper with the 82nd Airborne Division. Now I am a librarian. It hasn't been too much of a change. Both call for being well trained, aware of your environment, reacting quickly to changes, courage, initiative, resourcefulness, and dealing daily with people you otherwise wouldn't associate with.

Many librarians would agree other occupations they have worked in contributed to the development of their information management skills.

Our library skills could be divided into five separate areas: collection development, collection management, cataloging/indexing/abstraction, reference, and administrative management. Some transferable skills we all use are:

- **collection development:** gathering information, inventory management, comparing similarities or differences, compiling data, searching, or researching, studying, or observing things and people,

- **collection management:** analyzing, classifying, organizing, planning a goal-oriented process, prioritizing information, synthesizing, systematizing information,

- **cataloging/indexing/abstracting:** adapting, classifying, organizing, problem solving, record keeping, seeing patterns among data, systematizing information,

- **reference:** communication skills, searching or research, evaluation, making recommendations, memory skills, retrieving information in various forms, service orientation, taking instructions,

- **administrative management:** assessing & evaluating individuals, coaching, communication skills, conflict resolution, creating, designing, inventing, mentoring, negotiation skills, planning a goal-oriented process, problem solving, teaching.

You don't have to become an expert in all the tasks needed to perform the above processes, but you should be aware of them.

When I worked construction, I learned to see the big picture and how what I was doing fit into it. I was made aware of the values of planning, organization, design, and making lists of materials you need. Construction depends on teamwork and you gain insight into assessing and evaluating people and their skills. Construction also calls upon public contact as your management is constantly checking on your work and the people who you are doing the work for often come by to see how things are going.

I've worked as a factory watchman where I worked alone for long hours. Certain tasks had to be done by the end of shift, as well as hourly tasks such as checking doors and punching time clocks, which called for time-management skills. As did my jobs at a television station and as a disk jockey (DJ).

In the Army, everything depends on teamwork and relying upon other's skills & training. You may not like the people. You may even hate them. But you must rely upon their skills so the mission gets accomplished. Being in a unit with a wide spectrum of unique individuals gives you a great opportunity to study, observe and learn from people from all over the country.

You must know and trust the skill levels of your team and if you are a manager or leader, you must train your team, build up their skill levels and have them practice those skills.

You can't let the diverse personalities, backgrounds, or any ethnic, religious, or other factor affect the team. Always practice and preach you are all on the team together and the team survives or fails by everyone's actions. You practice mission planning & organizing so when you are called upon to move, you react instinctively.

The paratroopers always said the reason we jumped out of planes was because we didn't trust the Air Force pilot's driving. It was never said, but we knew if they were called upon to fly us to our drop zone, no matter what the obstacles, they would do it. And we put our trust in other paratrooper's bravery and skills to accomplish our missions. It's a good feeling knowing you are not alone.

I worked at a television station in Florida doing production. We were constantly working against deadlines, so it required quick thinking, innovation, and creativity to accomplish our work. It also let us use imagination in designing new ways of doing commercials and broadcasts. Keeping track of all the films, videos, slides, and recordings required an organized record keeping and filing system.

Being a disc jockey also required being organized. You had to know where to go when someone called in a song request. And with most songs being about 3 minutes long, you were under tight deadlines to get the next song cued up before one ended. Pre-planning, searching, or researching what songs went well with each other was a valuable skill. Dj'ing is mostly presentation skills, doing public speaking, and marketing yourself as an interesting, knowledgeable person. You also need to know when to keep your mouth shut.

Working as a short order cook is mostly public contact, public speaking, organization, and presentation skills while dealing with multiple projects within time constraints. You must be knowledgeable about food, and upcoming events. You must also remain calm when dealing with customers who range in age from children to senior citizens.

A real estate photographer takes pictures of property for real estate agencies. This involves much public contact and presentation skills so you can get the best pictures of the property and pre-planning your day to cover as many sites as possible with the least amount of driving. It, like being a disc jockey or working in television production, calls for creativity, innovation, and invention so your product always remains fresh and interesting.

Some leadership behaviors are customer focus, integrity, people orientation, teamwork, speed, innovation, and performance. Customer focus is valued in construction trades, radio, television, and photographic fields. At the building and remodeling company I worked for, I constantly saw the owner's integrity as he redid work or did extra work for his customers, regardless of the cost to him. He was one of the first to teach me people skills, which I further expanded upon in the Army, and the media trades. Teamwork is all important in construction, the Army, and when working on a production job for television. Speed has been valuable in all areas where I've worked, from delivering a customer's meal as a short order cook to fulfilling a rush job for a Library's customer. Innovation in your field keeps you offering new developments to your customers. Performance is what you ultimately get judged upon and what better way to perform than planning and laying out a step-by-step process for achieving a goal.

Reviewing some of the jobs I have had brought new insights into my transferable skills and are a reminder to me using these skills can expand my horizons. I urge you to do the same.

And as you read job descriptions and postings, collect the most often used keywords and use them in your resume if you have performed that function.

I did have here a 4½ page list of industries I've worked in, departments I provided services to, software and hardware I used, library functions I did and all the 'soft' skills I possess. But why read mine? Go list your own.

What skills do you have which are transferable from one organization to another? Don't just think about the industry you are in, most of your skills are transferable. Your organizational skills, your research skills, your interviewing technique skills, all of these are transferable.

Occasionally you should look over your previous jobs and your current job. Determine what skills in each position you enjoyed doing, what skills or tasks you did not enjoy, what skills you did not have in each position and what skills you want to and need to develop.

Every 2 to 3 years ask yourself "Who am I?" and "Where do I want to go and what do I want to do?" Especially after a promotion, a change in what you are doing at your present position, or a job change. Whatever you are doing, it is nice to know if you are maximizing your skills and interest.

Draw a grid of four boxes. Label them 'Like and do well', 'Like but don't do well yet', 'Don't like but do well', and 'Don't like and don't do well'.

List all your responsibilities in the boxes. This gives you a picture of what is expected of you. Now use this to determine how you can maximize the tasks you want to do and minimize the task you don't like. In the 'Like and do well box', keep doing these and maybe find others in this area. In the 'Like but don't do well yet' box, perhaps find training in these areas. In the 'Don't like but do well' box, either learn to like it or maybe delegate it to somebody else. And of course try to get away from everything in the 'Don't like and don't do well' box.

Do this for all your previous jobs. List each job, the skills you used in each, the skills you enjoyed and the skills you didn't enjoy. As well as the skills you want to develop. This shows throughout your career what you've like to do and the strengths in certain skills. You can use this when looking for a new position. I've always known I hated to do paperwork. But it's unavoidable and so I've become used to it.

When and if you delegate a task or project, you must sit with the person and cover these 5 steps:
1. Define what is to be done and by when.
2. Be certain the person knows and understand Number 1.
3. If you want it done in a certain manner, explain how it is to be done and why it must be done in that certain manner.
4. Teach the person how to do it and make sure they know and understand Number 3.
5. Make sure the person agrees with what is to be accomplished, how it is to be done and when by it must be done.

"How to Fireproof Your Career: Survival Strategies for Volatile Times" by Anne Baber and Lynne Waymon lists five good strategies. Liberate your mind, learn for mastery, lean out of specialization, line up your finances, and link up with people. I suggest you consider these. For example, I'm trying to earn more money by writing. What can you do to gather more income?

Librarians come to a job willing to share their expertise and knowledge. That is very unusual in most organizations and most often very appreciated. A lot of coworkers I've had prefer to keep their skills and expertise to themselves so they remain a highly valued employee. Rarely

I have found a coworker who is willing to teach their expertise to another. The first thing I said after being told I was being let go from The Medicines Company, was to offer to train my replacement so they would quickly come up to speed. The human resource person later told me it was the first time she ever heard anyone offer to train their replacement.

Your resume should show you have excellent customer service skills. This is highly desirable and you can present this in several ways. If you ask for thank you notes during your career, you can quote from them on your resume. Or show them during a job interview.

A recruiter or an interviewer wants to know 3 things. 'Can you do the job?' 'Will you do the job?' 'And will you fit in and can you fit in to the organization?'

A very good argument to use when applying for a position is to say, **"Give me the job because the operation will run better with me in charge because......"**

In your career, focus on skills and techniques you could use in any industry. I am talking about managing such tasks as budgeting expenses and savings, internal and external customer focus and services, the quality of the services you provide, and vitally important, relationships with management and coworkers.

If you become aware of and work to maximize your abilities in these areas, you can transfer those skills from position to position to make yourself a very useful and valuable information professional. I've always looked for ways to cut expenses in certain areas and then ways to use the money to provide other services. Not to cut my budget, but to use the money available most effectively and efficiently.

An often overlooked skill is the ability to quickly learn the jargon of an industry or a profession. I think one good way is to immerse yourself in the literature. Read everything you can, especially a basic introductory textbook, if you can find one. If you hear something you don't understand, say you are new and ask what it means. It is better to show you are willing to learn, then to try and hide your ignorance.

Always be a warrior for librarianship. If someone says something demeaning about librarians, ask "Who taught you to be organized? How many courses have you taken which specifically deal with organizing information so it can easily be accessed and used?"

"We're the only profession (librarians) in the world that if we keep up with our professional literature, we're only half informed. We not only have to keep up with our professional literature, we have to keep up with the literature of all the other professions."
Professor Ralph Black,
SUNY Geneseo Library Science Graduate School, 1979

Accomplishments

I served in the military, met guys from all social strata, educational levels, cultural & ethnic backgrounds and got along with most of them. I have been in 42 states (so far) & hitchhiked thru many seeing the country and meeting the locals. I worked for a living doing both blue & white collar and know how to report to different upper supervisory & management styles. I am aware of different cultural scenes and social changes. I lived on my own a great deal and have been a decent roommate at other times.

In graduate school I took the first ever computer course offered, which focused on programming and on-line database searching. I was amazed how quick and easy it was for me compared to others. I could see then the non-relevance of several courses and knew most students could use a practical business course.

At The Binghamton Public Library I saw right away the separation of the public service group and the administrators. The administration wanted nothing to do with the public because 'they're the ones messing up our nice library'. It felt good to be able to help everyone while working in the stacks.

At Singer-Link, I created a special projects library, created a database of department documents, instituted online searching, moved the library, and modernized their library. In all my years of managing classified documents, nothing was every misplaced or lost. I learned 'don't ask questions I don't want to know the answers to'. How to do financial juggling of expense reports as in 'don't leave a meal cost empty', and 'breakfast never cost more than dinner'. I found serving multiple departments difficult because of different wants, needs & desires. I saw how different the white-collar and blue-collar views were of the company and its actions.

For Bendix, I instituted online searching, created a database of library books and periodicals, modernized the library, moved the library, and brought in specifications and standards in digital format, as well as creating a library website. A computer software package (Bibliotech from Comstow) was purchased and installed to catalog and manage the library's holdings. I was also the leader and founder of a corporate wide total quality library modernization team. This team brought in corporate wide contracts from periodical and newspaper jobbers resulting in massive company-wide savings. I was sometimes amazed at the limited views of other corporate librarians who saw no reason to help or serve any department but their own.

Also at Bendix I continued to apply the 'don't ask questions I don't want to know the answers to' philosophy. And perfected the financial juggling of expense reports. Again, my manager Ed S only wanted me to serve the Engineering department which caused issues but I worked around them.

At the Lucent Whippany library, I weeded periodicals after user surveys to determine what wasn't being used, saving more money. I wrote and published well received library newsletters. I created a bibliography of telecommunications and science books for a divisional startup in India. I saw again the limited views of other corporate librarians and had problems with old, stodgy views of library network management. They marketed each library separately, did not like paper newsletters or the use of humor. They believed 'everyone knows the value of library' but didn't realize you have to keep reminding people of the value. Advertise, market, and publicize.

At Manchester and Right Management, I taught computer and online research skills. I created user guides for the online resources available to candidates. I created the library for a career center. I did the first ever survey of online recruiting processes and had it published in the Wall Street Journal. I believe I handled the emotional issues with clients in a positive, supportive way. I help the staff and the clients see how computers & WWW was changing job hunting & recruiting.

At The Medicines Company I created the corporate library, moved it and managed the finances and budget of the library.. I drove a rental truck to move corporate documents several times. I researched and brought in-house the computer software system for the library. I did database maintenance and data entry of all library materials. I digitized over a million pages of documentation. I did online research for multiple departments. I brought in-house the drug products alert service and modernized it.

Here at The New York State Academy of Fire Science I updated library resources, digitized older training materials and also digitized some older training videotapes.

In every position I presented training sessions on the resources available through the library, the skills I posses and how I can use them to help employees, useful WWW sites, and the advantages of using a trained researcher (me) to find information faster and cheaper than you doing it yourself.

I have helped countless (okay, a lot) of individuals rewrite or update their resumes and find jobs. I have done research for people in multiple areas such as financial planning, vacation planning, real estate, scientific and technical fields and "I like to read this so what should I read next?" I have helped build and remodeled houses, helped people move and helped raise children both related and non-related to me.

I have also taught fly-fishing skills.

Sometimes the non-library career tasks I have done have provided more satisfaction than my professional work.

> **"I couldn't live a week without a private library – indeed, I'd part with all my furniture and squat and sleep on the floor before I'd let go of the 1500 or so books I possess."**
> **H. P. Lovecraft**

Failures

I did not market myself as best as I could have. I have already mentioned I should have been involved in the professional associations more. I should have marketed myself more to upper management in every company. I should have gained more support for the libraries from all top management. And I should've marketed the library to all employees at every company. But I was too busy with other activities, including writing.

I could have risen higher in company management if I had moved out from being the librarian. But for sure I would not have been as happy. I know where my level of "The Peter Principle" is and have happily stayed there.

I also did not move geographically to where I could have made a greater salary. This was mostly because I wanted to stay were I could help my parents as they aged. Also I wanted to stay close to family and friends.

As I am a very good presenter and teacher of learning and training classes, I could have joined some of the big computer and firms as a trainer of their products. But life on the road, going from town to town giving classes, did not appeal to me. As above, I felt I needed to stay close and help my parents.

I worked with some ladies I think I could have had some good relationships with, but I refrained from dating them. I wonder what they are doing now. I look upon this as both a failure and an accomplishment. I failed to have some good relationships. But I also did not cause any heartache to any female co-workers. If any former co-workers read this and would like to get in touch, you can reach me through my publisher, Lies Told Press, LTD., or at LiesToldPress@mail.com.

The Special Library Association Has Lost Its Way

I have just received the ONLY communication from The Special Library Association (SLA) I receive each year. Their request for my yearly dues.

This has been about the ONLY communication from them for about the past 10 years.

I joined SLA while I was in graduate school in 1979. I have been a member for over 40 years.

Have I ever received a thank you, a notice of appreciation, or a discount in my dues for being a member so long? NO.

I truly believe they lost their way when they moved their headquarters to Virginia. They think they make a difference by being physically in the political arena near Washington, DC. But are most of the SLA members employed by government agencies? I don't think so. Why isn't SLA centered geographically for their American members?

They should be marketing to the industries who employ most of their members. But they do not. I have NEVER seen advertising from SLA aimed at showcasing what a librarian does or can do for a company.

How about using some of my examples?

"Librarian Dale Carpenter found a periodical in his library which enabled Allied-Signal to get a lawsuit against it dismissed. That is what librarians do."

"Librarian Dale Carpenter consolidated all periodical ordering within his library and saved the 3 company divisions at his location thousands of dollars a year. That is what librarian's do."

"Librarian Dale Carpenter reviewed Lucent's Whippany Wireless Network location library periodical usage and saved them over $93,000 in one year. That is what librarian's do."

Why not have all the industry divisions start a publicity campaign using examples like the above and advertise in all the industry periodicals? All the other vendors and suppliers do this. Why not us librarians?

Also, SLA has not published any magazines in years. I used to avidly read their stuff and share it with co-workers. I would clip and save articles for future reference. You can't find any of those on their website. Just go to the SLA website and try to find any articles written by Herb White, Stephen Abrams, or any other former writer.

Peter Drucker was the keynote speaker at the 2002 SLA Convention. Marjorie M.K. Hlava wrote a fine article detailing his presentation which was included in the 2002 Conference Wrap-Up published in Information Outlook. Can you find this article? I have it right here at hand. Because I tore it out of the magazine to keep and re-read over and over to inspire me. Why doesn't SLA have an "Inspiring Articles" section so this wisdom will always be available?

SLA does not do outreach. If they are my professional association, aren't they supposed to be supporting me? And helping me? They SHOULD NOT be expecting me to reach out to them. So why aren't they helping me by giving information and support?

The SLA job board should be FRONT and CENTER on their main page. Not buried somewhere.

Why does SLA have so much money in the bank? For a non-profit? They could pay for the entire yearly conference with their savings.

Part of our professional association's responsibility is communicating with its members. They must communicate what it is doing to maintain and increase the professional image of the profession to the public and to every industry.

I often see advertisements from other professions detailing the skills, knowledge, and experience of members in that profession. You want to hire just anybody to run electrical wiring in your house? No, you hire a trained licensed experienced professional electrician.

How often do you see any advertisements like that for librarians? I never do.

Why isn't SLA telling us what they're doing for us?

It is the responsibility of SLA to tell us what they're doing with the money we are paying them. We are busy professionals. We are too busy to go to the SLA website to look for this information. SLA MUST push this information out to us.

Who were they talking with? Where are they advocating legal requirements for the hiring of professional librarians? What industry publications have they advertised in in the last month?

They are not telling us. They have not told us this for years.

Since I have not been told us this for years, I'm assuming they have done nothing. So I'm done with SLA.

If you agree with anything I have said about SLA, why not ask others at professional librarianship meetings if they agree. Why not ask local chapter and national chapter officers to bring up these issues? If you don't get answers to satisfy you, find another professional association.

Pournelle's Iron Law of Bureaucracy states that in any bureaucratic organization there will be two kinds of people: those who work to further the actual goals of the organization, and those who work for the organization itself. Examples in education would be teachers who work and sacrifice to teach children, vs. union representative who work to protect any teacher including the most incompetent.

The Iron Law states that in all cases, the second type of person will always gain control of the organization, and will always write the rules under which the organization functions.

Where To From Here?

I will finish up my PhD degree at Miskatonic University. Just so I can be introduced as "Doctor Dale".

I plan to keep working as long as I can get paid for it. I am still doing consulting on process improvement for libraries and research for companies and individuals. I have several other books on which I am working. Perhaps this book and other writings will bring an offer to teach or give talks on library science. No one knows what the future may bring.

But I will always be collecting, reading and writing books.

Thanks for buying this book. I hope it was helpful.

If you think it was, please help pass the information on by:

    Recommending this book to friends, co-workers or anyone you think might find it useful.
    Write about this book on your social account, or book review sites such as Goodbooks.
    Tell everyone in the professional societies you belong to, especially the book reviewers.

You can also help me by emailing me at:
LiesToldPress@mail.com,
And telling me:

    How could I have made it better?
    Was there a question you wanted me to answer that went unanswered?
    How was the amount of detail in the book? Did you want less or more? And where and why?
    Were you inspired or motivated in some way?

Thanks. By doing this you will improve the future editions of this book and all other books I write.

Lies Told Press, LTD. is a non-profit company helping authors and artists publish and market their works. All profits, except for what is needed to keep us running, go directly back to the authors and artists. Lies Told Press, LTD. books are available at www.Lulu.com.

> **"I wanted to see my name on the cover of a book.**
> **If your name is in the Library of Congress, you're immortal."**
> **Tom Clancy**

Bibliography

I stopped working on the bibliography for this book when it became larger than the book.

I have been collecting and saving articles about library science, education and teaching, applicable technologies, management and marketing and publicity, and anything which could make me a better person, librarian, and educator for well over 40 years.

I have 3 4-drawer metal file cabinets bursting with articles and copies of articles. I don't know how many scanned articles reside in my computers. But I do know listing them would be an enormous job.

And if I did list them, they might not be available to you. I have done some online searching to find references only to find the magazine the article appeared in has never been made available. At least to my resources.

But maybe creating the bibliography will be another book. Or maybe I'll just start weeding and recycling the paper. What is relevant and useful to me might not be relevant and useful to you.

I hope the appendixes I include will be useful.

Sort of a Full Resume

What follows is my complete resume. Sort of. I left off several jobs because they were done confidentiality and I will not divulge the details. Other things I did to make money were done for cash and/or services rendered and I won't talk about those either. And I certainly won't put into writing any of the illegal money-making schemes I've been involved in. But look for them to appear in disguise in my fiction writing.

Certain of my writings and publications are not listed on this resume because they were written for a limited and specific audience and not for general distribution or public release. Others were "ghost" written and have been attributed to other authors.

Dale Carpenter

"I find things for people."
Information and Knowledge Manager

Multi-industry experiences providing reference and research services to all levels of an organization. Created 3, modernized 5 and moved 4 corporate libraries. Project management, budget management, contract negotiation, and training program development experience.

SUMMARY OF QUALIFICATIONS'
Information professional with over 40 years in academic, corporate, government, private, public, and special libraries providing business, science, and technology references services. Hands-on experience creating and modernizing corporate libraries in the pharmaceutical (The Medicines Company), and aerospace/defense industries (AlliedSignal Aerospace, Singer- Link Flight Simulation). Over 30 years' experience designing and presenting corporate training programs on research skills and the use of online resources to all disciplines and management levels (Right Management, Manchester International, Lucent Technologies, AlliedSignal Aerospace).

SELECTED ACCOMPLISHMENTS
RESEARCH: Research study of World Wide Web (WWW) based recruiting published in Wall Street Journal July 2000. First ever survey of recruiters (over 400) asking for the best way for candidates to work with them online.
TRAINING: Created and conducted in-house and distance learning sessions at Right, Manchester, Lucent, and AlliedSignal on the use of reference sources, various electronic databases, and WWW resources and services. Prepared instructional handouts and bibliographies in conjunction with instructional sessions.
MANAGEMENT: Managed operations and staff of Fortune 500 corporate libraries (AlliedSignal Aerospace and Lucent Technologies).

EXPERIENCE:
1965 to 1969 = Firsthand knowledge of construction trade obtained by working summers with a builder and re-modeler in the Binghamton, New York area.

1969 to 1972 = Military Service: US Army, 82nd Airborne Division. Artillery Surveyor, Burial Detail Honor Guard, Officer's Driver.

1972 = WINK-TV, Ft. Myers, Florida. PROGRAMMER. Responsible for broadcast of all programs, commercial breaks, and station ID's. Drew up and maintained program log for program department. Duties in the capacities of cameraman, audio man, and engineer involved extensive knowledge of video-tape recorders, film projectors, slide drums, video and sound consoles, Videocon cameras and other video and audio equipment.

1973 to 1976 = attended full time year around - State University of New York, College at Geneseo
Major: Speech Communication B.A. Minors: Studio Art, English
Graduate level courses taken in Educational Radio and Television, Film Instruction Media, Film Literature, Film; Form and Function, and Speech in Mass Media.

1973 to 1976 = KINO, SUNY at Geneseo, NY. - Involved in all aspects of campus film service, which included much public contact, from film selection and ordering, film request surveys, cashier, ticket taker, crowd control, clean-up, and some projectionist work. KINO vice-chairperson for 1 year.

1974 to 1975 = Foxfire, Fresh Air, and Freeway, Geneseo, NY. BAND TECHNICIAN. Responsible for the coordination of moving, maintenance, set-up, and operation of all band equipment, sound systems, and lighting systems for these three western New York State bands. Also did public relations, crowd control, and publicity and marketing. Part-time during college.

1974 to 1976 = WGSU-FM, SUNY at Geneseo, NY. - RADIO ANNOUNCER at campus radio station serving western New York.

1975 to 1976 = GSTV, SUNY at Geneseo, NY. - ART DIRECTOR for student owned and operated campus TV station - produced artwork for student shows such as graphics, credits, and sets along with advertising and publicity materials for display or publication in the weekly campus paper.

1977 = WKOP-AM, Binghamton, NY. RADIO ANNOUNCER ("DJ"). Responsible for engineering two weekly ethnic music shows with local hosts. Worked in production of local area business commercials. Sorted, inventoried, and produced shows highlighting old 78 RPMs from station's record library. Part-time winter and spring.

1977 = REAL ESTATE PHOTOGRAPHER. Homeowners, Inc., Binghamton, NY. Responsible for obtaining architectural and advertising photographs for a real estate firm advertising on cable television. Worked closely with firm's owner on production of video-taped programs by designing the graphics, credits, and advertising materials for public distribution. The position called for much public contact.

1977 to 1978 = REPRODUCTION PHOTOGRAPHER. Valley Design, Johnson City, NY. Supervised and prepared inventory system of all darkroom materials and supplies for a design and engineering shop. Prepared procedure manual for training of new personnel. Implemented procedures and practices for use in new products and materials testing. Aided in development to double firm's production capabilities. Classified Material Clearance. Perfect attendance record.

1979 = State University of New York, School of Library and Information Science, Geneseo, NY. Graduate course work in special and academic librarianship emphasizing information resources and database usage. Masters of Library Science degree granted 1981.

1979 = LIBRARY ASSISTANT. School of Library and Information Science, SUNY at Geneseo, Geneseo, NY. Responsible for total control of all periodicals received by library school library. Aided library faculty in preparing library material for courses. Located materials and answered inquiries for patrons. Perfect attendance record. Part-time during graduate school.

November 1979 = White House Conference on Library and Information Services, Washington, DC. As a volunteer from Geneseo's School of Library and Information Science, I worked with the conferences staff photographer, ushered in delegate sessions and meetings, and performed all other functions as requested.

1980 to 1982 = LIBRARY PAGE. Binghamton Public Library, Binghamton, NY. Answered inquiries and located material for patrons from stack area of over 150,000 volumes. Performed periodical and microfilm holdings check-in and control. "enthusiastic and dedicated employee". "provided helpful ideas for stack maintenance ". Perfect attendance record.

1982 to 1987 = INFORMATION SPECIALIST. Singer-Link Flight Simulation, Binghamton, NY. Aircraft and helicopter simulator manufacture. Created Information Center for company. Performed all online computer database searching for company. Acquired, indexed, and maintained technical manuals, documents, and government and industry specifications and standards. Controlled and maintained files of government and company classified documents. Classified Materials Clearance.

1987 to 1996 = ALLIEDSIGNAL AEROSPACE, Teterboro, New Jersey. Diversified technology and manufacturing company which merged with Honeywell in 1999.
CORPORATE LIBRARY MANAGER - Guidance & Control Systems Division

Provide business, science and technology research services to marketing, engineering, scientific, and administrative customers throughout AlliedSignal in person, via phone and email.
Implement digital access to government and industry specifications and standards while reducing budget by 29%.
Increased customer usage 30% by publicizing specific alert services (strategic planning, competitor intelligence, technology updates, etc.).
Create Library home page for internal company network using HTML.
Led Total Quality Library team to obtain corporate-wide agreements with book jobbers, subscription services and online service providers.
Consolidate and streamline for three divisions book and periodical ordering, invoicing, and payment.
Manage Library operations and staff of 3.

1996 to 1998 = LUCENT TECHNOLOGIES, Murray Hill, New Jersey. Provider of communications networks for communications service providers.
INFORMATION REFERENCE SPECIALIST, Corporate headquarters, Murray Hill, NJ
Respond to specific research and reference questions and prepare value-added research packages, which include competitive intelligence, market research, demographic services, and patent searches by utilizing a variety of bibliographic materials, online electronic database services, and outside sources.
CORPORATE LIBRARIAN, Wireless Network Systems, Whippany, NJ
Provide reference services to Lucent engineers, scientists, and departments in person, via phone and email.
Eliminate low-use periodicals within Library to produce savings of $93,904.98 (34% of periodical budget) in 1997.
Develop information literacy, marketing, and publicity materials to publicize and promote Library services and educate Lucent constituents about resources and advantages the Library can provide.
Manage library operations and staff of 4.

1999 to 2002 = REGIONAL RESEARCH DIRECTOR, MANCHESTER INTERNATIONAL, Parsippany, New Jersey. Provider of career transition and career consulting services.

Acquired by Right Management in 2003.
Performed first study of WWW based recruiting. Results published in The Wall Street Journal, July 2000.
Provided business, financial and industry market research to senior and mid-level executives in career transition.
Created and conducted training programs and workshops on World Wide Web (WWW); database search techniques; electronic resources and job-hunting skills at Parsippany Career FastTrack Center. Center serviced 700+ candidates with revenues in excess of $4 million.
Compiled bibliography of 500+ WWW websites useful for professional development and industry research.
Developed digital online training guides for company website to provide 24/7 customer support.
Managed 2 corporate Library's functions: acquisitions, budgets, collection development, public relations, purchasing, and vendor contracts.

2003 to 2004 = MARKET RESOURCE CONSULTANT (One year contract position) RIGHT MANAGEMENT CONSULTANTS, Parsippany, New Jersey.
"World's leading career transition and organizational consulting firm".
Provided career transition business, financial and industry market research to senior and mid-level executives and scientific and technical experts.
Created and conducted training programs and workshops at Career Center operated for mid and senior level executives affected by Pharmacia/Pfizer merger. Programs and workshops taught the use of the World Wide Web (WWW); database search techniques; electronic resources and job-hunting skills.
Liaison between corporate human resources departments, executive recruiters and industry executives and subject specialists.

2004 to 2013 = THE MEDICINES COMPANY, Parsippany, New Jersey
Pharmaceutical company developing direct-to-hospitals acute care pharmaceuticals.
KNOWLEDGE MANAGEMENT DUTIES
Hired to create and manage a secure, limited access corporate Library to meet Food and Drug Administration (FDA) and Health Insurance

Portability and Accountability Act (HIPAA) regulatory compliance and safety requirements.

Responded to customer's in-person, email, or phone requests for research, files, and information; analyzed and organized documents, and provided technical support for Library systems, including guidance to a variety of electronic database resources.

Wrote and administered Library Standard Operating Polices (SOPs) and Procedures for the use of Library materials. Managed repository of all worldwide corporate policies and SOPs.

Designed and managed digital weekly marketed product safely alerts in Dialog. Performed online business, scientific and technical searches to support researchers.

Member of Corporate Training and Development Team which developed a three-year plan for employee training and development which established the new position of Corporate Training Director. Plan accepted and implemented by Management Committee.

Prepared and presented training sessions on Library resources and World Wide Web (WWW) search techniques.

Oversaw logistical aspects of corporate Library move to new building including serving as point of contact for movers.

DIGITAL ASSETS MANAGEMENT DUTIES

Investigated over 50 vendors of document management software to find one which met our functional requirements and customer service metrics. Project written up in "Computer Software Evaluation: Balancing User's Needs & Wants".

Project manager for digitization of over 34,000 paper regulatory documents into digital records management and imaging software system. Database administrator and system troubleshooting for system. Assisted in conversion of all records and images into Microsoft SharePoint.

Software development of custom document databases used by Finance, Legal, Manufacturing, Quality Assurance, and Medical Writing groups.

ARCHIVIST DUTIES

Point-of-contact person for all corporate archiving. Contract negotiation and budget management with offsite storage vendor. Performed detailed inventory on all materials to be archived, coordinated, and tracked the retrieval and return of records.

Launched improved database of all archived materials. Archives inventory review resulted in 320.5 cubic feet weeded and merged into 114 cubic feet and over $100 monthly savings in rent gained.

2013 to 2016 = FREELANCE INFORMATION CONSULTANT
Provided business, scientific, and technical research services to individuals and organizations.
Did inventory management, organized information, and materials, and created content for individuals and organizations.
Regained over $6000.00 in state sales tax for one company by questioning invoice irregularities.

2016 to 2018 = PUBLIC SERVICES LIBRARIAN, WOODBOURNE CORRECTIONAL FACILITY, Woodbourne, New York
Receive, analyze, and respond to reference and research questions having broad scope and complex topics.
Manage, develop, and modernize Library services in a New York State facility serving over 1000 customers. Supervise and train staff of 6.
Responsible for acquisition, cataloging, and maintenance of all materials (books, subscriptions, service, and support contracts).

2018 to 2021 = SENIOR LIBRARIAN, New York State Academy of Fire Science, Montour Falls, New York.
State training facility for New York State fire fighters, first responders, rescue personnel, etc.
Manage facilities library.

PARTIAL LIST OF PUBLICATIONS:
Books available at www.Lulu.com

"Computer Software Evaluation: Balancing User's Needs & Wants"; LTP., Ltd. 2017.
"If Was Organized, I'd Be a Librarian: Organizational Tips From a Librarian"; LTP., Ltd. 2014
"Needs & Wants: The History of a Corporate Needs Analysis Project "; LTP, Ltd., 2014
"Hitchhiking in America: Using the Golden Thumb"; LTP, Ltd., Second Edition, 2014
"Hitchhiking in America: Using the Golden Thumb"; LTP, Ltd., First

Edition, 1992
"Cost of Cutting a Check: As Justification for Centralization of Information Purchases in the Library"; quoted from SOLOLIB-L in OPL: The One-Person Library, November 2005
"Advice for Working with Recruiters"; CapLits, Bulletin of the Pharmaceutical and Health Technology Division, Fall 2004
"Recruiting Advice"; Hudson Valley Views, Bulletin of the Hudson Valley Chapter/SLA, Winter 2005
"Working with Recruiters"; Upstate Update, Bulletin of the Upstate New York Chapter of the Special Libraries Association, Spring 2005
"Email is Best Way to Contact Recruiters", Wall Street Journal, June 2000. First ever survey of how recruiters were using the World Wide Web to connect with job seekers.
"Hints and Tips on Attending SLA Annual Conferences", New Jersey Chapter Bulletin, April 1991

EDUCATION
Master's Degree in Library Science (MLS), State University College, Geneseo, New York
Bachelor of Arts Degree in Speech Communications (BA), State University College, Geneseo, New York
New Jersey State Professional Librarian Certificate

MILITARY SERVICE
82nd Airborne Division Paratrooper
Third Generation Veteran, US Army
Honor Guard (Burial Detail: North Carolina, South Carolina, Virginia)
Commanding Officer's Driver

VOLUNTEER WORK
Performed online research for family, friends, and neighbors.
Performed resume review and resume writing service for family and friends.
Coached individuals in job hunting skills.
Coming Home dog rescue volunteer work.
Rockaway Borough River Cleanup volunteer.
Taught fly fishing skills.
Built 8×10-foot barn to replace shed damaged by Hurricane Sandy.

OTHER
Hitchhiker, paratrooper, librarian, fly-fisherman, author.
Secret Level Security Clearance

Professional career experience: academic library, public library, corporate library, special library, abstracts, acquisitions, administration, archives, archivist, bibliography, business researcher, cataloging, collection development, collection management, corporate trainer, database administrator, database searcher, database trainer, document control, government documents, indexing, information management, knowledge management, information literacy, instructor, information retrieval, instructional materials, Internet, knowledge worker, library instruction, library relocation, library renovation, library science, serials management, market research, marketing, multimedia, one person library, online services, online databases, public relations, public service, records management, records retention, reference, reference services, scientific researcher, special collections, special library, supervisor, teamwork, technical researcher, technical services, trainer, user education, World Wide Web (WWW), aerospace industry, simulation, defense industry, guidance systems, telecommunication industry, wireless industry, outplacement industry, career management, career guidance, career development, career transition, Dun & Bradstreet, DIALOG, Factiva, Lexis/Nexis, Dow Jones, OneSource, Microsoft Office (Excel, PowerPoint, Word), Outlook, Internet Explorer, Netscape, Lotus Notes.

> "In a job, what you need to know is,
> you need to know more than you know."
> **Kim Kolakowski**

How Recruiters Are Using the World Wide Web:
1999 Recruiter Survey and Articles

While at Manchester International, I often heard from other employees how recruiters wanted to receive information from job candidates. But often, the information varied. Some said the recruiters wanted paper copies of cover letters and resumes mailed to them, other staff said a lot of recruiters were going electronic and wanted electronic versions. Since I could not find an answer, I decided to survey recruiters and find out.

This is the survey I sent out in 1999.

> I am Dale Carpenter, a Regional Research Director for Manchester Partners International, one of the world's largest and best career change management and outplacement firms.
>
> I would like to make your job easier. As part of my job, I help our candidates prepare resumes and determine which executive recruiters to contact. With the increasing use of electronic communications, I am being asked if recruiters prefer receiving resumes and cover letters in paper or electronic format.
>
> If you would please take the time to answer the following questions, I will share the information gathered with all our candidates, counselors, and offices. We will then know the most efficient way to contact you, making your job easier. Of course, I will be glad to share this information with all the firms answering my questions.
>
> Dale Carpenter
> Regional Research Director
> Manchester Partners International
> Parsippany, NJ 07054
> myname@manchesterus.com
>
>   1. How do you prefer to receive resumes and cover letters?
> Paper   E-mail   It does not matter
>
>   2. Do you prefer the traditional 2-page resume or will you accept an expanded resume which explains in detail a person's skills, accomplishments, and employment history? Or would you like to receive both?

Alphabetical by Color   238

    3. Would you prefer receiving a resume in plain ASCII text, to make it easier to scan into your database, or doesn't it matter what typeface it is in?

    4. Would it make your job easier to receive a resume in both paper and electronic formats?

    5. Do you like candidates to have sections of their resumes detailing their skills and accomplishments?

    6. Do you like candidates to have a keyword section on their resume, to make it more searchable when entered a database?

This is the article I published internally for Manchester International in 1999 after doing the survey of executive recruiters. After Manchester made this information public, DowJones published a short article on this survey.

E-mail the Best Way to Contact Recruiters

Our company works with many individuals doing job searches and as the Research Director, I get asked for the best way to contact executive recruiters. So I electronically surveyed a sampling of recruiters to find out.

    416 recruiters provided useful data.
    81.8% said they preferred to be contacted by email. 7.28% wanted only a mailed resume and 8.01% said they preferred faxes. 5.10% said any of the three ways was fine.
    43.45% preferred attachments to be in the Microsoft Word format, while 5.34% wanted Rich Text Format (RTF). 4.61 desired resumes to be incorporated into the body of the email.
    Of those who expressed preference, 33.01% preferred the traditional, chronological resume instead of the accomplishment-oriented resume, which 1.70% liked.

The data is useful, but of far more use are the comments people responded with stating good and bad ways to approach them. These are actual comments from recruiter's email, edited for brevity.

General advice on ways to approach a recruiter:

"Listen to an agency's specialization and send ONLY targeted resumes."
"Take the time to identify the fields in which the recruiters work."
"when someone sends an unsolicited email with a generic cover letter and a resume as an attached document, we most likely will not even look at the resume."
"visit our Web site prior to resume submission."
"We do not have the time to assist people out of our field of expertise."

Contacting recruiters: the all-important first impression:
"Identify yourself clearly or the message will be deleted before being opened."
"Always indicate subject in subject line, otherwise it is automatically purged from email."
"subject line gives as much info as possible, particularly position title or function, industry, compensation level, whatever,"
"prefer to see a 2-line summary of type of position desired, industry, compensation range and geographical location or preferences."

"As with networking in general, referrals to search firms are powerful ways for candidates to get in the door. I will always go out of my way to provide whatever assistance I can to referrals from people who have been of help to me over the years."

What your cover letter must contain:
"I will not open an attachment that does not have a cover letter. Most often, I receive e-mail's that say, "executive resume." I have no idea what that means so I delete it and don't bother to read it. It is a waste of my time."
"Cover letters should be straight to the point"
"Always provide the following information:
   1) occupation, career, or current position title
   2) geographic preferences,
   3) reason for leaving current position
   4) current base salary/compensation,
   5) current bonus compensation
   6) expected compensation in new position.
   7) phone number
   8) email address"

Clear, concise, and readable resumes:
"Always make a habit of sending them in the mail as well."

"Forget about the "new Internet profile/accomplishments/keywords format" as these formats are so complicated and filled with useless self grandising statements as to make them very difficult to process and render them useless for key word searching. Finally everything gets stripped out but the chronological part."

"The biggest problem with resumes is that people don't describe the company. I get resumes every day, and I can't help the people because I don't know the company. List the company name and the length of time worked for the company. Then describe the company: size, products, markets, etc. List the various job titles and the length of time held. For each job title briefly describe duties & responsibilities...and then list the accomplishments achieved in that position, what kinds of projects did you do, how many people did you supervise, etc."

"Indicate experience but not tell a detailed story, that is what the interview is for. No one hires a resume. No one hires without an interview. Focus on getting in front of the hiring manager."
"The more information we have about a candidate, the better."
"Actions verbs help to show a doer, "hands on" self-start" etc. "
"A summary paragraph at the top of the page is time efficient but may not be possible for everyone's career."
"Keywords should already be incorporated into the body of the written resume, which is fully searchable. "Facts and figures are essential."
"No follow up telephone call asking, "did you get my resume."

Their worries about attached files:
"Scan document so that you are not transmitting viruses." "We routinely scan all incoming e-mail for viruses; when we detect a virus, we delete the file."

"If the person writes their name as the name of the document, I always give them ten points for awareness of who's on the other side of the communication line! (most people write "resume" or similar) very convenient if the applicant's last name is used to name the document (IE., Smith.doc)."

"But there is one basic rule. No Attachments. No Addenda. No Additions. No extra files to try to open."

"We have ALL kinds of computers here, and there are ALL kinds of resumes that never get seen because the candidate has sent the important stuff in an attachment that we CANNOT OPEN."

"hiring managers prefer ASCII text embedded into the email message. They do not wish to take the time to open formatted attachments suitable for printing out."

If you do mail a resume:
"We use OCR to convert and store resumes in our files. This allows high speed detail searching of the resumes. Since OCR software is not perfect yet, we hope for the following things in resumes that are mailed or faxed to us."

* An unfolded original or laser copy (this means Mail is better than Fax)
* A type font of at least 10 points, preferably one with no serifs such as Arial
* No use of underscore or lines (such as boxes) on the resume
* No use of italics
* No use of fancy fonts which don't read well
* No two or three "newspaper" column presentation
* No pictures -- just words
* If you want to attach fancy stuff or words make them supplemental to the resume, not a part of it. (We can and do scan these items as pictures that can be sent via email)."

Dale Carpenter
Manchester International

After I left Manchester and was working for The Medicines Company, I wrote this article for the library profession. It was sent to several state chapters or industry group's library newsletters and several published it.

My name is Dale Carpenter. I have a Masters Degree in Library and Information Science and have worked in public, academic and corporate libraries, including creating and managing corporate information centers for Fortune 500 companies. Before entering the pharmaceutical industry, where I am now, I spent several years working with two top international career transition companies (they don't like to be called "outplacement firms" anymore) working with individuals in transition and presenting training seminars on WWW usage.

This information was gathered from recruiters and a survey I did of recruiting firms asking how best to work with them. 416 firms replied and the results were publishing in the Wall Street Journal June 2000.

Very quickly, here is what I tell individuals about contacting recruiters using email.

1. Recruiters, like everyone else, fear computer viruses. Many companies automatically delete emails with attachments. Send your email in plain text format.

2. In the subject line of the email, put your profession or title and industry/company you worked in. (Example: "Senior HR, pharmaceutical industry" or "Molecular Biologist, Merck").

3. If you have a reference, put in the name. (Example: "Betty Judd suggested we should talk".)

4. In the cover letter of the email, put your profession, industry/company you worked in, and compensation. (Example: "I am a research professional who has worked in the aerospace, telecommunications and outplacement industries. I was the Research Director for Manchester Inc., an international career change counseling and outplacement company. My compensation over the last three years was between $63,000 and $67,000".) Compensation includes base salary, individual performance bonuses, year-end bonuses, etc. Don't put down anything about

where you want to work. The recruiter will ask you when they call you.

5. Paste your resume after your cover letter. If the recruiter wants a Word version of your resume, they will contact you and ask for it. If they see your resume on a jobsite, they will ask for a Word version because they do not want to bring a plain text resume into a company.

6. Some recruiters will automatically bounce your email and tell you to go to their website and post your resume into their resume database.

7. Recruiters get hundreds of resumes named "resume". Name your resume file with your name. My resume is called "Carpenter Dale 20040704.doc". When the recruiter saves it on their computer, they can easily find it by searching for my name. Also, when I send an updated resume, they will know which one is the most current.

8. Check what your resume looks like by sending your resume in both a plain text and a Word version attachment to several friends by e-mail. Have them print it out and send you the printed versions without changing them in any way. This is the only way to know what your resume and cover letter will look like when you send it electronically.

Two Types of Recruiters

The two types of recruiters are retained and contingency. Retained recruiters are hired by a company to fill a position and are paid whether they fill the position. Usually retained recruiters work at salary levels of $75,000 and above. Contingency recruiters are paid only if the candidate they put forward is hired. Often, contingency recruiters from different recruiting firms will be working to fill the same position at a company.

Finding Recruiters:

I will not list recruiting firms which work with librarians or information professionals because I am sure I cannot provide a comprehensive listing. You can find firms listed at The Riley Guide, 'www.rileyguide.com', at the ALA and SLA websites, and at job boards specific to our profession. While you are scanning the job banks make notes of which recruiters are handling the interesting sounding jobs. Probably the best way to find good recruiters is to talk with people in your industry to find out which recruiters they've worked with and ask for a referral.

The Directory of Executive Recruiters, published by Kennedy Publications, is a very useful tool to find recruiting firms which meet your criteria of industry and function.

Attend our professional association meetings and conferences and introduce yourself to the recruiters. They are there to scout for prime talent, and you should make them aware of you. Tell them right away you are willing to help them when they are searching for someone in your field. By doing so you just became a valuable resource for the recruiter and they will remember you. Exchange business cards with the recruiter and let them know what your specialties and functions are within your profession and industry. When the recruiter calls you, even if you are not interested in the position they tell you about, tell them you'll pass on the information and their name and address to your network. Nowadays you can do this electronically over the electronic Web sites of your local and national associations.

Also check your college alumni association to see if any alumni are recruiters. Often, they will be happy to help fellow alumni.

Contacting Recruiters

Probably the best way to get a recruiter's attention is to be referred by a professional colleague who has worked with them. You could also ask senior managers for names of recruiters. Then put that colleague or manager's name in the subject line of the e-mail you send to recruiters. Ask your Human Resources Department if your company works with any specific recruiting firms.

Other guidelines for dealing with recruiters:
- register on their Web sites to be included in their databases.
- don't spread your resume too wide because they are less likely to help you if you do.
- become a source for recruiters by passing on names of other likely candidates.

Stay away from services which offer to distribute your resume to multiple recruiters. Recruiters prefer to handle someone who is selective about passing out their resume.

If you are dealing with recruiters and posting your resume on company Web sites, keep track of all the sites you post on. Recruiters will ask you where you have posted your resume. If you post it on a lot of company job boards, they are less likely to work with you because if the company finds you in its database, they do not have to pay the recruiter fees.

You can approach a recruiter by telephone but be prepared to have your 30 second personal commercial ready. You want to quickly give them an overall view of who you are, your experience, and what you can do so they will be receptive to receiving e-mails from you.

Many recruiters work on a nationwide basis, so when you contact one let them know you are willing and where you would be willing to relocate.

Often your first contact with a recruiter may be an interview over the phone. Make sure you present a professional image from the first moment they hear your voice. Is the voice mail message on your answering machine professional sounding? Or is it the happy cheery "we're not home right now leave a message" message? Some job seekers use a specific phone number or cell phone for their job search which makes it easier to present a professional image. Make sure paper and pencils are next to the phone for taking messages.

When speaking with a recruiter, focus on specific accomplishments in the past five or ten years. Mention specifics of your experience instead of generalities. "Reduced a budget 24 percent while retaining essential services" sounds much better than "managed corporate library".

When the recruiter calls you need to convince them their client wants to speak with you. You will discuss your experience, your technical and managerial skills, and your salary and how it is related to a job opening. You want to get your name and resume in front of the hiring manager. Keep insisting you would like to meet with the recruiter and the hiring manager to learn more about the opportunity even if the salary range, the geographical location, or another factor is not precisely what you want. You want to contact the hiring manager because they can change salary ranges, locations, etc.

Keep in contact with recruiters. Who are you more excited to see, someone who has stayed in touch over the years and helped you, or someone who calls you after a long absence and ask for a favor? You want to help the people who stay in touch. When you have landed a job, send a friendly, personal letter to recruiters you worked with. Offer to be a source of job leads. Mention their name to your Human Resources department. Suggest you meet once or twice a year, if possible, to exchange information on trends in your industry. You also could invite a recruiter to attend one of your professional association meetings to help them enlarge their contact network. And of course send them articles of interest to them.

If you successfully work with a recruiter and land a fine position, please let me know. And of course, mention my name to the recruiter.

Happy Hunting
Dale Carpenter
Corporate Librarian, The Medicines Company

Policies and Standard Operating Procedures (SOPs)

Policies and Standard Operating Procedures (SOPs) are written statements detailing how an organization will operate using agreed upon methods and practices to conduct business in a select area. They provide an agreed upon and pre-planned course of actions during an incident. They are written to help a person, department, or organization function effectively and standardize certain processes. They answer what actions are to be taken, and why, in a certain situation. They train and educate personnel, new and old, in methods to best assure efficiency.

Policy Number: POL-LIB-001
Title: Library Collection Development Policy
Version: 1.0
Effective Date: Approved by:

Purpose:
The purpose of the Library Collection Development Policy is to guide the development and maintenance of an outstanding, well-balanced collection of the best and most useful materials available to meet the research and teaching needs of this organization.

Scope:
The policy is intended to guide Library staff in the selection of materials including what subject areas and material types to consider, and how much emphasis each should receive. This is done within the limits imposed by physical Library space and available funds.

Mission Statement:
Library Services are committed to serving the information needs of this organization's staff, through its own collection and by providing access to the resources of other libraries and networks throughout the world in a cost-effective manner. To achieve this goal, the Library will undertake to develop and maintain a collection of in-house materials in various formats, focused on the business goals and subject needs of the organization. As the business and research needs of the change, the Library will assess and adapt its collection to reflect the new and differing areas of interest and concern.

Collection Development Guidelines:
Materials to be acquired by the Library will meet one or more of the following criteria.

- a recognized training and certification requirement under this state's laws (if required).
- permanent value as a resource material.
- suitable subject and material related to business goals and subject needs.
- heavy demand:
- does the material fill an information gap within the in relation to the existing collection.
- does the information required already exist in the collection or within the organization.
- justifiable cost within the established budget for a given year.

Priority will be given to materials which have a significant importance to established department objectives and to materials which have the greatest value for the widest segment of staff.

The Library will also accept donations of books, serials, textbooks or training materials, and other materials, but these will be judged on the same basis as materials being considered for purchase. Retention and/or utilization of donated material is at the discretion of Library staff. The Library also readily welcomes purchase suggestions for books, serials, or other materials from staff, but the actual purchase of such materials will be based on the criteria above.

The Library does not purchase and pay for materials for individuals, departments, or other agencies within the organization. If the material(s) are not kept in the Library, the Library does not pay for the material(s). (Vitally important these statements are in your policies and procedures.)

Collection Management and Tracking:
Finance will inform the Librarian whenever funds are used to purchase any book, periodical subscription, access to electronic information system or membership in a professional organization. This will allow:

- Knowledge of what information resources are available to the

organization.
- Tracking of department funds spent on information resources.
- Elimination of duplication of information resources.
- Resources bought by the organization to be kept in-house when staff leaves the organization.

Finance will inform the Librarian what material was purchased, who purchased it, who it was purchased from, and if applicable, the start and stop dates of subscription, membership, or access.

The Librarian will keep an inventory of all information resources received in-house so staff may be informed what is available for their use.

Human Resources will inform the Librarian when an employee is leaving the organization so all purchased materials held by the individual may be retained by their department or brought to the Library.

Selection of Specific Materials:

Books
Points considered in book selection are the book's role in supporting research and development or business needs, authority and effectiveness of presentation, available funds, and space. Books will be selected by the Librarian based on their entire contents.

Textbooks and/or Training Materials
The Library will not purchase course or training textbooks or materials unless the book or material is kept in the Library for use by multiple users. Individuals and instructors must purchase training materials themselves or through their departments.

Serials (Journal Subscriptions)
Serials supplement the book collection by providing up-to-date information, covering current topics not yet available in books, and presenting a much less in-depth treatment of a subject than is usually found in books. Serials are generally acquired by paid subscription, but the Library will also accept gifts.

In general, the selection policies for serials are like those for books.

Selection factors include its usefulness in supporting research, business needs or regulatory requirements, accuracy and objectivity, or full-text availability through commercial vendors. Other factors will include format, price and coverage by similar titles already held at the organization.

The Librarian will review subscriptions on an annual basis to ensure they continue to provide on-going value to the organization.

Electronic Information Systems/Aggregated Databases
Electronic Information Systems/Databases save time and resources by collecting large amounts of information into a searchable database(s). Subscription to and renewal of these systems or the addition of new systems will be addressed annually by the Librarian, to ensure they are fulfilling the current needs of the within the established budget for a given year.

New systems of information delivery will be reviewed by the Librarian for possible use, as they become available. If their value appears appropriate and useful to the company, they will be incorporated into the selection of library materials, if the cost is justifiable.

Document Delivery
It is not cost-effective to spend large sums of money on little-used materials. The Library cannot purchase every item of value or all materials requested by staff. The Library will extend its resources with other libraries and networks, and access other available sources for material which may include interlibrary loan networks, document delivery services, or electronic information.

The Library will use every available format, electronic and paper, to provide information and services to associates.

Collection Maintenance:

Reference Materials:
Certain materials are of such high value to the Library, the staff, and researchers they are considered reference materials and as such do NOT circulate or leave the Library.
These include but are not limited to:

This; That; and the other.

Archiving
Important materials will be archived to preserve the history of the organization and the history of our industry. This will include teaching materials used in courses.

Weeding
To keep the collection current, materials will be re-evaluated on an ongoing basis, at which time decisions will be made whether to dispose of or repair damaged materials or dispose of outdated materials. In general, the same criteria apply to weeding as are used in the selection of new materials.

Definitions:
Materials: The word "materials" refers only to books, journal subscriptions, audio-visual resources, and electronic information resources. Media such as digital video disks (dvds) and video tapes are included in this definition. Other media resources shall be evaluated as they become available.

Revision of Policy:
This policy will be reviewed, and revised if necessary, no less frequently than every two years.
This Policy was last reviewed?

SOP Number: SOP-LIB-001
Title: Filing and Management of Materials in the Library
Version: 1.0
Effective date: Approved by:

Purpose:
The purpose of this Library procedure is to describe the procedure for organizing, maintaining, and archiving materials in the organization. This procedure will also describe the procedure for storing and controlling access to materials.

Alphabetical by Color

Scope:
This procedure covers all individuals who use or borrow materials held in the Library or held under the Library's control.

Process Description:
This procedure explains how materials are transferred to, classified, and archived within the Library. This procedure also describes how access to these materials are controlled as well as how retention and/or weeding measures are carried out.

Receive Materials into the Library:
Materials ordered by the Librarian, or donated by other individuals, groups, or departments, are received by the Librarian. The date of receipt is written upon the shipping paperwork. Paperwork is kept for inventory and tracking purposes.

Classify and Index Materials:
The material is classified using subject matter keywords, International Standard Book Number (ISBN) numbering and other criteria to create a unique identification for the item. It is then entered into a records database which provides item tracking as well as providing staff and researchers a way of seeing what is in the Library collection.

Place Materials into Library:
The materials are stamped with the organization's markings, book cards and spine labels are created and added to the materials and they are placed in the Library.

Gaining Access to Materials:
A staff member or researcher may request a specific item or item from the Library. If the person has the right to borrow the material, the Librarian will assist the employee in finding the item. The Librarian will sign-out the material(s) to the borrower. If necessary, the Librarian will package the requested item(s) and take them to Shipping to be sent to the borrower.

The Librarian will inform the employee how long the item may be borrowed, not to exceed 30 days. The borrower may request a loan renewal for another 30 days, which is granted by the Librarian unless someone else has requested the item. The Library will grant a grace period of 30 days after the item is due. If the item has not been returned within 60 days of the due date, a late notice is mailed to the borrower. If the item has not been returned 30 days after the mailing date of the overdue notice, the Library staff brings the overdue notice to the Administration Office staff who shall invoice the borrower for the replacement cost of the material(s).

A list is kept of all borrowers who do not return materials, keep materials long overdue, or return materials in a damaged state. Access to the Library materials and research will be refused to that individual.

Reference Materials:
Certain materials are of such high value to the Library, the staff, and researchers they are considered reference materials and as such do NOT circulate or leave the Library.
These include but are not limited to:
This; That; and the other.

Archive or Weed Materials
On an on-going basis, the Librarian will review the usage of all materials in the Library. If an item has not been borrowed or viewed in a long length of time (10 or more years for example) the Librarian may consider removing the item from the collection by weeding or archiving it. For example, workbooks for specific courses may be superseded by newer editions as the course content changes and the older workbooks may no longer be relevant. One copy may be placed into Archives for a historical record while other copies are discarded.

Revision of Policy
This policy will be reviewed, and revised if necessary, no less frequently than every two years.
This Policy was last reviewed?

SOP Number: SOP-LIB-002
Title: Managing Access to the Library
Version: 1.0
Effective Date: Approved by:

Purpose:
The purpose of this procedure is to describe how the Library provides access to the secure storage area known as the "the Library". The Library contains materials which have been obtained for teaching, reference, and research purposes and which may contain information which must not be released to unauthorized individuals inside or outside. Consequently, open unrestricted access to the Library is not permitted.

Scope:
This procedure applies to all staff as well as the public and covers access to the secure storage area known as the Library.

Process Description:
This procedure explains how authorization to enter the Library is granted to staff, students, or researchers.

Access to the Library:
The Library is always kept locked unless the Librarian is in the Library.

To limit access to the Library, keys to the Library shall be given only to the Librarian, other authorized Library staff, the manager whom the Librarian reports to, Security, Housekeeping and Maintenance.

If anyone desires access to the Library during off-duty hours, they must ask Security to let them in. Security will remain in the Library while the person uses the Library resources and ensure no Library materials leave the Library.

Revision of Policy
This policy will be reviewed, and revised if necessary, no less frequently than every two years.
This Policy was last reviewed?

SOP Number: SOP-LIB-003
Title: Loan and Retrieval of Library Materials
Version: 1.0
Effective Date: Approved by:

Purpose:
The purpose of this procedure is to describe how the Library safeguards the security of the teaching, reference and research materials kept in secure storage. Open access to them is not permitted.

Scope:
This procedure covers all materials in the Library or held under the Library's control and applies to anyone who want access to items held in the Library.

Process Description:
This procedure explains how materials are borrowed from the Library, how they are delivered to the reader and, if appropriate, how they are returned to the Library.

Reference Materials:
Certain materials are of such high value to the Library, the staff, and researchers they are considered reference materials and as such do NOT circulate or leave the Library.
These include but are not limited to:
This; That; and the other.

Request to View an Item Held by the Library:
An individual makes a request to the Librarian to look at or borrow an item or items. The request may be done in writing, by email, by phone or in person.

Review Request:
The Librarian reviews the requestor's right to view the item. They should have a legitimate reason for viewing or borrowing the item(s).

If the requester does not have permission to view the document, the Librarian informs them as such. This might be an individual who, because of prior refusal to follow Library procedures, is on the "No Services" list kept by the Library staff. (See SOP-LIB-001).

Assist Requester to Locate and Borrow Item(s):
The Librarian may allow the employee to sign out the item for 30 days. A maximum of five (5) items may be signed out at a time. The Librarian

will write down the borrower's name, home address and phone number and attach it to the book card. The book card is filed in the Loan File on the Librarian's desk. A due date slip with the date the item is to returned is placed into the book pocket in the book or with the item.

For accountability reasons, the borrow must provide a home address. The Library will not ship to a post office box, a fire station, or department address. The individual is accepting sole responsible for material(s) and so will provide their home address.

Return Materials to the Library:
Requester returns the original item to the Library:
After the requester is finished with the item(s) or after no more than 30 days, they must return it to the Library. The borrower may request a loan renewal for another 30 days, which is granted by the Librarian unless someone else has requested that item. The Librarian returns the book card to the book pocket and refiles the item(s) where it belongs.

The Library will grant a grace period of 30 days after the item is due. If the item has not been returned within 60 days of the due date, a late notice is mailed to the borrower. If the item has not been returned 30 days after the mailing date of the overdue notice, the Library staff brings the overdue notice to the Registration Office staff who shall invoice the borrower for the replacement cost of the material(s).

A list is kept of all borrowers who do not return materials, keep materials long overdue, or return materials in a damaged state. Access to the Library materials and services will be refused to those individuals.

Revision of Policy
This policy will be reviewed, and revised if necessary, no less frequently than every two years.
This Policy was last reviewed?

Creating a Library from the Ground Up

These are the notes and planning documents I wrote when planning the creation of a corporate library for "The Medicines Company" (TMC). Since the pharmaceutical industry has quite strict regulatory requirements, they entered greatly into the planning considerations. And since TMC never had a library or librarian before, I had to start from nothing. Like building a house I had to design from the foundation on up.

The existing materials for the library were all documents created in-house by TMC employees. Each company and every industry will have its own regulatory requirements and restrictions with which you must concern yourself while planning their library.

Building The Medicines Company's Corporate Library

1. Consult with key members of teams/departments to ensure all business requirements are documented –
 a. identify what regulatory documents will need to be filed and maintained
 b. identify what company/department documents will need to be filed and maintained
 c. identify what documents will be brought to Parsippany from other locations
 d. identify major document types
 e. identify requirements (legal, regulatory, retention, etc.) for document types

2. Business requirements must link with company strategic aims, policies, and procedures -
 a. document to be 'view' only unless permission granted by head of department owning document
 b. all changes or modifications to documents will be tracked by software
 c. originators will have final sign-off on all document content
 d. certain documents will be viewed only by the department which owns the document, IE. Sales and ad agreements, contracts, legal, etc.
 e. templates for company forms and documents available to all thru

SharePoint
   f. creation of Library SOPs:
   g. document filing and retrieval method
   h. document control methods (check-in, check-out etc.) including version control
i. document archiving and retention procedure (includes legal requirements for each document type and solutions for security of documents)

3. Implement design solution in agreement with infrastructure and resources -
   a. classification solution (developed in-house or purchased from outside vendor) must co-exist seamlessly with current TMC software
   b. training sessions on Library system will be developed and presented to TMC employees so they may learn to use the system to access documents
   c. what software package is the company using now for information and documentation both structured and unstructured?

   4. Manage Library to ensure -
   a. regulatory requirements are met;
   b. ensure return on investment;
   c. productivity and performance measures are met;
   d. overall customer satisfaction is realized

   5. Any plan must address these essential processes:
   a. identifies and capture relevant knowledge
   b. store, organize and classify information in a central repository
   c. provide knowledge to users thru easy automated access
d. interacts with knowledge and users creating a feedback loop to beginning (number 1)

Classification Scheme must cover these items and answer these questions to be useful:

Three main classes of documents: What falls into my area of responsibility? (What else will be my responsibility? Research, document acquisition and delivery, etc.?)

1. Documents published in-house – 3 types:

regulatory documents – required for regulatory approval
external documents – created for external release, (marketing or sales materials), etc.
internal documents – policies, procedures, memos, etc.

2. Documents received from outside sources - clinical study materials, etc.

3. Reference materials purchased for in-house use: Held by departments?

Documents created in house: (David M says company policy is "paper copies are the official copy")
    What are they?
    Who creates them and who owns them?
    How are they used and by whom?
    How often are they used or accessed? Does this change over time?
    What regulatory requirements pertain, IE. retention period, original copy, paper or electronic?
    Is version control needed?
    Is access control needed?
    Are they available in paper or electronic format (Internet, databases, CD-ROM, email) or both?
    Are they stored in paper or electronic format or both?
    How long do they need to be retained?
    Do they need to be in the Library?

Documents or reference materials received from outside sources:
    What are they?
    Where do we obtain them?
    Who obtains them for company or department?
    How are they used and by whom?
    Are they shared among departments?
    How often are they used or accessed? Does this change over time?
    What regulatory requirements pertain? IE. Do we need updated versions on a regular basis?
    Is version control needed?
    Is access control needed?

Are they available in paper or electronic format (Internet, databases, CD-ROM, email) or both?
Are they stored in paper or electronic format or both?
How long do they need to be retained?
Do they need to be in the Library?

QUESTIONS AND ISSUES

1. TMC organizational chart is needed so I may meet with department heads and group managers.
   a. introduce myself and offer whatever help I can to assist them in their jobs
   b. learn what they do and how they do it
   c. learn what they create and how it is used
   d. learn what information they need to function and where and how they obtain that info
   e. find out if they have and use a classification scheme for dept. documents

2. A procedure is needed which mandates all departments to provide Library with documents required for the regulatory process and auditing process.
   a. how do we determine what documents these are?
   b. how do we determine what version of document is required?
   c. keep only final, or all versions?
   d. how can we be sure Library receives all documents from every department?

3. These other procedures will be needed:
   a. procedure detailing process by which Library receives, classifies, securely stores, retains, and provides knowledge of (database or index), company and external documents and records.
   b. procedure detailing how Library provides access to documents – sign-out procedure
   c. procedure detailing records retention and archiving by Library, either in house or off site
   d. Policy and SOP updating procedure
   e. disaster recovery plan

4. Are we concerned with only paper documents or both paper and

electronic forms of documents?
   a. if electronic version, how do we maintain access control?
   b. done thru SharePoint?

5. Classification system should include any existing department classification system which will be placed into a searchable subfield. Create taxonomy in-house or purchase from outside source?

   6. Storage space must be secure and restricted to Library staff only.

   7. Library must provide to TMC a searchable electronic database and index of their holdings.
   a. how? thru SharePoint?
   b. searchable by what terms? And to what depth? (full text?)
   c. ability to request documents thru database?

   8. How does Library provide access to the documents when required by staff?
   a. do we provide the original or a copy?
   b. do we provide a paper or electronic version?

   9. How do we determine the retention schedule for each item?
   a. by department procedures, by market lifetime of the product, or regulatory requirements?

   10. How does a TMC employee request access to a document?
   a. by paper form, email, electronic form?

   11. How long will an employee be able to sign a document out of the Library?
   a. how do we enforce this?

   12. Will we need to retain sign-out forms showing who looked at what document? A good idea.
   a. how long will we have to retain sign-out forms?

13. How do we determine if an employee has the right to view a document?
   a. by SharePoint reader/author/approver/coordinator function?
   b. or by department manager approval?

14. What level of detail must the classification scheme show?
   a. more levels of detail the better storage & retrieval but more detail adds more work
   b. must we go down to table of contents level as shown in TMC-CL-002 addendum?

15. What departments have functions which may overlap the document control function or have functions which might become my responsibility? Who are they, where are they, what do they do?
   a. Knowledge Management
   b. Medical Affairs Information
   c. others?

Here I am thinking about how the documents should be classified, both on paper and then electronically.

FIELDS NEEDED IN CLASSIFICATION – all should be searchable -

Document source
Title
Study name
Study number/amendment/supplement
Date
Author(s)
Country(s)
State(s)
Hospital(s)
Number of pages
Number of volumes
Agency form # (IE. FDA 3397)
Subject
Product name: chemical name, trial name, trade name, generic name
Keywords
Table of contents?
Existing department classification code
Version number
Which version number is official legal copy?
Frequency of updates

Retention period
Date of document for retention calculation
Related documents in process
Indication of content subject to regulatory compliance
Company confidentiality
Information which potentially could be used in identity theft or company fraud
Publisher
Notes
ISBN
Location within facility

Possible Classification Scheme – draft
Tracked by Product (chemical name, trial name, trade name, generic) and by Time

ACQUISITION OF PRODUCT - materials relating to identification and acquisition by TMC

Initial New Drug (IND) – materials relating to the period of study trials
- protocols
- reports
- Clinical study numbers 1 to ?
- synopsis
- study report
- data listing
- publications

New Drug Application (NDA) – materials relating to submission of drug and passage thru regulatory process

NDA submission sections
- manufacturing
- safety
- investigation
- protocols
- study reports

Alphabetical by Color

- statistical data
- administrative
- quality
- clinical
- labeling
- chemistry
- investigative information
- promotional materials
- correspondence - Dear Doctor letters, etc.
- annual reports
- periodic SAEs
- safety information - MedWatch
- protocols
- trial master file
- contracts
- ERB approval letters
- electronic signature forms
- signature pages

MARKETING of PRODUCT – materials relating to period drug is on the market
FDA requirements

All other materials

Since The Medicines Company (TMC) would eventually have several or many products, the classification scheme had to take that into consideration. A firm in another industry might track by project, materials, employee or group, geography or something else.

The next planning was done after I learned a bit more about TMC. I wrote this out to clarify my thoughts about what the library's mission, services, goals, and objectives were to be. It helped greatly when discussing the library with TMC employees.

Inside the Library: updated 8/3/04

Has TMC ever had a library/librarian before? - No, I was hired to create and run the library.

What services did/will the library offer?
- "Primary function is to be document storage and retrieval with security for company documents" according to David M (my manager, the VP of IT)
- Secondly it will provide electronic document management company wide
- Third it will "interact with all teams to provide a full range of reference and information services, from directional assistance to online/internet searching and research" Jane P thinks this is her turf and no one else should do this – see her email of 7/28/04

Start out with the first function and expand into the second and third. Talk about the second and third to everyone to implant the idea, find out user's needs and desires, current resources used, and gain support.

What sort of cataloging, shelving, classifying, etc., will be used in the library?
Shelving is movable shelving housed in a secure (electronic passkey protected) room. (Designed and built before I was hired.)
Cataloging and classification systems are still unknown and will probably be home grown as I have not found any system which fits what we are doing. Still need to look more at Mesh headings and vendor offerings: Tab, Merrill, AskSam, First Consulting Group, etc. – look at CTD format from FDC for possible system (See my book "Computer Software Evaluation: Balancing User's Needs & Wants" which detailed the process I used to evaluate and select software.)

Are there any partnerships, formal or informal, between your company's library and outside sources?
Waltham group has some. Michael M and Greg F have some. Need to review what they have access to. Barbi A is pushing to get access to online services and will keep me informed. Jane P does not want to share – see email of 7/21/04

To whom do you report? To whom does your supervisor report? David M, head of IT. He reports to Steve K, head of Finance

How does your supervisor feel about the library? Big supporter but views it as archive only for documents submitted for regulatory purposes, not doing active document management function. Does not want to get anywhere near the issue of electronic documents because of validation issues.

Will you have control over the library budget? Unknown, but I should have.

Will the library budget be part of a departmental budget or be a separate entity? Unknown

What expenses is the library budget expected to cover? Unknown

What kind of staff will you have? None foreseen in the near future. Likely outside vendors will be hired to do efforts such as imaging and scanning of documents. (No, I ended up doing it all.)

What kinds of materials are there/will you obtain for your library?
- Company documents created for regulatory submissions: NDA, sNDA, MAA, clinical case report forms; reports; study documents; regulatory files; manufacturing records; computer software; annual reports; financial reports; etc. Most will come from Waltham and NZ and perhaps some from Great Britain. Others will come from internal groups such as Legal, Finance, Safety, etc.
 - Government documents such as FDA and SEC files
 - Access to databases & online services, print publications
 - Periodicals?
Local maps and phone books are needed. Also post a NJ and metro NYC area map for all to view. Karen suggests it should be framed. Prices are about $100 to purchase them at Hagstrom. Framing estimate at $90 apiece so total is about $500

Which departments are expected to use the library?
All but it's likely Regulatory, Publishing and Safety will use it the most. When information services come under my responsibility, more functions will use it.

What is the relationship between the library and the other departments in

the company?
Unknown because they do not know what functions I will be able to perform for them. Keep marketing me.

What are you planning to do to help the library get started?
- Be outgoing, make myself known to all, by responding to requests in person and hand carrying requested documents to people,
- Ask questions to learn the business
- Have maps and phone books, local info materials
- Be the 'go to person' for reference/information services. This will step on Jane P's toes so caution is advised until formal backing gained from management.
- Make available reports, lists of websites (emerging trends sites; pharma & biotech sites; etc.), local items of interests; interesting items to create buzz
- hold educational/training sessions on library services, WWW use, etc. – ask John P
- ask about infrastructure team meetings – what can I contribute?

What are the next steps needed to be taken?
1. Materials need to come from Waltham and NZ to file in the library. Prepare an inventory and make it easily available thru the desktop to all TMC employees – how? Not with SharePoint but by some other database, perhaps Access. Ask Bob D after making rough drafts of screens.
2. Look at software packages for the library. Liberty NET from Info Solutions is a possibility.
3. Look at imaging services for the library – what should be scanned? I think as much as possible but what do others think? 8/13/04 Information Solutions meeting might help.
4. Gently talk up document management efforts and document and file naming conventions – working company wide. Monica said Joan must have process on Clive's desk by 7/22
5. Ask around about email management solutions – anyone thinking about this? Anyone think this function is useful?
6. Gather support from key individuals such as Paul A (Legal), Steve K (Finance), Dennis R for "virtual document library"
7. Write up mission statement, prepare goals and objectives, and design programs and services the library will offer.
8. Ask questions about who is currently doing reference and research

services, what they are doing, and what resources they are using. Ask Gina Z in Waltham, knowing Jane P does not want to share.

Mission Statement draft:

The Medicines Company (TMC) mission statement "meet the demands of the world's most advanced medical practitioners by developing products that improve hospital acute care".

The TMC Library reflects the company's purpose and functions as an integral part of the information flow. We strive to support the information needs of the company by:
- collecting, preserving, storing, and cataloging all materials acquired or purchased for the collection, especially those documents produced in-house.
- providing information resources and services to meet the demands and needs of TMC employees.
- working in collaboration with the Information Technology department to construct, maintain, and update a library intranet.
- educating company employees as needed on proper use of materials and information as dictated by copyright, trademark, FCC, and privacy laws.
- purchasing and acquiring materials such as but not limited to books, periodicals, videos, films, electronic media, viewing devices, equipment, software, etc., as needed to maintain, update, or enhance the collection.

Library Goals and Objectives
Primary Long-Term Goals
1. Review Library Policies and Standard Operating Procedures (SOPs) to ensure they are consistent with company needs and practices. This review will be conducted at the start of every calendar year.

2. Review Library Plan to ensure company and staff needs are being efficiently and effectively met. Twice a year, librarian and staff will discuss company resources and information needs.

3. Build and maintain the collection in accordance with company needs.

An informal user advisory committee consisting of 3 to 10 TMC employees will meet no fewer than 3 times a year to provide input and suggestions on what would be useful in the collection. At least once a week, update the catalog with any newly arrived materials.

4. Promote and market Library services company-wide. Quarterly, newsletters shall be distributed to TMC staff and employees worldwide. This may be done by electronic or paper means.

5. Maintain the electronic resources necessary for maintaining the Library collection and providing services to the company.
Perform cataloging of new materials at least once a week.
Perform yearly checks on all electronic subscriptions to outside information sources and periodicals.
Create an intranet for access to Library holdings and information.

Primary Short-Term Goals
1. Develop a catalog and classification system or purchase one from an outside vendor. This may have to wait until materials are onsite from Waltham to give me an idea of what I will be working with.
By August 31, 2004: Decide which classification system to use – CTD?
By September 30, 2004: In collaboration with the IT department, purchase or implement system.

2. Decide which library software system to use. As above, may have to wait until material onsite. Check LibertyNET functions on 8/13/04
By August 31, 2004: Develop, in collaboration with IT dept., an RFP to send to library software vendors,
By September 30, 2004: In collaboration with the IT dept., review proposals sent in by vendors, and arrange for in-house demos.
By October 31, 2004: purchase library software system.

3. Purchase materials. Ask for suggestions from employees.
By September 30, 2004: Prepare a list of materials needed for library
By October 31, 2004: Purchase or subscribe to needed library materials

Program Designs

Who will be the primary users of the library? People looking for regulatory materials: Safety, Regulatory, Documentation, Finance, Legal,

What kinds of materials will they use? Mostly print at first, then electronic later as we put more documents virtual

Major areas: reference, consultation, technology, and education.
What will you do in each area to provide maximum service for TMC? For each area, establish goals and objectives, the end results you wish to accomplish, and a tentative schedule of implementation or evaluation.

For each service
who will the service be for? - TMC employees
what do you hope to accomplish with each service? -
when will the service be implemented/evaluated? -
where will the service be setup/started? - in Parsippany serving worldwide
why are you starting this service? - needed by TMC
how will the service be implemented/evaluated? - user survey feedback

Here are the services in the major areas of the library.

Reference:
Provide research services to TMC
Allow librarian to learn industry
Assist employees to perform job
Order what resources?
Collection Development Policy written after materials come from Waltham and NZ

Consultation:
Assist in company decision making
Join committees and teams
Market services
Create working relationships
Maintain visual presence
Librarian gets to know everyone

Keep current on entire company
First consultation programs will begin no later than 3 months after library is set up (Dec?)

Technology:
Provide services to TMC
Develop & maintain easy desktop access to inventory
Update catalog weekly
Design and maintain reference library
Enable employees to find documents easily
Employees can search easily
Will provide reference materials
Catalog system and database will be up and running by?
Intranet will be up by?

Education:
Provide opportunities for employees to learn how to use library services
Develop series of workshops
Create desktop tutorials
Create pathfinders
Will allow employees to find documents easily
Will teach employees to find documents easily
Educational courses will be conducted in house by me
Formal instructional sessions will be developed when necessary
Pathfinders and bibliographies will be created after materials in database

Document storage, retrieval, and archiving:
Provide secure storage for regulatory documents
Provide access to copies of regulatory documents
Allow employees to find documents during audits
Provide documents to be used as templates for future documents
After materials arrive from Waltham and NZ
Ask groups what documents they need to place in Library – finance, legal, etc.

Alphabetical by Color 272

I sent this email to the main process owners within TMC to set up meetings to learn how their departments create, use and store information. After each meeting, I wrote up their answers and sent them back, asking if I had missed anything or made a mistake writing down the information they gave. Always a good practice to follow, because they could never in the future claim they said something different which sometimes happened.

Hello,
I need to find out how information is created, moves, and is used within The Medicines Company so when the company library is created, it meets regulatory requirements, ensures return on investment, and provides overall customer satisfaction. Since you are one of the main sequence process owners, could we please set up a time to meet? If you are very busy this week and next, perhaps you could suggest a key member of your department who could meet with me.

Dale Carpenter MLS
Corporate Librarian
The Medicines Company
Parsippany, NJ 07054
973-647-DDDD
dale.carpenter@TMC.com

These are the issues I am interested in:

Meet with department heads and group managers:
a. learn what they do and how they do it
b. learn what they create and how it is used (in relation to regulatory documents)
c. learn what information is used (in relation to regulatory documents)
d. where and how that info is obtained (in relation to regulatory documents)
e. does a classification scheme exist for dept documents (in relation to regulatory documents)?
f. what library function or functions would provide the greatest return to you and your department?

Documents created in house:
  What are they?
  Who creates them and who owns them?
  How are they used and by whom?
  How often are they used or accessed? Does this change over time?
  What regulatory requirements, IE. retention period, original copy, paper or electronic?
  Is version control needed?
  Is access control needed?
  Are they available in paper or electronic format (Internet, databases, CD-ROM, email) or both?
  Are they stored in paper or electronic format or both?
  What software systems are used to create, maintain, and store the documents?
  How long do they need to be retained?
  Do they need to be in the Library?

Here is the question & answer sheet I made for each process owner interview. (From their answers I wrote up my notes and the email to send them.)

NAME: DEPT:

This discussion is primarily concerned with the legislative, audit, quality, regulatory and corporate requirements to maintain and preserve access to corporate information.

What documents do you or your group create in house?

Who creates the documents and who owns the documents?

Where do you obtain the information to create the documents?

How are they used and by whom?

How often are the documents used or accessed? Does this change over time?

What regulatory requirements pertain to them, IE. retention period, original copy, paper or electronic?

Have you written formal retention policies for your documents?

Do you need document version control?

Do you need access control?

Your documents are in what format? (paper, electronic format (Internet, databases, CD-ROM, email), both or all?

Are they stored in paper or electronic format or both?

Do you manage paper records and electronic documents in separate systems?

What software do you use to create, maintain, and store the documents?

Do they need to be in the Library?

Does your department create or use any other information or materials we have not discussed?

Roughly, by your estimate, how many documents does your department control?
In regulatory area: all others:

Does a classification scheme exist for your documents?

What expectations do you have of the Library?

What Library function or functions would provide the greatest return to you and your department?

This was written when planning to move to a new building.

The Medicines Company Library & Clinical Trial Documents Secure Storage Space Planning

MDCO receives clinical trial documents with personal information (doctor and patient names, social security numbers, date of birth, addresses, etc.) which must be kept secure. Combining a secure storage space with a work area for the product team members will limit physical access while allowing authorized access.

Specific recommendations:

1. Create a secure storage area for Cangrelor documentation with 1500 linear feet of shelving for all Bridge, Platform PK/PD, PCI, Platform and Phoenix documents.

2. The secure storage area must be a storage AND work area. Requiring documents to be removed for any purpose GREATLY increases the possibility of loss, damage, HIPAA violations and audit problems.

3. The secure storage area must limit access only to those product team members working on the documents stored in the area and the Corporate Librarian.

4. The building fire suppression system contains water sprinklers. Water damage to documents will certainly occur if it is activated. All documents should be under cover or the shelf units must have tops to reduce water damage.

5. Documents should not be placed on bottom shelves in case of flooding.

6. Shelving units do not have to be movable but must be sturdy enough to hold heavy volumes of paper either in folders or binders, both 8.5" by 11" and A4 formats. Shelves should be adjustable.

Current usage factors:

Cangrelor documentation currently occupies over 975 linear feet of shelves in the MDCO Library.

It is unknown how much space the incoming Phoenix trial materials will require.

It is unknown how much space the incoming Recothrom documentation will require.

It is unknown if any documentation is coming from Incline Therapeutics.

Documents from completed clinical trials are held until after publication of trial results. After the clinical trial manager approves archiving, then documents are sent to secure off-site storage. Regulatory submissions are not sent off site.

The fire suppression system is water based. Therefore all documents should be covered on shelves to avoid water damage. (We were extremely lucky the flooding in February 2011 did not affect the Library.)

General Recommendations for Secure Storage Space Planning:

Square footage required depends on the type of shelving: height, width, length and if shelves are adjustable. Aisle space must also be included unless movable shelving units are used.

If documents are kept in a secure storage with no workspace, MDCO associates will bring them to their work area. This is in-efficient and WILL lead to lapses in security.

A secure storage area could be for one product documents only or multiple products documentations. A one product document area would be most efficient as it would impact the fewest MDCO associates. Since Cangrelor currently takes up most storage space, it is the logical choice for now.

Wireless computer access throughout the area would be useful for individuals working on secure documents. Multiple computer network connections and power outlets should be available.

A workspace for individuals or groups to review (QA & QC) documents is needed. (Tables, chairs, etc.)

A copier/scanner and office supplies such as a 3-hole punch, staplers, and storage space for papers, boxes, binders, would be useful so documents do not need to be removed. A shredding bin should also be close by.

Lighting should be planned so aisles are not in shadow. It should also be designed for the work areas. Motion sensors are needed for the lights, so they will automatically turn off when no one is in the area.

There should be an area for boxes in transit to offsite archiving comprising a storage area for packing boxes, a work area for inventorying/packing/marking the boxes and a space to store packed boxes until the shipment is ready to be picked up.

Please look at "Computer Software Evaluation: Balancing User's Needs & Wants" for information on the process I used to determine what software was needed at TMC. What, you haven't yet? It's available at www.Lulu.com.

> "A man should keep his little brain attic stocked with
> all the furniture that he is likely to use,
> and the rest he can put away in the lumber-room of his library,
> where he can get it if he wants it."
> Arthur Conan Doyle

www.ingramcontent.com/pod-product-compliance
Lightning Source LLC
Chambersburg PA
CBHW070529090426
42735CB00013B/2918